Kinnor

The Biblical Lyre in History, Thought, and Culture

Books in This Series

Partners with God
Theological and Critical Readings of the Bible in Honor of
Marvin A. Sweeney

Qol Tamid
The Shofar in Ritual, History and Culture

Kinnor

The Biblical Lyre in History, Thought, and Culture

Edited By
Jonathan L. Friedmann
and
Joel Gereboff

CLAREMONT STUDIES IN
HEBREW BIBLE AND SEPTUAGINT 4

Kinnor

The Biblical Lyre in History, Thought, and Culture

©2020 Claremont Press
1325 N. College Ave
Claremont, CA 91711

ISBN 978-1-946230-46-1

Library of Congress Cataloging-in-Publication Data

Kinnor The Biblical Lyre in History, Thought, and Culture/Jonathan L. Friedmann
     viii + 193 pp. 22 x 15 cm. –(Claremont Studies in Hebrew Bible and
     Septuagint 4)
     Includes bibliographical references and index.
     ISBN 978-1-946230-46-1

     1. Music in the Bible.
     2. Musical Instruments, Ancient Israel.
     3. Jews, Israel, Music, History and Criticism.
     BS 2361.2 C739 2019

To Jeremy Montagu (1927–2020), whose important work in organology and the study of biblical instruments – including his chapter in this book – has expanded our knowledge and inspired our hearts.

Table of Contents

Preface   *ix*

Introduction   **1**
     Joel Gereboff and Jonathan L. Friedmann

The Kinnor   **19**
     Jeremy Montagu

The Kinnor in the Bible   **31**
Instrument of the Divine
     Marvin A. Sweeney

The Character of the Kinnor   **43**
An Instrument of Joy
     Jonathan L. Friedmann

The Kinnor as a Symbol of Joy of the Past and   **61**
Future Messianic Eternal Eras
     Joel Gereboff

The Kinnor in Jewish Thought   **77**
Some Remarks
     Dov Schwartz

Artistic Depictions of David and the Kinnor   **87**
     Siobhán Dowling Long

Handel's Harpists and the Morals of Music   **123**
     Ruth Smith

Studies on the Kinnor and Ancient Lyres   **145**
An Annotated Bibliography
     Jonathan L. Friedmann and Joel Gereboff

List of Contributors   *163*

Bibliography   *165*

Indices   *181*

Preface

This volume brings together essays on diverse historical, musical, spiritual, intellectual, and artistic views and representations of the biblical kinnor, commonly understood to have been a lyre. The interdisciplinary chapters are a testament to the instrument's lasting religious and cultural importance.

Joel's research on the history of the use and understanding of the kinnor arises from four interests: material culture and religion; embodiment as a dimension of religion and culture; the dynamics of resignification; and the comparison of Jewish and Christian appropriations and interpretations of texts and practices from the Hebrew Bible. Religions are not merely systems of ideas or direct experiences of the divine; they are primarily social phenomena transmitted and lived through embodied practices involving material objects. The diverse ways in which music and musical instruments, sung and played, have been part of religious life are vital examples of embodied actions performed through such objects. But these practices do not stand alone. They are intertwined with multiple and changing meanings over the course of time, as Jews, Christians, and others ascribe different and expanding significance to such behaviors and physical items.

Jonathan's interest in the kinnor is also fourfold: the symbolic and functional uses of music in biblical life; the cross-cultural and cross-historical ubiquity of music in human societies; the field of organology, which deals with the evolution, classification, and technical aspects of musical instruments; and efforts of religious communities to keep ancient symbols alive by ascribing new meanings, and, in the case of the kinnor, new identities. Although the original instrument did not survive its ancient setting, the kinnor has been interpreted and reinterpreted by regionally dispersed communities through the ages. As the Bible's most elevated instrument, the kinnor has been associated with a range of culturally valued string instruments, including the lyre, harp, psaltery, lute, oud, and violin. The instrument's name and prestige have lived on in varied sounds.

The editors are grateful to Thomas E. Philips and the staff at Claremont Press for guiding this book through the stages of production, and to the contributors for sharing their wisdom, creativity, passion, and expertise.

Introduction

Joel Gereboff and Jonathan L. Friedmann

This book explores wide-ranging conceptual and sonic resonances of the biblical kinnor and its ancient Near Eastern and Mediterranean counterparts. Collecting interdisciplinary studies from historical, theological, musicological, artistic, and cultural perspectives, it is a follow-up to *Qol Tamid: The Shofar in Ritual, History, and Culture* (2017), also published by Claremont Press, and covers similarly broad territory. The chapters discuss literary and artistic renderings of the kinnor in selected works and periods, including analyses of references in the Bible and classical rabbinic texts, selections from medieval and early modern Jewish philosophical and kabbalistic writings, and examples of Christian and Jewish art and music from medieval to modern times.

Like the shofar, the kinnor has a rich historical, interpretive, and cultural legacy that persists to this day. Its association with the primordial musician Jubal, Levitical musician-priests, and especially with King David made it the "foremost instrument among Jews"[1] and "the noblest of musical instruments."[2] However, unlike the crude shofar, which rabbinic sources considered "unmusical," the melodious kinnor was prohibited, along with other musical instruments, from being played on Shabbat and holy days. As a result, while the shofar—a natural animal horn—has retained its shape, sound, and Jewish ceremonial usage over the millennia, the biblical kinnor is essentially extinct.

Mysteries surrounding the kinnor have not deterred artists and interpreters from hypothesizing about its construction and sonic qualities, depicting it in art and music, and connecting it to an assortment of symbolic and allegorical meanings. This introduction

---

[1] Macy Nulman, *Concise Encyclopedia of Jewish Music* (New York: McGraw-Hill, 1975), 134.

[2] Manuel Jinbachian, "Music and Musical Instruments in the Septuagint, the Peshitta and the Armenian Psalms," *Text Theology & Translation: Essays in Honour of Jan de Waard* (eds. Simon Crisp and Manuel Jinbachian; London: United Bible Societies, 2004), 64–67.

aims to acquaint readers with this long history of creative engagement. Section one asks the fundamental question, "What is the kinnor?" Section two explores, "What does the kinnor represent?" A third section offers brief summaries of the book's contents.

What Is the Kinnor?

The Hebrew Bible mentions some sixteen musical instruments by name. Various attempts to positively identify, describe, and classify these instruments have been made over the centuries, beginning with Roman authors, the Mishnah and Talmud, and church fathers. While the earliest sources, composed during or shortly after the late Second Temple period, contain some contemporaneous musical information, they are mostly concerned with meaning, interpretation, and symbolism, rather than detailed or objective descriptions. Theologically, ideologically, and culturally slanted assumptions regarding biblical instruments persist to this day, despite more recent interest in archaeological and iconographic evidence. As Joachim Braun opines in his book, *Music in Ancient Israel/Palestine*, "Of all pre-Christian cultures, none has a music history as burdened by one-sided and subjective perspectives and prejudices as that of ancient Israel/Palestine. Research into other high cultures of the ancient world has never been as plagued by a neglect of scientific principles or by unscientific arguments as is the case with this region."[3]

The academic impulse to categorize and typologize has yielded several attempts to group biblical instruments based on hints found in the text. For instance, pioneer Israeli musicologist Edith Gerson-Kiwi proposed three categories: sacerdotal (high priest) horns (shofar and *hatzotzrah*); Levitical (secondary priest) instruments (kinnor and *nevel*); and lay instruments (*ugav, halil,* etc.).[4] Gerson-Kiwi's colleague, Hancoh Avenary, offered a different classification: magical instruments of the nomadic period (shofar, *hatzotzrah, toph, metziltayim*); urban aesthetic instruments during the monarchic period (kinnor, *nevel, halil*); and Temple instruments

---

[3] Joachim Braun, *Music in Ancient Israel/Palestine: Archaeological, Written, and Comparative Sources* (tr. Douglas W. Stott; Grand Rapids: Wm. B. Eerdmans, 2002), 1.

[4] Edith Gerson-Kiwi, "Musique dans la bible," *Dictionnaire de la Bible*, supp. 5 (Paris: Letouzey and Ané, 1957), 1411–68.

(shofar, *ḥatzotzrah, ḥalil, kinnor, nevel, metziltayim*).[5] Such grouping do not hold up well under scrutiny, as musical instruments are not typically confined to a single use, single context, or single class of player. Like modern-day instruments, biblical instruments appear to have been versatile and multifunctional. For instance, the Bible includes references to the shofar in cultic ceremonies and on the battlefield but excludes its likely use as a shepherd's horn and non-cultic communal alarm (functions outside of the Bible's narrow theological scope).

A more profitable typology, though not Bible-specific, is a system devised by Erich Moritz von Hornbostel and Curts Sachs, which categorizes the world's musical instruments as idiophones (percussion instruments with vibrating bodies), membranophones (drums with membranes), chordophones (string instruments), and aerophones (wind instruments).[6] Instead of focusing on problematic areas of symbolism and meaning, which are more contextually, sonically, historically, and functionally diverse than any typology can account for, the Hornbostel-Sachs system allows for objective and inclusive groupings arranged by family resemblance. Biblical instruments are attested in each of the four categories of the Hornbostel-Sachs system, with paradigmatic examples being: *pa'amonim* (priestly bells) — idiophone; *toph* (frame drum) — membranophone; kinnor — chordophone; and shofar — aerophone. Yet, even in an inclusive system, ambiguities arise. Some biblical instruments remain difficult to classify. For example, the *mena'anim*, mentioned only in 2 Samuel 6:5, derive from a Hebrew verb meaning "shake" or "tremble" (*nua*). Whereas the Greek Septuagint and Latin Vulgate identify the instrument as a cymbal or rattle, and thus an idiophone, the Aramaic Targum and *Pistis Sophia* (Coptic gnostic text) translate it as "drum," making it a membranophone. Other historical translations include "trumpet," an aerophone.[7]

---

[5] Hanoch Avenary, "Jüdische Musik," *Die Musik in Geschichte und Gegenwart: allgemeine Enzyklopädie der Musik* (Kassel: Bärenreiter-Verlag, 1958), 7:224–32.

[6] Erich Moritz von Hornbostel and Curt Sachs, "Systematik der Musikinstrumente," *Zeitschrift für Ethnologie* 46 (1914): 553–90. Sachs added eletrophones in 1940. A later modification divides wind instruments into horn/trumpets and woodwinds. D. A. Foxvog and A. D. Kilmer, "Music," *International Study Bible Encyclopedia* (Grand Rapids, MI: W. B. Eerdmans, 1980), 3:436–49.

[7] Braun, *Music in Ancient Israel/Palestine*, 19.

Such difficulties do not apply to the kinnor, the Bible's second most frequently mentioned instrument, after the shofar. Occurring forty-two times in eleven books, the kinnor is almost universally understood to be a chordophone and, most often, a lyre.[8] Still, we cannot claim with absolute certainty the precise construction or design of the kinnor, which, depending on the biblical verse, may have been a specific instrument, a catchall name for lyre variants, or a generic term for chordophone. The introduction of Jubal as the father of the kinnor and *ugav* (pipe) in Genesis 4:21 is likely a merism: a pairing of contrasting things to imply "everything," or, in this case, "all instruments." As category markers, the kinnor represents all chordophones (string instruments), while the *ugav* encompasses all aerophones (wind instruments). Braun includes thirty-four lyre sketches reproduced from etchings, jars, stands, seals, figurines, coins, plaques, mosaics, and gems from the second millennium BCE to the sixth century CE.[9] All share the basic characteristics of a lyre—sound box, two arms, a crossbar, and strings—but no two images are exactly the same. They vary in almost every conceivable way: shape, size, construction, component materials, ornaments (or lack thereof), number of strings, etc. It is possible that, in the biblical nomenclature, each version would have been called "kinnor." *Musical Instruments of the World*, a widely cited visual encyclopedia, broadens the view by including images of ancient lyres, European lyres, and African lyres, as well as closely related folk harps, historical harps, and orchestral harps.[10]

Complicating the kinnor's interpretive history is the tendency of translators, commentators, and authors to identity instruments according to their own time and place. In the period from the mid-third century BCE until the destruction of the Second Temple in 70 CE, a limited number of written works refer to the kinnor. The most extensive references are in the Septuagint's

---

[8] The kinnor is mentioned in these biblical verses: Gen 4:21; 31:27; 1 Sam 10:5; 16:16, 23; 2 Sam 6:5; 1 Kgs 10:12; Isa 5:12; 16:11; 23:16; 24:8; 30:32; Ezek 26:13; Pss 33:2; 43:4; 49:5; 57:9; 71:22; 81:3; 92:4; 98:5; 108:3; 137:2; 147:7; 149:3; 150:3; Job 21:12; 30:31; Neh 12:27; 1 Chr 13:8; 15:16, 21, 28; 16:5; 25:1, 3, 6; 2 Chr 5:12, 9:11; 20:28; 29:25.

[9] Braun, *Music in Ancient Israel/Palestine*, xxxii–xxxvi.

[10] Diagram Group, *Musical Instruments of the World: An Illustrated Encyclopedia* (New York: Paddington, 1976), 168–77.

translation of the Hebrew Bible into Greek.[11] It renders kinnor as *kithara* (lyre) twenty times, *kinura* (a reproduction of the Hebrew term) seventeen times, *psalmterion* (psaltery) four times, and once as *organon* (a generic term for musical instrument).[12] The text also translates *nevel* eight times as *psalmterion*, twice as *organon*, and in fourteen occurrences as *nabla* (harp), showing that the two instruments were sometimes treated as interchangeable. The fifth-century Armenian Bible, which tends to eliminate references to musical instruments, calls the kinnor a "song of praise," "testament," and "proverb of praise." These substitutions likely stemmed from the view that instruments were too pagan or hedonistic to include in a Christian text.[13] Spanish medieval Hebrew poetry imagines the kinnor as an oud (short-necked lute), the principal instrument of the Muslim world.[14] Several Hebrew dictionaries from Renaissance Italy describe the kinnor as a lute (*lutio*).[15] A sermon by Italian rabbi Judah Moscato (c. 1530–c. 1593), *Higgayon BeKhinnor* ("Sounds for the Contemplation of a Kinnor"), portrays the instrument as a harp in accordance with musical preferences of his day.[16] The King James Bible (1611) likewise translates kinnor as "harp." The harp, lyre, and lute are sometimes employed as synonyms in English librettos of George Frideric Handel dealing with biblical themes. However, the harp and, for a

---

[11] For general comments on music among the Jews during this period, see Emmanuel Friedheim, "Jewish Society in the Land of Israel and the Challenge of Music in the Roman Period," *Review of Rabbinic Judaism* 15 (2012): 69–88 and John Arthur Smith, *Music in Ancient Judaism and Early Christianity* (Burlington, VT: Ashgate, 2013).

[12] On these comments, see Sol Baruch Finesinger, "Musical Instruments in the OT," *Hebrew Union College Annual* 3 (1926): 27, 37. See also Jinbachian, "Music and Musical Instruments."

[13] Jinbachian, "Music and Musical Instruments," 64–67.

[14] Yosef Tobi, *Between Hebrew and Arabic Poetry: Studies in Spanish Medieval Hebrew Poetry* (Boston: Brill, 2010), 151–52.

[15] *Makrei dardekei* (Naples: Joseph ben Jacob Ashkenazi Gunzenhauser, 1488); David de Pomis, *Tzemach David: Dittionario novo hebraico, molto copioso, dechiarato in tre lingue* (Venice: Juan de Gara, 1587); and Leon Modena, *Galut Yehudah: Novo dittionario hebraico et italiano cioè Dichiaratione di tutte le voci hebraiche più difficili delle scritture hebree nella volgar lingua italiana* (Padua: Giulio Crivellari, 1640).

[16] BT *Berakhot* 3b–4a. See Don Harrán, "The Levi Dynasty: Three Generations of Jewish Musicians in Sixteenth-century Mantua," *Rabbi Judah Moscato and the Jewish Intellectual World of Mantua in the 16th–17th Centuries* (eds. Giuseppe Veltri and Gianfranco Miletto; Boston: Brill, 2012), 186–95 and Don Harrán, *Three Early Modern Hebrew Scholars on the Mysteries of Song* (Boston: Brill, 2014), 47–128.

brief time, the lyre guitar (a guitar with wings and a crosspiece in vogue from around 1785 to 1815), were instruments of choice for classical composers. In Modern Hebrew, kinnor means "violin." The term figures prominently in "Yerushalayim shel Zahav," Naomi Shemer's secular-religious anthem (or *shir koddesh*[17]) of the Six-Day War: "Jerusalem of Gold, and of bronze, and of light; Behold I am a violin (kinnor) of all your songs." Still, modern Israelis have not lost sight of the historical instrument of the same name. For example, a color image of David and his lyre, reproduced from a Gaza synagogue mosaic (early sixth century CE), is featured on an official Israeli commemorative coin from 2013.[18]

Divergent translations are visualized in several paintings, sculptures, etchings, and illuminated manuscripts reproduced in Moshe Gorali's *The Old Testament in Music*.[19] As both a stand-alone instrument and an instrument played by Jubal and King David, the kinnor sometimes appears as a lyre, more often as a harp, and other times as a psaltery. Such depictions have a long history, which extends into modern fine art and even comic books. For example, several paintings by Marc Chagall portray David and Solomon playing the kinnor.[20] *King David*, Kyle Baker's raucous graphic novel adaptation of the biblical narrative, begins with a young David entering Saul's court with a lyre (called a harp in the text).[21] R. Crumb's *The Book of Genesis Illustrated*, a verse-by-verse of rendering of the Book of Genesis, includes a drawing of Jubal,

---

[17] Natan Greenboym, "Yerushalayim Shel Zahav Ke'shir Koddesh," *Mayim Midalav* (1933): 27–32 [Heb.]. See also Meeka Simerly, "Naomi Shemer's Artistic Expression: Poetry, Prayer, or Both?" *Emotions in Jewish Music: Personal and Scholarly Reflections* (ed. Jonathan L. Friedmann; Lanham, MD: University Press of America, 2012), 5–29. For a discussion of the violin (kinnor) in modern Israeli literature, see Michal Ben-Horin, "Musical Discourse and Historical Narratives in Hebrew Literature: Senaz's *Musical Moment* and Shaham's *Rosendoft Quartet*," *Israel Studies Forum* 21.2 (2006): 85–101.

[18] See Mel Wacks, "Music to Sooth a Troubled King: David's Harp on Coins Old & New," *Shekel: The Journal of Israel and Jewish History and Numismatics* 47.2/3 (2014): 47–50.

[19] Moshe Gorali, *The Old Testament in Music* (Jerusalem: Maron, 1993).

[20] See, for example, David L. Petersen, "Portraits of David: Canonical and Otherwise," *Interpretation* 40.2 (1986): 130–42 and Liliya Garifullovna Safiullinna and Gulnara Ibragimovna Batyrshina, "Musical Images as a Reflection of the Artistic Universalism of Marc Chagall," *Terra Sebus: Acta Musei Sabesiensis* (2014): 67–104.

[21] Kyle Baker, *King David* (New York: DC Comics, 2002).

dressed in rags, playing a rugged kinnor and leaning against a brick wall.[22] (Two panels later, Jubal plays an *ugav*, drawn as a Middle Eastern *mijwiz*, a double pipe made of short, parallel stocks of bamboo.) *Asterix*, a French comic book series created by writer René Goscinny and illustrator Albert Uderzo, follows the adventures of Gaulish warriors fighting the Roman Empire during the reign of Julius Caesar.[23] Among its characters is Cacofonix the Bard, whose favored instrument is a lyre made from two bull horns and some metal work.

Other popular culture occurrences of the ancient lyre include appearances in scores and diegetic (source) music for Hollywood Bible and Roman epics, such as *King of Kings* (1927), *Cleopatra* (1934), *David and Bathsheba* (1951), *The Robe* (1953), and *Demetrius and the Gladiators* (1954), as well as in fantasy and science-fiction television series, such as the original *Star Trek*, where it appears as Spock's Vulcan harp, and *Xena: Warrior Princess*, where a golden lyre is the prize in an epic battle of the bands.[24]

Advances in archaeomusicology—the application of archaeological methods to the study of music—have enabled intriguing attempts at reconstructing the kinnor and other biblical instruments.[25] These efforts remain speculative, despite a handful of contemporary players who claim to have retrieved the kinnor's original design, determined its tuning, and deciphered the few extant notations from the ancient Near East and Mediterranean. While musically interesting and aesthetically appealing, these reconstructions, like the historical translations of kinnor, tend to mirror the tastes and preferences of our own time.[26]

What Does the Kinnor Represent?

Historically, writers and renderers have focused more on the kinnor's symbolic and allegorical purposes than on the instrument's

---

[22] R. Crumb, *The Book of Genesis Illustrated* (New York: W.W. Norton, 2009).

[23] René Goscinny and Albert Uderzo, *The Complete Asterix* (New York: Hachette, 2013).

[24] Aaron Fruchtman intended to write a chapter on the kinnor in film music for this book, but his schedule prevented him from doing so.

[25] Theodore W. Burgh, *Listening to the Artifacts: Music Culture in Ancient Israel* (New York: T & T Clark, 2006), 153–56, details a sophisticated attempt at reconstructing a kinnor and the problems encountered.

[26] See, for instance, the music and research of composer and lyre player Michael Levy: https://ancientlyre.com/

physical attributes. The dominant symbolism in the Hebrew Bible is joy, and particularly joy associated with the cultic ritual. The few references in Greek Jewish literature, including 1 Maccabees (3:45; 4:54; and 13:51), likewise link the instrument with joy and the Temple. The *Sibylline Oracles*, which collect Greek oracular utterances, mentions the *kithara* in 8:119 and 12:92. The first of these affirms the classical Greek view of the lyre as the most elevated instrument. Philo of Alexandria, a first century Jewish thinker, made extensive references to the *kithara*, declaring it as the supreme instrument and connecting its harmonious tuning to the harmonious soul.[27]

The kinnor appears in a handful of comments in the Dead Sea Scrolls, most of which depict it as a symbol of joy (1QS 10:9; 1QM 21:23–25; IQH 10:13; 19:23). However, two comments describe it being played in a sad manner (1QH 19:23; 4Q437 1,4). The most controversial Qumran text is 11QPs 28:3–12, which parallels Psalm 151 in the Septuagint. The initial interpretation of the text by James Sanders portrays King David as an Orphic figure, with David charming animals and trees with the music of his kinnor.[28] A number of scholars object to the notion that Jews, at this early date, were drawing on conceptions of Orpheus as the creator of harmony among living creatures.[29] While several Jewish writers, such as

---

[27] For Philo's views on music, see Louis H. Feldman, *Studies in Hellenistic Judaism* (Leiden: Brill, 1996), 504–28 and Siegmund Levarie, "Philo on Music," *Journal of Musicology* 9 (1991): 124–30.

[28] James Sanders, *The Psalms Scroll of Qumran Cave 11*, Discoveries in the Judean Desert 4 (Oxford: Clarendon, 1965), 61.

[29] Opposing views include: Isaac Rabinowitz, "The Alleged Orphism of 11 Q Pss 28:8–12," *Zeitschrift fur die Alttestamentliche Wissenschaft* 76 (1964): 193–200; Frank Moore Cross, "David, Orpheus and Psalm 151:3–4," *Bulletin of the American Schools of Oriental Research* 231 (1978): 69–71; Morton Smith, "Psalm 151, David, Jesus and Orpheus," *Zeitschrift fur die Alttestamentliche Wissenschaft* 93.2 (1981): 247–53; Natalio Fernandez-Marcos, "David the Adolescent: On Psalm 151," *The Old Greek Psalter: Studies in Honour of Natalio Albert Pietersman* (ed. Robert J. V. Hiebert; London: Bloomsbury, 2001), 205–17; and Devorah Dimant, "David's Youth in the Qumran Context (11 QPs 28:3-12)," *Prayer and Poetry in the Dead Sea Scrolls and Related Literature: Essays in Honor of Eileen Schuller on the Occasion of Her 65th Birthday* (eds. Jeremy Pener et al.; Leiden: Brill, 2012), 97–114. Dimant reads the text of line 4–6 to say, "My hand has made a harp and my finger a lute (kinnor). And [so] I have rendered glory to the Lord. I said to my soul, 'The mountains do not bear witness for me, the hills will not report about me, nor the trees my words, nor the flock my deeds.'" This contrasts with Sanders, who renders line 6, "The trees have cherished my words and the flocks my works," resulting in his Orphic

Aristobulos (second century BCE) and Artapanus (c. 100 BCE), had made connections to Orpheus as the father of esoteric knowledge, they did not depict him in his musical role as charmer of animals.[30] Also disputed are Orphic interpretations of the kinnor in paintings and mosaics in Jewish locations from the third to sixth centuries CE.

Early Christian writers, like Philo before them, mostly read "Old Testament" references to music and musical instruments allegorically. James K. McKinnon provides a rich collection of such writings from church fathers, arguing that, as part of their general rejection of cultic references in the Old Testament, they focused on spiritual messages encoded in the Temple's instrumental music. An alternative approach was to frame religious practices of the ancient Jews as evidence of their inferior spiritual development, including their use of instruments in ritual contexts. Christian rites during these early years lacked all instrumental music and even singing.[31]

The kinnor appears in Jewish literary, numismatic, and artistic works from the destruction of the Second Temple in 70 CE until the close of the classical rabbinic era and the rise of the Geonim in the seventh century. Among the assorted coins minted during the Bar Kokhba revolt (c. 132–136 CE) are bronze coins featuring a lyre. Hanan Eshel provides a detailed analysis of the various coins, the heaviest of which date from the first year of the revolt.[32] The obverse of the coin has a palm branch encircled by a wreath and the inscription, "Shimon, prince (*nasi*) of Israel." The reverse contains a lyre or harp with the inscription, "Year one of the redemption of Israel." In the second year of the revolt, two different bronze coins were produced. The first was very much like those of the first year, but the reverse stated, "Year two of the freedom of

---

interpretation.

[30] In an apologetic vein, Artapanus identifies Moses with Mousaios, Orpheus' master, thus claiming that a Jew originated esoteric knowledge.

[31] See James W. McKinnon, *Music in Early Christian Literature* (Cambridge: Cambridge University Press, 1989). David John Shirt, "'Sing Psalms to the Lord with the Harp': Attitudes toward Musical Instruments in Early Christianity – 680 AD," *Journal of Early Christian History* 6 (2016): 97–115, challenges McKinnon's claim that all forms of early Christianity rejected the use of music in ritual settings, drawing on evidence from Christian communities beyond the Mediterranean basin.

[32] Hanan Eshel, "On Harps and Lyres: A Note on the Bronze Coins of the Bar Kokhba Administration," *Israel Numismatic Journal* 16 (2007–08): 118–30.

Israel." The second coin from year two had a different wording on the obverse, "For the freedom of Jerusalem." The obverse of harp-imprinted bronze coins from the third year were also imprinted with "For the freedom of Jerusalem." Eshel notes a number of differences among these coins in regard to their weight and the instruments they depict, and speculates that, to reduce the confusion, the depiction of the lyre (harp) was altered in the third year because the coins were similar in weight to those of the second year, which were also lighter than those of the first year. Whereas the lyre (harp) of the first two years had a sound chest with the shape of a goatskin, the lyre in the third year took a wood sound-chest. According to Eshel, the goatskin-shaped instrument is a *nevel*, while the one with a wooden sound chest is a kinnor. Whatever the case, the coins were meant to inspire the rebels with images of Israel's "glory days," when these instruments were heard in the Temple and were linked to King David, the national hero *par excellence*.

Several paintings and mosaics from this period also feature the lyre. Two such mosaics have been found in Sepphoris (central Galilee region), one of which is in a synagogue. Two other lyre images appear in synagogues: one from Dura-Europos (Syria) and the other from Gaza. As with the aforementioned Dead Sea Scrolls, the most debated issue regarding these finds is whether they depict David playing the lyre in a manner equating him with Orpheus, the magician who charms the animals, creates harmony, and perhaps brings salvation. Sepphoris, which had a large Jewish population but was also home to many Christians and pagans (Romans), contains the only known zodiac featuring a lyre (in the sign of Gemini). The early fifth-century image is consistent with the zodiac's other surviving signs, which also use Greek mythological figures and label each sign in Hebrew with its astrological name and the name of the month.[33] The second find from Sepphoris is a domestic mosaic depicting a figure playing a lyre surrounded by animals. The figure is clearly Orpheus, though no label appears, and

---

[33] See the comments by Sonia Mucznik, "Musicians and Musical Instruments in Roman and Early Byzantine Mosaics of the Land of Israel: Sources, Precursors and Significance," *Gerion* 29.1 (2011): 278–80 and Mira Warner, "Aspects of Music Culture in the Land of Israel during the Hellenistic, Roman and Byzantine Periods: Sepphoris as a Case Study," *Music in Antiquity: The Near East and Mediterranean* (eds. Joan Goodnick Westenholz et al.; Berlin: De Gruyter, 2014), 288–89.

there is no reason to presume an equation with King David. It is unclear who owned or lived in the house, but it, along with the House of Dionysus in Sepphoris, has elegant mosaics presenting various Greek mythological scenes and myths.[34]

An unlabeled figure in a wall painting from Dura, dating from the third century, is widely thought to be David. Carl H. Kraeling, who published his findings on the Dura synagogue in the mid-1950s, connected the image of David to Orpheus.[35] Erwin Goodenough elaborated on this association, viewing it as part of the larger influence of paganism on Greco-Roman Jews who lived outside the rabbinic orbit of influence.[36] However, based on a computer analysis of the painting, Paul Flesher argues that it is not a single work, but has been redone at several stages. He contends that the images that appear include only two animals, while a third, interpreted by others as an eagle, is actually the top of a shepherd's crook, thus challenging perceived associations with Orpheus.[37]

A Gaza painting, which contains the date 508/509 CE in the mosaic itself, identifies the lyre-player as David (in Hebrew). That mosaic is also incomplete. Asher Ovadiah, the publisher of the finds, asserts that the mosaic's creator used elements associated with Orpheus in depicting the seated lyre player, who is explicitly identified as David. Ovadiah suggests that the figure is a metaphor for the messianic hope for the end of days, which the figure of

---

[34] See Zeev Weiss, "'The House of Orpheus': Another Villa from the Late Roman Period in Sepphoris," *Qadmoniot: A Journal for the Antiquities of Eretz-Israel and Bible Lands* 126 (2003): 94–101 and Warner, "Aspects of Music Culture," 287–88.

[35] Carl H. Kraeling, *The Synagogue: Excavations at Dura-Europos, Final Report 8, Part I* (New Haven, CT: Yale University Press, 1956).

[36] Erwin R. Goodenough, *Jewish Symbols in the Greco-Roman Period,* vols. IX–XI: *Symbolism in the Dura Synagogue* (New York: Pantheon, 1964).

[37] See Paul V. M. Flesher, "Rereading the Reredos: David, Orpheus, and Messianism in the Dura Europos Synagogue," *Ancient Synagogues: Historical, Analysis and Archaeological Discovery*, vol. 2 (eds. Dan Urman et al.; Leiden: Brill, 1995), 2346–66, who cites all the important earlier scholarship. A similar position is advanced by Geza Xeravits, "The Reception of the Figure of David in Late Antique Synagogue Art," *Figures who Shaped Scriptures, Scriptures that Shaped Figures: Essays in Honour of Benjamin G. Wright III* (eds. Geza Xeravits et al.; Berlin: De Gruyter, 2018), 71–90. The alternative view of seeing the David figure as a fusing with Orpheus is advanced by Paul Corby Finney, "Orpheus David: A Connection in Iconography Between Greco-Roman Judaism and Early Christianity," *Journal of Jewish Art* 5 (1978): 6–15, and Asher Ovadiah, "The Symbolic Meaning of the David-Orpheus Images in the Gaza Synagogue Mosaic," *Liber Annuus* 59 (2009): 301–07.

David represents.[38] Both Flesher and Geza Xeravits challenge this conclusion. According to Flesher, the mosaic is too damaged and incomplete to support claims of the assimilation of Orphic elements.[39] Xeravits contends that the presence of the Orphic features may be due to the non-Jewish artists who possibly laid the mosaic and were familiar with Greek mythology. For Xeravits, the David figure reflects his depiction as a psalm composer and, by extension, his role in shaping synagogue liturgy. As for the animals: "They have just a subsidiary or marginal role as compared to David in the mosaic. Their presence might express the cosmic aspects of Jewish worship."[40]

The proposed connections between David and Orpheus tie into broader issues regarding Jews of this era. First, there is evidence of Jewish appropriation of various aspects of pagan Greco-Roman culture. To what extent this points to the "assimilation" of Jews into the larger, dominant culture is a disputed point among scholars. Second, the association of David and Orpheus raises questions about Christian adaptations of Orpheus in art and written works. Clement, a late second-century church father, associated Jesus with Orpheus for the purpose of presenting Jesus as the superior figure, while still adopting aspects of the Orphic mythos, including connections to mystery cults of salvation.[41] Flesher notes the influence of Christianity in conflating David with Orpheus and (Christian) messianism:

> Essentially what has happened is that the messianic character has been read back from Christianity onto Orpheus and then onto David. Christ as Orpheus became Orpheus as Christ, i.e., Orpheus the messiah. Once the Dura synagogue's David was identified as Orpheus, it was only a short step to identifying "Orphic" David as David

---

[38] Ovadiah, "The Symbolic Meaning of the David-Orpheus Images." Sonia Mucznik, "Musicians and Musical Instruments," 271–73, also accepts this identification, but assigns to it a somewhat different meaning.

[39] Flesher, "Reading the Reredo," 358–59.

[40] Xeravits, "The Reception of the Figure of David," 76–77.

[41] Miguel Herrero de Jauregi, *Orphism and Christianity in Late Antiquity* (Berlin: De Gruyter, 2010) presents the most thorough and recent discussion of the issue. Simon Collier's unpublished BA Honor's thesis, "An Exploration into the Reception of Orpheus in the Early Christian Period and the Christian Middle Ages" (University of Warwick, 2014), provides a thorough analysis of the artistic remains connecting Orpheus and Jesus.

the messiah. This faulty link was strengthened by Christian practice of also linking David—as a messianic forerunner—to Orpheus.[42]

Both Flesher and Xeravits caution that one should not read messianism into all Jewish expressions in late antiquity. Instead, David and his lyre are an "indication of the national unity of the Jewish people, despite their scattered circumstances across the diaspora. The unity comes from the past—the nationhood and the peoplehood—and unites them under their first king, King David, rather than the multiplicity of twelve tribes."[43]

The kinnor, and music in general, appears sporadically in Jewish legal (halakhic), poetic, philosophical, and kabbalistic writings and artistic works from the time of the early Geonim (seventh-century Babylonia) until the beginning of the modern era in the eighteenth century. There is also evidence of an instrument called "kinnor" being played in Jewish settings during this period of more than one thousand years.

Systematic legal discussions of musical instruments did not emerge until the time of Hai b. Sherira, the last of the Geonim. Hai assumed the office of the geonate in 997 and held that position until his death in 1038. He penned two responsa on various questions related to the use of music in diverse settings, both vocal and instrumental. These two responsa, which draw upon numerous and conflicting statements about music in classical rabbinic sources— and especially in the Mishnah and Babylonian Talmud—serve as the foundation of all subsequent major halakhic rulings on music. Hai also takes note of music-related practices of Jewish communities throughout the Near East, North Africa, and Spain, over which the Gaon held much authority. Don Harrán has presented a careful analysis of these responsa,[44] underscoring the somewhat ambiguous rulings on music in the first responsum, which appears to allow for some use of music, especially vocal, while limiting musical instruments to weddings. The second responsum holds a much more negative view of music, prohibiting rejoicing while the Jews remain in exile. Harrán explains that Hai is

---

[42] Flesher, "Reading the Reredo," 359.

[43] Flesher, "Reading the Reredo," 366, and Xeravits, "The Reception of the Figure of David," 88.

[44] Don Harrán, ""What Does Halakhah Say about Music? Two Early Rabbinic Writings on Music by Hai b. Sherira," Hebrew Union College Annual 81 (2014): 49–87.

not fully clear on the use of the four key biblical instruments—kinnor, *nevel*, *toph*, and *ḥalil*—but nevertheless prohibits them on occasions when wine is drunk and bars women from playing them. Harrán also discusses the views of later *halakhic* authorities, such as Isaac Alfasi, Moses Maimonides, and Joseph Karo. These later authorities restate many of Hai's negative views, while similarly allowing for music at weddings. The sources agree that the content of the music matters and aim much of their concern at "frivolous" (i.e., non-religious) songs.

The musical practices of some Jewish communities may have impinged on these authoritative decisions. Joseph Tobi comments: "The practice of singing songs to instrumental accompaniment at social gatherings of the Jewish community, in both East and West, is well-documented in the *halakhic* responsa [of leading rabbis]."[45] In his essay, which analyzes references to music and musical instruments in Spanish medieval Hebrew poetry, Tobi observes: "The element of instrumental music returned to Hebrew poetry only in the 10th century, with the flowering of a new school that was greatly influenced by Arabic poetry."[46] This is especially true of "wine songs," poems chanted at parties where wine was drunk. Many of these poems, along with more religious ones, are imbued with allusions to musical instruments. Chief among them is the kinnor. Dumas b. Labrats (920–985), Solomon ibn Gabirol (1021–1070), Moses ibn Ezra (1055/1060–1138), Judah Halevi (1075–1141), and others speak of the kinnor in the course of their poems.

Dumas b. Labrats, the earliest of the Andalusian poets to write under the influence of Arabic poetry, describes a wine party in the garden of Chisdai ibn Shaprut, the Jewish vizier of Cordoba, in his poem *Ve-omer al tishan*. The kinnor is the first of several instruments mentioned in this celebration of the sounds of music:

> To the hum of fountain and the throbs of the lutes [*kinnorim*], to the sound of singers, flutes and lyres [*nevalim*]
> There every tree is tall, branches are fair with fruit, and winged birds of every kind sing among the leaves

---

[45] Tobi, *Between Hebrew and Arabic Poetry*, 149.

[46] In his very detailed discussion of pre-expulsion Iberian Jewish life, Edwin Seroussi remarks, "When it was chanted, secular strophic poetry in Hebrew might have been accompanied by musical instruments in unison." Edwin Seroussi, "Music in Medieval Ibero-Jewish Society," *Hispania Judaic* 5 (2007): 20.

The doves moan melodiously, and the turtle-doves reply, cooing like reed pipes [ḥalilim][47]

Solomon ibn Gabirol, in his wine poem *Yigzol shena*, also extolls wine and music. Allusions in the poem celebrate connections between music and the vine, and, like a biblical psalm, bring them together in rendering praise to God:

> Let us sing to the vine-shoot a song, and come! Let us bow-down to God and kneel to Him!
> We shall come out before Him with the lute [kinnor], like [the playing of] a pipe it shall make a doleful sound opposite the summer cloud, like the bellowing of an ox.
> The musicians have brought to my heart's desire! For they have made the musical note rest, opposite the note which moves!

Moshe ibn Ezra composed the first known Hebrew poem in praise of the oud, *Esh Qadechu*. It opens with the following:

> Play for me, minstrel, for you vanquish my thoughts of grief and sorrow
> Your lute [kinnor] is like a leg joined to the hip, without a thigh to divide them
> My heart leaps out to the lute's [kinnor's] stings — now some of them are in motion and some at rest.

The kinnor also served as a metaphor for addressing the pain of Israel's exile and the hope for return. Jewish mystical writings fixate on this theme and its reflection in the disruption of the universe. Judah Halevi, in his poem *Tsiyyon halo tishali* ("Zion will you not inquire about the fate of your captives"), alludes to Psalm 137, which recounts the exiles in Babylonia choosing not to play their *kinnorim* (pl.). Halevi imagines himself as a kinnor in the poem's opening verse: "My voice is like a jackal's when I mourn your suffering; But when I dream of how you will return, I turn into a kinnor."[48] Later Hebrew poetry and mystical thought builds on this imagery, connecting the longing for Zion, ending of exile, and joyous playing of the kinnor in a restored Jerusalem inhabited by the people of Israel.

---

[47] Tobi, *Between Hebrew and Arabic Poetry*, 151. All translations are from Tobi.
[48] Tobi, *Between Hebrew and Arabic Poetry*, 167.

These few examples demonstrate that the kinnor, understood as an oud by Andalusian poets, figured prominently in medieval Hebrew (and Arabic) thought of the region. Tobi concludes his discussion by noting:

> [N]otwithstanding the explicitly negative attitude towards music on the part of leading religious figures, particularly Maimonides, due to its supposedly destructive influence on ethical life, Jewish scholars and Hebrew poets in the medieval Muslim world did not refrain from writing about music in a positive manner....Nevertheless, one discerns certain social reservations regarding the fact that the one playing the instrument—whom in our day we would call a musician—was not from the highest level of Jewish society in the Muslim lands, as opposed to other poets and composers.[49]

Jewish philosophers and mystics also expressed their views on music in treatises, exegetical works, and liturgical creations. In this volume, Dov Schwartz discusses a number of such remarks with particular attention to the conceptual role of the kinnor. Schwartz explores these matters in greater depth in his Hebrew book, *Kinor Nishmati*.[50] Moshe Idel has produced several essays analyzing and sorting out diverse reflections on music found in Jewish mystical and philosophical texts from the Middle Ages to the early years of Hasidism.[51] Idel elucidates the different goals of musical thought and practice, including playing the kinnor and singing. Some saw music as a means of attaining mystical experiences, while others valued music for its magical or theurgical potency.

Both Idel and Schwartz, along with Harrán and Gianfranco Miletto, highlight Jews living in Italy during the Renaissance. Judah Moscato, an Italian preacher and kabbalist mentioned earlier, is a

---

[49] Tobi, *Between Hebrew and Arabic Poetry*, 189.

[50] Dov Schwartz, *Kinor Nishmati: HaMusika BeHagut HaYehudit* (Ramat Gan: Bar Ilan University Press, 2012) [Heb.].

[51] Moshe Idel, "Music and Prophetic Kabbalah," *Yuval: Studies of the Jewish Music Research Center* 4 (1982): 150–69; Moshe Idel, "The Magical and Theurgical Interpretations of Music from the Renaissance to Hasidism," *Yuval: Studies of the Jewish Music Research Center* 4 (1982): 33–62 [Heb.]; and Moshe Idel, "Music in Sixteenth Century Kabbalah in North Africa," *Yuval: Studies of the Jewish Music Research Center* 7 (2002): 154–70.

focal point of these expositions.[52] His sermon, *Higgayon BeKhinnor*, plays on the dual meaning of the word *higgayon*, which connotes the sounds of words and pitches, as well as reflections on such sounds. The sermon alludes to the *midrash* in which David, awakened by the sound of his kinnor played by the north wind, responds: "Awake my honor (*kevodi*)." Moscato understands this to mean: "Awake my soul, which as a lyre is prepared to receive the efflux of the divine spirit." Here, the kinnor and its strings serve as a metaphor for the interactive resonance between the supernal realm and the soul in this world. In subsequent eras, kabbalists, philosophers, and poets continued to rely on kinnor symbolism to express their place in the universe and to enrich the lives of readers.

Chapter Overviews

The chapters in this book attest to the kinnor's important place in history, thought, and culture. Jeremy Montagu offers an examination of the instrument itself, drawing on biblical and extra-biblical accounts to argue that the kinnor was, in fact, a lyre. Marvin A. Sweeney follows with an analysis of the kinnor as the Hebrew Bible's "divine instrument," played in liturgical and prophetic contexts to communicate between human beings and God. Jonathan L. Friedmann engages the biblical conception of the kinnor as an instrument of joy, grouping the references into five subcategories: tranquility, pleasure, gladness, excitement, and ecstasy. Joel Gereboff takes the discussion into the rabbinic realm, where the kinnor was not only conceived as a symbol of joy, but also of the future messianic era. Dov Schwartz surveys Jewish theological and philosophical views of the kinnor from various perspectives, including the Talmud, Kabbalah, Italian Renaissance sources, and modern-day Israeli discourse. Siobhán Dowling Long analyzes numerous artistic representations of David and his kinnor through the ages. Ruth Smith concludes the book with an examination of George Frideric Handel's symbolic representation of the kinnor in different works. These chapters are followed by an annotated bibliography, which lists one hundred books, articles, and chapters

---

[52] Harrán, "The Levi Dynasty," 161–97; Harrán, *Three Early Modern Hebrew Scholars on the Mystery of Song*, 47–128; and Gianfranco Miletto, "The Human Body as a Musical Instrument in the Sermons of Judah Moscato," *The Jewish Body: Corporality, Society and Identity in the Renaissance and Early Modern Period* (eds. Maria Diemling and Giuseppe Veltri; Leiden: Brill, 2009), 277–

addressing the kinnor and related lyres of the ancient world. The chapters and bibliography illustrate the continued significance of the kinnor, a long-silenced biblical instrument.

The Kinnor

Jeremy Montagu

The kinnor is the archetypal string instrument of the Bible. It permeates the Tanakh (Hebrew Bible) from Genesis 4:21 onwards, and in the New Testament appears both in First Corinthians 14:7 and near the end of Revelation (18:22).

So, what was the kinnor? Undoubtedly it was a lyre, the same sort of instrument as those that we see on ancient Greek vases and on statues of Apollo; the same sort but not the same shapes. This is a problem for us because we have no clear representations from the period of the Tanakh. The earliest we have are in mosaics from early synagogues of the first centuries CE and on coins of the Bar Kokhba Revolt of around 135 CE. There are some earlier Mesopotamian reliefs and there is an Egyptian wall painting of prisoners of war carrying a lyre, who may or may not have been Israelites; but we have no certainty for these.

We can say for certain that the kinnor had a body, usually of wood but perhaps sometimes of gourd, and that in ancient Greece, in its simplest form, it had a body of a tortoise shell and a skin belly as a soundboard, and that for serious music the Greeks also had larger lyres with bodies of wood. All of them had an arm reaching up on each side. The top of each arm was joined by a crossbar called a yoke, from which the strings descended, across a bridge on the soundboard, to the bottom of the body. The strings were plucked, either by a plectrum or by the player's fingers. The player could either pluck strings individually with both hands or strum across them with one hand from in front, while muting any unwanted strings with the fingers of the other hand from behind. We have illustrations on ancient Greek pots showing both techniques and, as we shall see, such techniques survive in Scandinavia, or did so until very recent times, and they still persist in East Africa today.

This was the instrument that Jubal was said to have played as the father of all who make music in Genesis 4:21. It wasn't a harp, it wasn't a psaltery; it was a lyre.

We meet the kinnor again in the first book of Samuel, in chapter 10, verse 5. It is there in an interesting context. The prophet Samuel had just chosen Saul and anointed him to be the first king of the Israelites, and had told him that, after two somewhat mystic encounters, he would meet a band of prophets playing the *nevel*, *toph*, *ḥalil*, and kinnor.

The *toph*, a frame drum like our tambourine, though without its jingles, had already been well-established in biblical contexts. It was often a woman's instrument, and thus it was played by Miriam and her ladies after the crossing of the Reed Sea (Exod 15:20). As we shall see, the kinnor must also have already been well-established. But the other two are new to us. The *ḥalil* was a woodwind instrument of some sort, but not the archetypal one that Jubal had played as well as the kinnor—that was the *ugav*. The other new instrument was the *nevel*, and this was also a lyre: a lower pitched one with a sack-shaped body and more and thicker strings than those of the kinnor, as we shall see in due course.

Where had the kinnor been all this time? While it may actually be unreasonable to trace it as far back as Cain's remote descendant Jubal, had it been one of the instruments of the Levites in the Tabernacle of the Exodus? It was certainly one of the Levitical instruments in Solomon's Temple two generations after Saul, and it was clearly David's instrument as a shepherd in the fields near Bethlehem. This is our next reference from 1 Samuel 16:16.

Saul was still king, even though the "Spirit of the Lord" had left him and he was prone to depression and fits of bad temper. His servants said to him: "Let us find a man who is a clever player on the kinnor, and then when you are in bad spirits he will play with his hand and you will be well." The prophet Samuel had already picked David out from all the sons of Jesse, so Saul's servants, who had probably been forewarned by Samuel to choose him, led him to Saul and "David took a kinnor and played with his hand, so Saul was refreshed and his evil spirits left him."

David had been a shepherd, and like all animal herdsmen he played music, not just to pass the time while alone on the hills, but because playing music soothes herds of animals and keeps them calm and contented. The singing cowboy is by no means a Hollywood myth; it has been true in all pastoral communities around the world. One could suspect that David's kinnor on the hills had been a simpler instrument than that which was thrust into his hands at Saul's court, but it would have been basically the same instrument, perhaps with a tortoise-shell body, like the simpler Greek *lyra*, or perhaps with a gourd body like those lyres that survive in East Africa today, with a skin belly. And this is likely where the lyre had been for all those past centuries, as a shepherd's instrument. Additionally, it was probably used as a bardic instrument, as it was for Homer to chant the *Iliad* and the *Odyssey*, and for itinerant musicians among the villages and towns, and for casual music, just as the guitar is with us for wandering musicians today.

One important detail is the emphasis that David played with his hand. While a plectrum will sweep the strings, plucking with the fingers is more delicate — much better for soothing King Saul, and better, too, for quiet music soothing the sheep. A bard would be more likely to play more strongly with a plectrum, partly so that a crowd in the village square could hear him, and partly to emphasize the dramatic accompaniment to his stories and his heroic lays. But David was chosen because he played "*b'yado*," with his hand.

The next reference, 2 Samuel 6:5, may perhaps tell us a little more about the kinnor, but, unfortunately, it is somewhat confusing. David was now the king and had taken Jerusalem as his capital, and he wanted to move the Ark of the Lord up to Jerusalem. So, he and all the house of Israel played before the Lord "on all manner of instruments made of wood of *roshim*, even on *kinnorot* and *nevalim*, *tuppim* and *mena'anim*." All of these words are plurals, suggesting that this was a large band. The first problem is what "wood of *roshim*" was. As so often with the Bible, we are uncertain; it may have been fir wood or it may have been cypress. Both of these are instrument-making woods, and these two are the common translations of *roshim*, but, nevertheless, they are guesswork. *Nevalim* we have met already, and also *tuppim*, the plural of *toph*, the frame drum. The last instrument, *mena'anim*, appears only this once in the Bible, so its meaning is obscure. However, the root of the word means shake or vibrate, so it was presumably some sort of rattle; it was not the cornets which the King James Bible (AV) translates it as.

Wood comes up again as the material for the kinnor in the next book of the Tanakh, after Solomon had succeeded David as king and had built both the Temple and his own palace. The Queen of Sheba came to visit him and brought gold and many exotic materials from East Africa. King Hiram of Tyre had also been down to that coast and had brought gold and also "almug" trees. "And the king made of the almug trees, pillars for the Temple and for his palace; *kinnorot* [pl.] also and *nevalim* [pl.] for singers" (I Kgs 10:12). The trouble is that neither we nor any other translators know what "*atsey almugim*" were. The AV simply uses almug as pseudo-English, and so does the New Revised Standard and, as the original text states, no more such trees were ever seen.

The books of Chronicles, which were written very much later, do amplify things and tell us much more of what went on in the Temple. These texts are somewhat problematic, though, for they tend to exaggeration as they try to show how much more wonderful and more impressive everything was in Jerusalem than in any other place. Even before Solomon built the Temple, King David spoke to the chief of the Levites to appoint their brethren to be the singers with musical instruments, *nevalim, kinnorot,* and cymbals, "to play and to sing with joy" (1 Chr 15:16).

There were two classes of priests, each of them the descendants of the tribe of Levi: the Kohanim, the descendants of Aaron, the brother of Moses, were the priesthood proper, and the Levites (Levi'im), who were the descendants of any of the other members of that tribe of Levi, were their assistants in the desert Tabernacle and later in the Temple. The priests, the Kohanim (Kohen in the singular, spelled Cohen more often as a name today) made the sacrifices, and the Levites did all the other work, including singing and playing the instruments.

1 Chronicles 15 goes on (vv. 19–22) to list the names of those who were singers, the three who played the cymbals, the eight who played *nevalim,* the six who played *kinnorot,* and their chief, Khenanyahu, who both sang and taught the others, because "he was skillful." Verse 24 also lists the seven who blew the silver trumpets. This was not what we would think of as a well-balanced band. It becomes even worse when King Solomon inaugurated the Temple, for in 2 Chronicles 5:12, there were singers, players of cymbals, *nevalim,* and *kinnorot,* and 120 priests blowing the silver trumpets, and, as the book goes on, the numbers ever increase.

Exaggeration or not, the text at least tells us that the Levites were musicians in the Temple, and also which instruments they played there: the kinnor, the *nevel,* the cymbals (*metzilta'im*), and the silver trumpets (*hatzotzerot*). At the end of Chronicles, and in Ezra and Nehemiah, we have further references to kinnor and *nevel*, and also interestingly to men and women singers, the latter presumably the daughters of Levites, something that would not be permitted in Orthodox synagogues today.

The kinnor, throughout all this Temple use, remained also a secular instrument, as it had been for David on the hills and at King Saul's court. This is confirmed for us in Job 21:12 and 30:31, where the kinnor is coupled with the *ugav*, that woodwind instrument which was the other musical archetype—that for all wind instruments—with Jubal in Genesis 4:21.

We now come to the Book of Psalms, which are referred to here by their number in the AV, for those are the same as in the Tanakh. (Those who read in the Vulgate, for example, will have to adjust to the preceding or succeeding psalm.) We do not know which psalms may or may not have been written by David himself, though many are attributed to him. Nor do we know which were sung in the Temple by the Levites, nor whether they were accompanied by the instruments, though, since the Levites were both singers and players of the instruments noted above, it would seem probable that they did sing psalms and accompany them with *kinnorot, nevalim*, and so on. One such psalm is number 30, for the dedication of the Temple, which is read near the beginning of every morning service in the synagogue to this day. Another, Psalm 136, is so obviously a call-and-response, that surely it must have been sung in the Temple. But others are less certain, partly because we cannot be sure that their incipits in the AV and their first verse in the Hebrew actually belonged to the psalm to which they are attached today. We do not know what the original order of the psalms was, nor indeed whether there was any standard order at all, before the order of our modern Tanakh was fixed by the Masoretes in the ninth century CE. It seems possible, too, as we can see in some other places in the Tanakh (Habakkuk, for example), that what appears as an incipit to a psalm today may have rather been the postscript to a preceding psalm, and we have no way to tell whether that preceding psalm was that which precedes it today. There is not even internal evidence in that group of psalms, the Psalms of Ascents (*Shirei ha-Ma'alot*), that it was actually those psalms that were sung on the steps leading up to the Temple, though we have long assumed that this was so.

However, we do have a number of psalms that mention the kinnor and the *nevel*, and we do have, as we shall see, so strong a traditional attribution to David that later mediaeval Christian iconography does almost invariably show King David tuning (more often than playing) a kinnor, very frequently combined with the B of *Beatus vir*, the first letter of Psalm 1 (a mistranslation, incidentally, of the Hebrew *Ashrei ha-ish*, "Happy the man," rather than *Beatus*, "Blessed the man").

The first psalm to mention the instruments is Psalm 33:2: "Praise the Lord with a kinnor, with a *nevel asor* sing to Him." This is our first reference to *asor*, and it is normally translated as ten-stringed. This is contrasted with Psalm 92:3: "the sound of the *asor*, the sound of the *nevel*, the sound of the music of the kinnor." This raises the question of whether *nevel asor* was one instrument or two, or whether this is a poetic duplication, as, for example, instead of *nevel asor* and kinnor, in Psalm 33, we might say "a scholar and a faithful pupil," and then in Psalm 92, "the faith, the pupil, and the learning of the scholar." My inclination is that it is such a poetic duplication, for we do have many references to *nevel asor* both in the Bible and later in the Talmud.

The Talmud does ask what the difference was between the two instruments: the kinnor and the *nevel asor*. In the Jerusalem Talmud (*Suk.* 5, 6), Rav Hiyya bar Abba says that the *nevel* and the kinnor are identical types of instrument (i.e., they are both lyres), the only difference being the larger number of strings, with the *nevel* having more strings than the kinnor. Rav Hunna says, in the name of Rav Joseph, that because the *nevel* was of untanned leather and had more strings, it used to put all other instruments to shame. The only useful information in the Babylonian Talmud comes from *Arakhin* 13b, where Rav Papa said that the two instruments are different, and that Rabbi Judah had said that the kinnor of the Temple had seven strings. However, because he goes on to say that the kinnor of the messianic age would have eight strings, and that in "the world to come" it would have ten and bases these numbers on selected irrelevant psalm and other numerical quotations, this is not really helpful.

Still, we can, I think, assume that the *nevel* did indeed have ten strings and that the kinnor had fewer, and seven is a likely number if—and this we do not know—they might then have had a seven-note scale as we do.

24

We do know more about the shapes of the instrument from coins of the Bar Kokhba rebellion. The kinnor had a slender and rather elegant body, whereas the *nevel* had a rather squat one that seemed to have resembled a sack. We also know from the Mishnah (*Kin.* 3:6) that the strings of the *nevel* were made from the large intestines and that those of the kinnor were made from the small intestines. This tells us that the *nevel* had thicker strings, and so a lower pitch than the kinnor, which had thinner strings and a higher pitch.

This is about as much as we do know of their physical characteristics. There are mosaics from the early Christian era, laid as synagogue floors, as noted earlier. No two are the same and some are quite clearly imaginary, as though the mosaicist had heard of the kinnor but had never actually seen one. It is probable that the mosaicists were specialists in laying the little stones to make patterns and pictures, rather than musicians, and that they often came from abroad and were not Jewish. Since most, and probably all, such mosaics were created after the destruction of the Temple and the laying waste of Jerusalem by the Romans, the departure from any probable reality is not surprising.

Returning to Psalms, there are a number of passing references which need not detain us. One that is perhaps worth mentioning is Psalm 137:2. This psalm is a part of the evidence that David did not write all the psalms, since it clearly dates from the time of the captivity in Babylon, several centuries after him, but it does have a link with him. Hanging the *kinnorot* on trees was a sign of mourning in that psalm, but when that is done, the wind will blow through them, softly sounding the strings—a gentle sigh of Israel sorrowing in its exile. One of the Talmudic legends is that David also hung up his kinnor overnight, and when the dawn breeze began, as it does on the hills in that climate, the sound of the kinnor singing to itself woke him each day in time to say his morning prayers.

The last three psalms are very specifically praises of God: Psalm 148 with all creation doing so; Psalm 149 with the people and especially the righteous; and in Psalm 150, the climax, with musicians leading everything that breathes in praise.

There are no further references of any significance in the Tanakh, save for the eternal problem of Nebuchadrezzar's orchestra in the book of Daniel, chapter 3. And this is the point where we must confront the problems of translation, for Daniel is not written in Hebrew; it is in Aramaic, the language that was spoken in Babylon and that became the common language in the land of Israel in the last few centuries BCE.

All our texts, save for the Tanakh in Hebrew and the Apocrypha in Greek, are translations; even the New Testament, which is in Greek, is thought likely to have had the Gospels, at least, originally in Aramaic before they were translated into Greek. There were two early translations of the Tanakh in the second century or so BCE, one into Greek for the communities in Hellenistic Egypt, known as the Septuagint or LXX for short, and the other, the Targum, into Aramaic (of which there are several different versions) for the local communities who had forgotten Hebrew. Then in Christian times came the Vulgate, the Latin translation made mostly by St. Jerome in the late fourth century. From this text stem all other translations before modern times, up to and even beyond the AV, though many of these translators did also look to the Greek and the Hebrew.

Returning to Daniel, we have to consider whether, despite the fact that the book was written some centuries after the events it purports to tell, any of the instrument names were those which might have been current in Nebuchadrezzar's time. Two are possible. The first, *karna*, is one of those few words which transcend the divide between the Semitic and the Indo-European language worlds (another of them is *sack*, a bag). *Karna* is *keren* in Hebrew, *keras* in Greek, *cornu* in Latin, horn in German and English, and is certainly here a horn. The other is *sab'cha*, a lyre in Assyrian and Aramaic. What of the others? None seems to relate to the *nevel*, so we might leave the rest of them were it not for the fact that two seem to resemble Greek. One of these is *kaithros*, a word that might have been an attempt at *kithara*, that word which the Septuagint and the New Testament consistently use for kinnor. The other is *p'santerin*, which seems to resemble Greek *psalterion*, the latter of which the LXX uses consistently for the *nevel*.

Turning now to the Apocrypha, the books of which may well have been written in Greek. (Even if some of them might originally have been in Hebrew or Aramaic, there is no trace of any version other than the Greek.) The only two references of any substance come in the first book of Maccabees. The first is from 4:54: Judas, then the leader of the Maccabees, had conquered the Greek armies and, having reoccupied Jerusalem, was preparing to rededicate the Temple "with songs and *citherns*, and harps, and cymbals." In the Greek we have *ōdais, kitharais, kinurais, kumbalois.* This immediately raises a problem. The Septuagint consistently translates the Hebrew kinnor as the Greek *kithara,* but here we have both *kitharais* (the plural) and *kinurais.* We can, I think, assume that the writer was referring back to normal Temple instruments, which would have been the kinnor and *nevel,* but it seems unlikely that the word *nevel* would have been forgotten. The Maccabees were, after all, Kohanim who had served in the Temple before it had been desecrated by the Greeks, so why they should have used two names for one instrument seems odd when describing the use of two instruments. This becomes especially so when we reach chapter 13, verse 51. The Temple had again been desecrated, and now Simon, the last of the Maccabean brothers and who had become the High Priest, was again rededicating it with "harps, and cymbals, and with viols and hymns, and songs": *kinurais, kumbalois, nablais, humnois, ōdais.* Here we do have the kinnor and the *nabla.* All that we can say is that the writer was a historian and not a musicologist!

At last we reach the New Testament. Here the only stringed instrument that is mentioned is the *kithara,* which, as we have already established, is the term invariably used both in the Septuagint and in the New Testament for the kinnor. There is a passing reference in 1 Corinthians 14:7, but it is only there to represent sound. Where we find the word again and again is in Revelation. In chapter 4, verse 4, there is a throne with round it twenty-four seats and sitting in each seat was an elder. In 5:8 those twenty-four elders fall down before the Lamb, having every one of them *kitharan* and golden vials. It is these elders that we see carved round the porticos of many churches in Spain, Portugal, and southern France, each of them sitting with a vial, a jar or vase, in one hand, and in the other hand a musical instrument. On some of these porticos, each is holding a similar instrument, usually a small fiddle such as a rebec, but in others there is a wide variety of instruments in their hands.

In Revelation, the English word for the *kithara* in the AV is invariably "harps," while in other earlier books of the Bible there is some variation, though in the majority of cases the kinnor is normally translated as harp. This is, as we shall see, because of the link with King David, who by that time was always portrayed with a harp, as he had been for some five centuries before that translation, which dates from the early 1600s.

In chapter 14, verse 2, we read: "I heard the voice of harpers (*kitharōdōn*) harping (*kitharazonton*) with their harps (*kitharais*)"; in 15:2 we have harps of God; and, finally, in 18:22 we have the fall of Babylon and, with it, the end of the voice of harpers, musicians, pipers, and trumpeters.

Thus, from the beginning to the end of the Bible, we have the kinnor/*kithara*, first as the emblem of the first of all musicians, then of King David, then of the Levites, and finally of the Elders of the Apocalypse and the harps of God.

It is clear that the kinnor/*kithara* is the great emblem of music, so why did it, in most translations, change from its original meaning of a lyre to that of a harp? Quite simply because of a change in musical fashion and taste. The lyre was in ancient times the great instrument of music and song. In Greek legend, it was invented by Hermes, the messenger of the gods, stolen from him by Apollo, used by Homer and all the other bards to accompany their lays, just as it was by David to his sheep, to King Saul, and to accompany his psalms, taught to all children in schools in Athens, played by Nero while Rome burned, and carried to Byzantium where Constantine established Christianity as the state religion of the Roman Empire.

In Byzantium, the most trusted soldiers were the Norse, those great warriors, some of them Vikings, who traveled down through what was to become Russia to Byzantium in search of lucrative employment. It was they, who returning home after their years of duty, carried the lyre back through Novgorod and Danzig, where early medieval examples have been found, and home to Scandinavia where various forms of the lyre are still played. It spread through Germany as well, where the single survivor of the early medieval lyre was the so-called Alemannic lyre. This was destroyed in Berlin during the Second World War, but it served as the model for the British Museum's reconstruction of the sixth-century Anglo-Saxon lyre that was found in the great ship burial at Sutton Hoo. It spread even further to Wales, where a bowed lyre, the *crwth*, was still being played into the eighteenth century.

It is this lyre, usually plucked but occasionally bowed, that can be seen in the illuminations of early psalters, often tuned or played by King David. However, by the twelfth century the harp was becoming more fashionable, and by the thirteenth century the lyre was pretty well extinct. One of the problems in trying to sort out why this was is the instrument's name: the lyre was, in Anglo-Saxon and in Early English, called the *hearpe*, and the name stuck even when the instrument changed its shape. So, this is why our English Bibles almost all use the word "harp" for the kinnor.

The Kinnor in the Bible
Instrument of the Divine

Marvin A. Sweeney

I. Introduction

The kinnor (*kinnôr*), often translated as "harp" or "lyre," is perhaps the best-known musical instrument in the Hebrew Bible. Josephus describes the kinnor as a ten-stringed instrument that is played with a bow (*Ant.* 7.305; 7.12.3), although its construction varied, and it could be played by plucking its strings with the fingers or plectrum as well. Indeed, the ubiquitous presence and reputation of kinnor in the Bible and later in Jewish history is such that it has come to be recognized as the national instrument of modern Israel, although the modern Hebrew word has now come to mean "violin."[1]

Despite its association with the Jewish people, the kinnor is attested throughout the ancient Near Eastern world well before ancient Israel and Judah were formed at the beginning of the Iron Age, ca. 1200 B.C.E.[2] The earliest known reference to the kinnor appears in the Mari archives in a letter from Mukannišum to King Zimri-Lim of Mari in which he employs the Akkadian term, *giškinnarātim*, a plural form of *giškinnaru*, "lyre." The Hurrian term, *kinnaruḫli*, denotes a "lyre player," and the Ugaritic term, *knr*, likewise denotes a "lyre." Forms of the term appear in early Aramaic (*knr*) and Phoenician (*kinnûr*), as well as in all later forms of the Semitic languages with the exception of Ethiopic (e.g., Jewish

---

[1] See Ludwig Koehler and Walter Baumgartner, *The Hebrew and Aramaic Lexicon of the Old Testament* (Leiden: Brill, 1995), 2:484; Reuben Alcalay, *The Complete Hebrew-English Dictionary* (Ramat-Gan and Jerusalem: Massada, n.d.), 1038; and Avraham Even-Shoshan, ed., *Ha-Millon Ha-'Ivri HaMrukaz* (Jerusalem: Kiriyat Sepher, 1988), 299 [Heb.].

[2] For surveys of the usage of cognate terminology in ancient Near Eastern and other texts, see M. Görg, "כִּנּוֹר, Kinnôr," *Theological Dictionary of the Old Testament* (eds. G. J. Botterweck et al.; Grand Rapids, MI: Eerdmans, 1995), 7:197–203; Koehler and Baumgartner, *The Hebrew and Aramaic Lexicon of the Old Testament*, 2:484.

Aramaic, *kinnārā'*, Syriac, *kennāarā'*, and Arabic, *kannārat* and *kinnārat*). As a loanword, it appears in non-Semitic languages as well, including Egyptian (*knwrw*), Coptic (*ginēra, genēre*), Hittite (*lukinirtalla*), Sanskrit (*kinnarî*), and Greek (*kinúra, kinnúras*). The origins of the term are uncertain, but it appears likely that it originated in the Semitic languages from which it was then incorporated into the non-Semitic languages mentioned here.

Although the term and the instrument were widely known throughout the ancient world both prior to and following the periods of the ancient Israelite and Judean monarchies, references to the kinnor in the Bible indicate that the instrument could play a very common role as a musical instrument. But a number of texts indicate that the kinnor played a very special role as an instrument associated especially with the divine. A survey of the usage of the term, *kînnôr*, in the Bible will demonstrate these roles. Discussion will include instances of the term in the narrative literature of the Pentateuch, where Jubal is identified in Genesis 4:21 as the inventor of the instrument, and the Former Prophets, where it is played by a band of roaming prophets in 1 Samuel 10:5, David in his efforts to relieve the distressed Saul in 1 Samuel 16:16–23, and perhaps in relation to Elisha's prophecy concerning Moab when he requests a musician in 2 Kings 3 to accompany his prophecies. The term also appears frequently in the Poetic and Narrative literature of the Latter Prophets, where it appears at various points in Isaiah, such as his oracles against the allegedly corrupt leadership of the nation in Isaiah 5 and the metaphorical portrayal of a prostitute to advertise her profession in Isaiah 23; and the Writings, especially throughout the Psalms and the Chronicles where it is employed for the performance of the Temple liturgy.

Examination of these key texts indicates that the kinnor in the Bible functions as an instrument of the divine, insofar as its application represents a primary means to give expression to the voice of the divine and the voice of the people when addressing the divine.

II. The Narrative Literature of the Pentateuch and Former Prophets

The first instance of the Hebrew word, *kinnôr*, in the Bible appears in Genesis 4:21, which identifies Jubal ben Lamech, born to Lamech's wife, Adah, as the inventor of the kinnor, "lyre," and the *ugav*, "pipe," the two major stringed and wind instruments of ancient Israel and Judah and perhaps the ancient Near Eastern world at large. Most interpreters recognize this statement to be a part of the larger text in Genesis 4:17–26, which relates the initial descendants of Adam and Eve, who originated many of the early social patterns and cultural inventions of humanity, such as city and nomadic life, musical instruments, and metal implements, and thereby became the early cultural heroes of the world.[3] Genesis 4:17–26 is generally viewed as the product of the J source of the Pentateuch, which was formerly considered to be the earliest stage of the literary composition of the Pentateuch, although more recent scholarship has recognized that Assyrian and Babylonian influence indicates that its origins are to be found in the late-monarchic or early-exilic periods.[4] When read in the context of the Pentateuch's presentation of Human Origins in Genesis 2:4–4:26, this segment points to the earliest achievement of human beings, whom G-d had blessed and declared to be very good in Genesis 1:26–31.[5] Such achievement was therefore presented in the final form of the Genesis narrative as in keeping with divine intentions in the creation of the world with humans at its center. Although many interpreters maintain that Eve's eating of the fruit of the tree in the Garden of Eden in Genesis 3 constitutes an original sin, they generally overlook the fact that Eve is the one who introduces the knowledge of good and evil to humanity, and the early cultural heroes noted in Genesis 4:17–26 exhibit traits of the knowledge of good rather than of evil. The invention of musical instruments, such as the kinnor, thereby gives humanity the capacity to express itself in extraordinary form, which will later be recognized in the Bible as the means to communicate with and to hear the expression of the divine.[6]

---

[3] E.g., Claus Westermann, *Genesis 1–11: A Commentary* (Continental Commentary; Minneapolis: Augsburg, 1984), 321–344 and Nahum Sarna, *Genesis* (JPS Torah Commentary; Philadelphia: Jewish Publication Society, 1989/5749), 35–40.

[4] Antony F. Campbell and Mark A. O'Brien, *Sources of the Pentateuch: Texts, Introductions, Annotations* (Minneapolis: Fortress, 1993), 94–95, 261; cf. Thomas B. Dozeman, *The Pentateuch: Introducing the Torah* (Minneapolis: Fortress, 2017), 135–199; Marvin A. Sweeney, *The Pentateuch* (Core Biblical Studies; Nashville, TN: Abingdon, 2017), xvii–xxix.

[5] See Sweeney, *The Pentateuch*, xxvii–xxix.

[6] The reference to the kinnor in Gen 31:27 simply relates Laban's professed intention to send off Jacob and his family from Aram with rejoicing and music,

First Samuel 10:5 presents the second major reference to the kinnor to be considered, where it functions as a means for Samuel to inform Saul that he will encounter a band of prophets at Giveat ha-Eloqim, presumably Gibeon, whose music and ecstatic prophesying will confirm the divine selection of Saul as the first King of Israel. The verse is part of the larger narrative in 1 Samuel 9:1–10:16, which presents an early account concerning the unexpected selection of Saul as King when he goes out in quest of his father's lost asses, but finds instead by means of the priest and prophet, Samuel, that he will become King of Israel. Although the narrative appears within the narrative segment of 1 Samuel 8–12, which has been heavily edited by the Deuteronomistic historians to portray Saul as an unfit King, it apparently originated during the reign of Saul to identify him as YHWH's first choice to become King of Israel.[7] Within this context, the association between the prophets' playing of musical instruments, including the kinnor, and their uttering ecstatic prophecy, constitutes evidence that they speak on behalf of YHWH, and Samuel's instruction to Saul in the narrative thereby confirms Samuel's authorization to speak on behalf of YHWH as well. The narrative does not state that the prophets will confirm YHWH's choice of Saul with their own prophesying, but it nevertheless associates the narrative portrayal of the kinnor with the phenomenon of prophecy in ancient Israel which functions as a means to convey the words of the divine.

First Samuel 16:23 narrates how David would take up the kinnor and play for Saul at times when the King suffered from what the narrative describes as "an evil spirit from YHWH" in 1 Samuel 16:14. The verse appears in the context of 1 Samuel 16:14–23, which functions together with 1 Samuel 16:1–13 and 1 Samuel 17:1–58 as one of three episodes that introduce David to the reader as the next King of Israel in place of Saul. Within the larger framework of the DtrH, these narratives serve as the introduction to the so-called History of David's Rise in 1 Samuel 16–2 Samuel 8, which recount

---

ostensibly to indicate his support and high esteem.

   [7] For discussion of the Deuteronomistic History, see Martin Noth, *The Deuteronomistic History* (Journal for the Study of the Old Testament Supplement Series 15; Sheffield: Journal for the Study of the Old Testament Press, 1981), esp. 54–62; Marvin A. Sweeney, *King Josiah of Judah: The Lost Messiah of Israel* (Oxford: Oxford University Press, 2001), 33–177, esp. 110–24; cf. Thomas Römer, *The So-Called Deuteronomistic History: A Sociological, Historical, and Literary Introduction* (London: T & T Clark, 2007), esp. 91–97.

David's rise to power as the King of Israel with the blessing and support of YHWH.[8] The purpose of these narratives also includes attempts to undermine Saul by demonstrating that he is not fit to serve as King. In 1 Samuel 16:14–23, the narrative depicts Saul as afflicted by an evil spirit from YHWH, which moderns might readily attribute to manic-depressive behavior. Saul has every reason to be depressed. His primary task as King of Israel is to defend the nation against its enemies — the primary enemy being the Philistines — and throughout the accounts of his reign he fails at every turn, culminating in his defeat and suicide in battle against the Philistines at Mt. Gilboa in 1 Samuel 30–31. Throughout the narratives, Saul is portrayed as an incompetent leader and military commander who is continually surpassed by his own son, Jonathan, and his son-in-law, David. The narrative in 1 Samuel 16:14–23 portrays David as someone who can relieve Saul's depression by the playing of the kinnor. Insofar as David's playing of the kinnor relieves the so-called evil spirit from YHWH, the kinnor becomes the means to reverse the effects of the evil spirit from YHWH on Saul. By countering the effects of the evil spirit from YHWH, the kinnor thereby functions as an instrument of the divine to relieve YHWH's attempt to afflict Saul.

Second Samuel 6:5 refers to the kinnor as one of the musical instruments that is played to accompany the journey of the Ark of the Covenant of YHWH from its resting place at Kiriath-Jearim in the territory of Benjamin following its capture by the Philistines during the battle with Israel at Aphek years before. The verse appears in the context of 2 Samuel 6, which functions as the concluding episode of the so-called Ark Narrative in 1 Samuel 4–6; 2 Samuel 6, which recounts how the Ark of the Covenant, signifying the divine presence of YHWH, moved from the sanctuary at Shiloh during the time of Samuel to Jerusalem during the reign of David, when David reunited the tribes of Israel and established his capital at Jerusalem. The Ark Narrative is understood to be an independent account that was ultimately incorporated into the DtrH as part of the means to recount David's rise to power.[9] When read in context,

---

[8] See Jakob H. Grønbæk, *Die Geschichte vom Aufstieg Davids (1. Sam. 15–2 Sam. 5). Tradition und Komposition* (Acta Theologica Danica X; Copenhagen: Munksgaard, 1971); cf. Antony F. Campbell, S.J., *1 Samuel* (Forms of the Old Testament Literature 7; Grand Rapids, MI and Cambridge, UK: Eerdmans, 2003), esp. 1–21, 134–93.

[9] Antony F. Campbell, *The Ark Narrative (1 Sam 4–6; 2 Sam 6): A Form-Critical and*

the reference to the playing of the kinnor and the other musical instruments that accompanied the journey of the Ark to its new home in Jerusalem is intended to convey the celebration of the people of Israel as they return the Ark to full Israelite control and prepare for its function as the representation of the holy presence of YHWH in Jerusalem, thereby identifying the city as the new holy city of Israel and Judah. Although the Samuel narrative does not identify the music that is played, the Chronicler's account in 1 Chronicles 16 (see esp. verse 5), indicates that the people played Hymns of Praise, including elements from Psalms 96; 105; and 106, as examples of the music that would have been played. Chronicles is a priestly history of Israel from creation through the reign of Cyrus the Great of Babylon that often attempts to correct problems in the earlier DtrH and focuses especially on the role of the Jerusalem Temple in the history of Israel. Although readers will never know if these psalms were actually played at the time, the Chronicler's intent is to illustrate the holy procession with an appropriate portrayal of how the holy Ark of the Covenant should have taken place. In doing so, it points to the kinnor and the other instruments as means to give expression to the liturgical expression of the voice of the people to YHWH, indicating that the kinnor is once again an instrument of the divine.

First Kings 10:12 notes that Solomon used almug wood for the decoration of the Temple and the royal palace as well as to construct musical instruments, including the kinnor, for the musicians who would have played in the Temple and elsewhere. Insofar as the passage is part of the Queen of Sheba narrative in 1 Kings 10, intended to demonstrate Solomon's wealth and power, its association with the Temple is incidental, but it nevertheless demonstrates the role of the kinnor in relation to the Temple and therefore its role as an instrument of the divine.

The final narrative to be considered in the Pentateuch and Former Prophets is 2 Kings 3, which recounts the invasion of Moab by an allied coalition including King Jehoram ben Ahab of Israel, King Jehoshaphat ben Asa of Judah, and an unnamed King of Edom to attack King Mesha of Moab who had rebelled against Israel. The

Tradition-Historical Study (Society of Biblical Literature Dissertation Series 16; Missoula, MT: Scholars Press, 1975); idem, *1 Samuel*, 60–84; idem, *2 Samuel* (Forms of the Old Testament Literature 8; Grand Rapids, MI, and Cambridge, UK: Eerdmans, 2005), 53–86.

narrative is part of the early Dynastic History of the House of Jehu in 1 Kings 12–2 Kings 14, which included the narratives concerning the prophets Elijah and Elisha of Israel in 1 Kings 16–2 Kings 13. The Jehu Dynastic History was later incorporated into the DtrH.[10] As the allied coalition journeys through the wilderness of Edom along the southern edges of the Dead Sea to attack Mesha from the south, King Jehoshaphat of Judah proposed that a prophet be asked to inquire of YHWH concerning the success of their undertaking, particularly since the region lacked water for the men and their animals. The prophet Elisha had accompanied the expedition, but at first he demurred from speaking an oracle and demanded that the King of Israel get his own prophets to perform the task much as his father Ahab had done in 1 Kings 22. But due to their continued urging and his respect for King Jehoshaphat, Elisha agreed to undertake the oracular inquiry provided that a musician might accompany his words. The result was an oracle that promised water for the army and victory over Moab, both of which were realized in the narrative. But Israel ultimately withdrew in disgust when Mesha reportedly sacrifices his own first-born son as an offering to his god. The narrative never mentions the kinnor as the instrument played by the musician, but it nevertheless illustrates the role of musical instruments in the prophet's attempt to inquire of YHWH. In keeping with earlier observations concerning the role of multiple musical instruments to express human communication with YHWH, the kinnor would be but one of the instruments of the divine.

III. The Poetic and Narrative Literature of the Latter Prophets and the Writings

The term, *kinnôr*, appears frequently in the Latter Prophets and the Writings. It is clear, however, that the references in the Latter Prophets focus on the non-religious use of the instrument, whereas the citations in the Writings tend to support the hypothesis that the kinnor is an instrument intended to express the divine.

The Latter Prophets include five citations in Isaiah, all in the first part of the book, and one in Ezekiel. For the most part, they present a non-religious or what moderns might consider a secular

---

[10] Marvin A. Sweeney, *1 and 2 Kings: A Commentary* (Old Testament Library; Louisville, KY: Westminster John Knox, 2007), 26–30, 276–84.

understanding of the term and its function. Isaiah 5:12 appears as part of Isaiah's Woe oracle sequence in Isaiah 5:8–30, which is designed to condemn the powerful in Israel and Judah and those who doubt the power of YHWH to do justice and defend the nation.[11] Here, the kinnor is one of the instruments played to entertain those who drink a lot of wine at their banquets, but never give any thought to the work of YHWH in the world. Isaiah 16:11 refers to the kinnor as an instrument that will be played in relation to mourning over the destruction of Moab in Isaiah 15–16.[12] Isaiah 23:16 portrays a prostitute playing the kinnor as she goes about in search of customers to portray Tyre metaphorically when she is restored and in search of trade in Isaiah 23.[13] Isaiah 24:8 depicts the cessation of celebration with music, including the kinnor, when the earth languishes in drought due to the alleged violation of the covenant with YHWH by the people in Isaiah 24:1–23.[14] Isaiah 30:32, an apparently difficult verse to understand, depicts YHWH's punishment of Assyria with the celebration of musical instruments, including the kinnor for its maltreatment of Zion in Isaiah 30.[15] At least in this case, kinnor gives voice to hymns of praise for YHWH in the context of battle. Finally, Ezekiel 26:13 refers to the kinnor in announcing the end of music when Tyre is destroyed in Ezekiel 26.[16]

The thirteen references to the kinnor in Psalms demonstrate the role of the instrument in giving voice to the people at times of worship in the Jerusalem Temple and perhaps elsewhere. Such a role is particularly important insofar as Psalms is a key work in which the people address YHWH with praise, complaint, thanksgiving, and lament, indicating the kinnor's function as an instrument of the divine. Ps 33:2 names the kinnor in the context of

---

[11] Marvin A. Sweeney, *Isaiah 1–39, with an Introduction to Prophetic Literature* (Forms of the Old Testament Literature 16; Grand Rapids, MI, and Cambridge, UK: Eerdmans, 1996), 121–130.

[12] Sweeney, *Isaiah 1–39*, 240–52.

[13] Sweeney, *Isaiah 1–39*, 302–11.

[14] Sweeney, *Isaiah 1–39*, 325–33.

[15] Sweeney, *Isaiah 1–39*, 386–401; for discussion of the role of instruments in YHWH's battle against Assyria, see Willem A. M. Beuken, *Isaiah II: Isaiah 28–39* (Historical Commentary on the Old Testament; Leuven: Peeters, 2000), 184–86. One might consider the potential role of hymns of praise to YHWH, e.g., Exodus 15 or Deborah 5, in battle or the playing of bagpipes by the British army when marching into battle.

[16] Marvin A. Sweeney, *Reading Ezekiel: A Literary and Theological Commentary* (Reading the Old Testament; Macon, GA: Mercer University Press, 2013), 132–35.

a community hymn of praise to YHWH in Psalm 33.[17] Ps 43:4 names the kinnor in the context of an individual complaint in Psalms 42–43 in which the psalmist asks for relief from distress while expressing the desire to approach YHWH's altar with praise accompanied by the kinnor.[18] Ps 49:5 presents a proposal to play the kinnor in the context of a Meditation and Instruction on the part of the psalmist who, in a manner much like Qohelet, reminds his listeners that wealth and honor are wonderful, but one will ultimately reside in Sheol.[19] Ps 57:9 proposes a hymn of praise accompanied by the kinnor for YHWH in the context of a Complaint asking for divine mercy and deliverance in Psalm 57.[20] Ps 71:22 proposes to respond to YHWH's deliverance with song and the playing of the kinnor in the context of a Complaint in Psalm 71.[21] Ps 81:3 calls upon the people to sing with instrumentation, including the kinnor, as YHWH presents a divine oracle to the people in Psalm 81, which apparently relates the setting in which oracular prophecy is heard.[22] Ps 92:4 calls for the singing of hymns accompanied by the kinnor and other instruments to celebrate the Shabbat at a time when the Temple was standing.[23] Ps 98:5 calls for the playing of the kinnor and trumpets to accompany a hymn to celebrate YHWH's kingship in Psalm 98.[24] Ps 108:3 calls for the playing of the kinnor and the harp to accompany a hymn to YHWH to plead for assistance from YHWH against enemies in a complaint in Psalm 108.[25] Ps 137:2 depicts the people hanging up their *kinnōrôt* in sorrow when their captives demand that they sing songs of Zion while in Babylonian captivity in the community complaint in Psalm 137.[26] Ps 147:7 calls for a hymn of praise to YHWH at the time of the rebuilding of

---

[17] Erhard S. Gerstenberger, *Psalms, Part 1, with an Introduction to Cultic Poetry* (Forms of the Old Testament Litrature 14; Grand Rapids, MI: Eerdmans, 1988), 143–46.

[18] Gerstenberger, *Psalms, Part 1*, 178–82.

[19] Gerstenberger, *Psalms, Part 1*, 202–07.

[20] Gerstenberger, *Psalms, Part 1*, 229–32.

[21] Erhard S. Gerstenberger, *Psalms, Part 2, Lamentations* (Forms of the Old Testament Literature 15; Grand Rapids, MI, and Cambridge, UK: Eerdmans, 2001), 58–64.

[22] Gerstenberger, *Psalms 2*, 107–13.

[23] Gerstenberger, *Psalms 2*, 168–73.

[24] Gerstenberger, *Psalms 2*, 195–98.

[25] Gerstenberger, *Psalms 2*, 253–56.

[26] Gerstenberger, *Psalms 2*, 290–306.

Jerusalem in Psalm 147.[27] Ps 149:3 likewise calls for the kinnor to accompany dance and song in praise of YHWH in Psalm 149.[28] And finally, Ps 150:3 concludes Psalms with calls to praise YHWH accompanied by song, dance, and instrumental music, including the kinnor in Psalm 150.[29] Every citation of the kinnor in the Psalms points to the role of the instrument as a means to address YHWH or to hear directly from the divine.

Only two references to the kinnor appear in the wisdom literature in the Book of Job. Job is mundane in his response to Zophar the Naamathite in Job 21:12, where he refers to song, dance, and instrumentation of the wicked as they celebrate by ignoring YHWH.[30] But Job 30:31 expresses Job's frustration with his lot when he devotes his kinnor and his pipe to mourning in his final response to his three friends in Job 29–31.[31]

The references to kinnor in Nehemiah and Chronicles once again point to the instrument as the means to address the divine. Nehemiah 12:27 refers to the kinnor among the instruments played by the Levites at the dedication of the newly rebuilt Jerusalem wall.[32] Like 2 Samuel 6:5, 1 Chronicles 13:8 refers to David and all Israel dancing before the Ark to the music of the kinnor and other instruments as the Ark was carried to its new location in Jerusalem.[33] First Chronicles 15:16, 21, 25, and 16:5 refer to the kinnor repeatedly in the account of David's appointment of the Levitical musicians who will play in the Temple before YHWH and the people.[34] First Chronicles 25:1, 3, and 6 again refers to the kinnor repeatedly in the account of David's appointment of the Sons of Asaph, Heman, and Jeduthun, who will prophesy to the accompaniment of music on behalf of YHWH before the people in the Temple, again indicating the role of the kinnor as an instrument

---

[27] Gerstenberger, *Psalms 2*, 442–47.

[28] Gerstenberger, *Psalms 2*, 452–57.

[29] Gerstenberger, *Psalms 2*, 458–61.

[30] Norman Habel, *Job: A Commentary* (Old Testament Library; Philadelphia: Westminster, 1985), 320–30.

[31] Habel, *Job*, 413–22.

[32] Joseph Blenkinsopp, *Ezra-Nehemiah: A Commentary* (Old Testament Library; Philadelphia: Westminster, 1988), 344.

[33] Sara Japhet, *1 and 2 Chronicles: A Commentary* (Old Testament Library; Louisville: Westminster John Knox, 1993), 279–80.

[34] Japhet, *1–2 Chronicles*, 302–04, 314–15.

of the divine.[35] Second Chronicles 5:12 shows the Levitical singers in action with the kinnor as they celebrate Sukkot before the Ark of the Covenant during the reign of Solomon in 2 Chronicles 5:2–6:2.[36] Second Chronicles 9:11 repeats the earlier reference in 1 Kings 10:11–12 concerning the almug wood used to make musical instruments, such as the kinnor, brought by the Queen of Sheba to King Solomon.[37] Second Chronicles 20:28 refers to the kinnor as one of the instruments played on the journey of the men of Jerusalem and Judah to the Jerusalem Temple following King Jehoshaphat's defeat of Edom in the Valley of Blessing according to 2 Chronicles 20.[38] And finally, 2 Chronicles 29:25 refers to King Hezekiah's stationing of the Levitical musicians with their instruments, including the kinnor, as part of his Temple purging in 2 Chronicles 29.[39] Although some of these references indicate mundane usage of the kinnor, most demonstrate the liturgical usage of the instrument, thereby pointing to the kinnor as an instrument of the divine.

IV. Conclusion

The kinnor is perhaps the most ubiquitous musical instrument of ancient Israel and Judah, so much so that it now functions as a national symbol of the Jewish people. As the above discussion shows, it functions not only in mundane settings of celebration, drunkenness, and even prostitution, but it serves most prominently in the liturgical and prophetic realms in which it gives expression to communication by humans with YHWH and by YHWH with humans. It thereby functions as an instrument of the divine. May its music speak forever to the ongoing relationship between G-d and the Jewish people.

---

[35] Japhet, *1–2 Chronicles*, 435–439; on the role of Temple Levites as prophets, see David L. Petersen, *Late Israelite Prophecy* (Society of Biblical Literature Monograph Series 23; Missoula, MT: Scholars Press, 1977), 55–87.

[36] Japhet, *1–2 Chronicles*, 572–81.

[37] Japhet, *1–2 Chronicles*, 638.

[38] Japhet, *1 and 2 Chronicles*, 780–803.

[39] Japhet, *1 and 2 Chronicles*, 910–32.

The Character of the Kinnor
An Instrument of Joy

Jonathan L. Friedmann

This chapter reevaluates the common conception of the kinnor as an instrument of joy. Although the generalization is well-founded, it overlooks the various types and levels of positive emotions associated with the kinnor in the Hebrew Bible. The forty-two occurrences of the instrument suggest a nuanced typology comprising five subcategories or "shades" of joy: tranquility, pleasure, gladness, excitement, and ecstasy. These categories are examined below, along with the challenges of reading modern understandings of emotions into the Bible and relying on biblical texts to ascertain responses of ancient listeners.

Deciphering the Kinnor

The exploration of music in the Hebrew Bible is a silent endeavor. With the exception of the shofar, an organic signal horn blown since ancient times,[1] the lack of details concerning the construction, performance, tuning, and timbres of biblical instruments has made their identification notoriously difficult. Despite the discovery of numerous Near Eastern artifacts, including reliefs, murals, figurines, seals, carvings, mosaics, coins, and occasional instruments (esp., bone flutes, clay rattles, and small metal cymbals and bells), debate surrounds linking these artifacts to biblical terms and matching biblical instruments with evidence spanning such a large timeframe (Bronze Age, 3200–1200 BCE, to the Hellenistic-Roman period, fourth century BCE to fourth century CE).[2] Sophisticated reconstructions notwithstanding, the skeptical

---

[1] For the shofar's multifaceted role in ritual practice, textual traditions, and cultural imagination, see Jonathan L. Friedmann and Joel Gereboff, eds., *Qol Tamid: The Shofar in Ritual, History, and Culture* (Claremont: Claremont Press, 2017).

[2] It is tempting to fall back on the notion of the "eternal East" when imagining artifacts of the ancient Near East. Although the region may have been conservative in its customs and institutions, musical instruments were likely subject to more frequent modifications and embellishments. The basic types persisted for long

observer minimally concedes that biblical instruments bore a family resemblance to roughly contemporaneous instruments found elsewhere in the region.[3]

The biblical authors apparently considered musical information to be unnecessary. As Alfred Sendrey and Mildred Norton explain in their book, *David's Harp* (the title of which misidentifies David's instrument as a harp, although the book itself describes it as a lyre): "The biblical chroniclers wrote for a contemporary audience. It never occurred to them that 3,000 years later people would be trying to puzzle out the meaning of musical terms that to them were household words.... Nowhere is it described."[4] The disinclination to record musical minutia is not unique to the distant past. Even today, the experiential nature of music makes description seem superfluous. According to Joachim Braun, an Israeli musicologist who specializes in the archeology and iconography of ancient Israel/Palestine, "musical periods documented much more richly than those of the ancient world can leave us in uncertainty. How were Beethoven's works actually performed? How were the harmony and melody of Corelli's *basso continuo* realized? What was the correct interpretation of neumatic systems?"[5]

---

periods, but their features were not static. Alfred Sendrey, *Music in Ancient Israel* (New York: Philosophical Library, 1969), 270.

[3] See Richard J. Dumbrill, *The Archaeomusicology of the Ancient Near East* (Victoria, BC: Trafford, 2005). For a comparative analysis of archaeological findings, see Bo Lawergren, "Distinctions between Canaanite, Philistine, and Israelite Lyres, and Their Global Lyrical Contexts," *Bulletin of the American Schools of Oriental Research* 309 (1998): 41–68. Biblical instruments conform to the four categories of the Hornbostel-Sachs system: idiophones (percussion instruments with vibrating bodies), membranophones (drums with membranes), chordophones (string instruments), and aerophones (wind instruments). Erich Moritz von Hornbostel and Curt Sachs, "Systematik der Musikinstrumente," *Zeitschrift für Ethnologie* 46 (1914): 553–90. Sachs added a fifth category, electrophone, in 1940.

[4] Alfred Sendrey and Mildred Norton, *David's Harp: The Story of Music in Biblical Times* (New York: New American Library, 1964), 113. Physical differences between the harp and lyre should be noted. The arms of a harp are angular and connect at the point. The strings are attached to the arms and shorten in length as they approach the connecting points of the angle. In contrast, the arms of the lyre are parallel, forming a U-shape, with a crossbar across the top between the two arms. Theodore W. Burgh, *Listening to the Artifacts: Music Culture in Ancient Palestine* (New York: T & T Clark, 2006), 110.

[5] Joachim Braun, *Music in Ancient Israel/Palestine: Archaeological, Written, and Comparative Sources* (tr. Douglas W. Stott; Grand Rapids: Wm. B. Eerdmans, 2002),

Musical materials, contexts, and preferences become more uncertain the further back we look. Without the luxury of rich descriptions, recordings, or conclusively decipherable notations, we cannot know for sure which scales or modes were used, how ensembles were constructed, what symbolism was attached to certain sounds, how instruments were played, or how listeners responded to specific musical stimuli. The performance settings, social circumstances, and psychological dispositions evade restoration. Even if we could accurately recreate an ancient melody and perform it on an authentically reproduced period instrument, our responses would likely be out of sync with those of the original audiences. Disparities of perception between insiders and outsiders are common in modern cross-cultural listening experiences and would only be amplified when listening to music from a time and place wholly at variance with our own.[6]

The situation is complicated by the linguistic economy of biblical texts. The Hebrew Bible mentions sixteen instruments or instrument groupings but tells us precious little about their sounds. For example, Numbers 10:1-10 depicts God commanding Moses to make two silver trumpets (הצוצרות) to be blown by priests for the purpose of gathering an assembly; but the passage divulges nothing of the nature of the blasts. Still, from the divine command, function of the instrument, status of the players, and (imperfect) comparisons with modern trumpets, one can deduce that the trumpets were attention-grabbing and represented the voice of authority.

Piecing together an instrument's character is perhaps best realized with the kinnor, the biblical lyre. Although questions remain regarding its shape(s), size(s), tuning(s), number of strings, and performance technique(s) — and how these might have changed over time — nearly all of the combined references attribute positive emotions to the kinnor. According to Curt Sachs, a pioneer of modern organology (the study of musical instruments):

> The melodies that the kinnor played or accompanied were gay, and unsuited to sorrow; the Jews refused to play that instrument during the Babylonian exile. They suspended their kinnorim on the willows; how should they "sing the

xi.
[6] Steven J. Morrison and Steven M. Demerost, "Cultural Constraints on Music Perception and Cognition," *Progress in Brain Research* 178 (2009): 67-77.

Lord's song in a strange land?" The kinnor was gay, and when the prophets admonished the people they threatened that the kinnor, symbol of joy and happiness, would be silenced unless the people desisted from sin.[7]

Musicologist and conductor Alfred Sendrey concurred, calling the kinnor "the instrument of joy and gaiety" and dispenser of "gladness and delight."[8] Sendrey opined elsewhere: "The lyre was a musical companion of joyous occasions, and the melodies played on it were mostly of a sweet, bright character."[9]

The certainty with which Sachs and Sendrey characterized the kinnor might raise eyebrows. After all, neither scholar heard the instrument in its native setting. Yet, such confidence is perhaps more justified with the kinnor than it is with most biblical instruments. The assumed qualities of other instruments derive mostly from performance contexts and functions (if their qualities are retrievable at all).[10] Contrastingly, the kinnor occasionally receives descriptors. Isaiah 24:8, for instance, links the kinnor with "joy" or "merriment" (כנור משוש). Psalm 81:3 calls the instrument "pleasant" or "melodious" (כנור נעים). Based on these descriptors, Sachs concluded that, in the biblical *Sitz im Leben*, instruments "were bound to well-defined occasions and moods."[11]

To be sure, the Bible gives a very limited view of the world that produced it, ignoring the lives of ordinary people and cultural meanings and functions that did not fit the authors' agendas.[12] Writers in antiquity composed texts for narrow purposes, not for posterity. Restricting our understanding of musical instruments to carefully crafted narratives and poetic verses is necessarily incomplete. Surely, the affective range of the kinnor exceeded the

---

[7] Curt Sachs, *The History of Musical Instruments* (New York: W. W. Norton, 1940), 108.

[8] Sendrey, *Music in Ancient Israel*, 276–77.

[9] Sendrey and Norton, *David's Harp*, 115.

[10] For example, the timbrel (תוף), a frame drum played mostly by women in non-Temple cultic settings and communal celebrations—including dance processions (e.g., Exod 15:20; 1 Sam 18:6) and celebratory meals (Gen 31:27)—accompanied joyful songs of feasting, praise, and military victory. Isaiah 24:8 links the timbrel with "merriment" (משוש תפים), just as it does the kinnor.

[11] Sachs, *The History of Musical Instruments*, 108.

[12] See Paul J. King and Lawrence E. Stager, *Life in Biblical Israel* (Louisville: Westminster John Knox, 2001), and William G. Dever, *The Lives of Ordinary People in Ancient Israel: Where Archaeology and the Bible Intersect* (Grand Rapids: Wm. B. Eerdmans, 2012).

joyful image conveyed in biblical texts. Even so, the association of instruments with stereotyped moods is still common today. Composers regularly use specific instruments to evoke desired responses, exploiting their tones and timbres for immediate effect. According to a recent psychological study of the affective qualities of string, percussion, brass, and woodwind instruments, listeners reported strings as having the most positive emotional valence.[13] At the risk of conflating contemporary instruments and auditors with those of ancient Israel, the study supports, at least superficially, the positive portrayal of the kinnor — the Bible's chief string instrument.

An Instrument of Joy

In modern usage, joy is one of several positive affective states in the range of human emotions, residing alongside happiness, gladness, contentment, satisfaction, pleasure, excitement, ecstasy, and so on.[14] Sachs and Sendrey included five synonyms in their statements on the kinnor, each presumably having a nuanced meaning: joy, gaiety, happiness, gladness, and delight. Sendrey extrapolated that melodies stimulating these emotions "were mostly of a sweet, bright character."[15] Much of what the Bible divulges about the kinnor's character is situational. Its presence at victory dances, communal feasts, cultic celebrations, and scenes of prophetic ecstasy give a strong impression of its positive associations. Additionally, three terms are directly applied to the kinnor: "joy" (משוש, Isa 24:8); "pleasant" (נעים, Ps 81:3); and "gladness" (שמחה, Gen 31:27; 1 Chr 15:16).[16]

Literature on the kinnor typically uses "joy" to encompass the variety of positive arousals.[17] However, this broad term conceals

---

[13] Stephen McAdams, Chelsea Douglas, and Naresh M. Vempala, "Perception and Modeling of Affective Qualities of Musical Instrument Sounds Across Pitch Registers," *Frontiers in Psychology* 8 (2018): 1–19.

[14] Gretchen M. Reevy, *Encyclopedia of Emotion* (Santa Barbara: Greenwood, 2010), 338. The English language contains roughly forty words describing positive states. See R. P. Bagozzi, "Happiness," *Encyclopedia of Human Emotions* (eds. D. Levinson, J. J. Ponzetti, and P. F. Jorgenson; New York: Macmillan, 1999), 317–24.

[15] Sendrey and Norton, *David's Harp*, 115.

[16] שמחה has numerous possible translations encompassing a range of positive emotional states: happiness, joy, felicity, gaiety, exhilaration, cheer, glee, mirth, and so on.

[17] Albert Barnes, an influential Presbyterian theologian, wrote representatively: "The harp [kinnor] is used on occasions of joy." Albert Barnes, *Notes, Critical, Explanatory, and Practical on the Book of the Prophet Isaiah*, vol. 1 (New York: Levitt &

shades of emotion. For instance, some psychologists view joy as a medium arousal state, somewhere between ecstasy (high arousal state) and tranquility (low arousal state). Nevertheless, because the kinnor inspired and accompanied a range of positive feelings—including ecstasy and tranquility—joy became the convenient, though untechnical, catchall emotion. Moreover, joy is often associated with transcendent experiences of a religious/cultic or spiritual sort,[18] which would include most biblical references to the instrument.

An area of agreement between psychologists and Bible interpreters concerns the temporary, stimulant-dependent nature of joy. Joy is generally recognized as a positive response to a particular event or stimulant, whereas happiness refers to a more consistent state of being.[19] In the Hebrew Bible, the kinnor is played to stimulate, accompany, or respond to a fleeting positive state, such as those experienced during a military victory, banquet, or cultic ceremony.

Additionally, recent scholarship contends that emotions in the biblical text include complex external dimensions, rather than internal or spontaneous feelings alone.[20] Some even question the

---

Allen, 1860), 137. More than one hundred years later, Nahman Avigad wrote, "It was a gay instrument and a symbol of joy and happiness." Nahman Avigad, "The King's Daughter and the Lyre," *Israel Exploration Journal* 28.3 (1978): 151.

[18] Reevy, *Encyclopedia of Emotion*, 339 and W. R. Schumm, "Satisfaction," *Encyclopedia of Human Emotions* (eds. D. Levinson, J. J. Ponzetti, and P. F. Jorgenson; New York: Macmillan, 1999), 583–90.

[19] J. W. Kalat and M. N. Shiota, *Emotion* (Belmont, CA: Thompson Wadsworth, 2007). For distinctions between joy and happiness in biblical texts, see Christine Abart, "Moments of Joy and Lasting Happiness: Examples from the Psalms," *Ancient Jewish Prayers and Emotions: Emotions Associated with Jewish Prayer in and Around the Second Temple Period* (eds. Stefan C. Reif and Renate Egger-Wentzel; Berlin: de Gruyter, 2015), 19–40.

[20] Contemporary discourse on biblical emotions focuses on interrelated concerns: terminological-taxonomic concerns (Which biblical terms, if any, reflect experiences of emotions in the modern sense?); textual-generic concerns (How do the different biblical genres disclose and describe emotional experience?); cross-cultural concerns (Do people across time and cultures experience universal and biologically determined emotions, or are emotions culturally defined and shaped?); cross-disciplinary concerns (How can biblical scholars possibly keep up with the deluge of books and articles on emotions from sundry fields and languages?). F. Scott Spencer, "Getting a Feel for the 'Mixed' and 'Vexed' Study of Emotions in Biblical Literature," *Mixed Feelings and Vexed Passions: Exploring Emotions in Biblical Literature* (ed. F. Scott Spencer; Atlanta: Society for Biblical Literature, 2017), 3–4.

validity of reading emotions, in the limited modern sense, into the biblical world.[21] Although emotion terms are used, such as love (אהב) and fear (ירא), they should not be read exclusively as feelings or isolated sentiments. Instead, as Françoise Mirguet explains, the terms "also include actions, movements, ritual gestures, and physical sensations, without strict dissociation among those different dimensions."[22] The modern dichotomy between emotions and rationality, popularized by Scottish philosophers David Hume and Thomas Brown,[23] do not hold for biblical contexts, where emotions were evidently synonymous with ritualized behaviors and calculated choreographies, and the types of expressive behaviors differed according to the expectations of a particular setting, event, or activity. As such, the command "You shall be glad" (sg. ושמחת, pl. ושמחתם) is perhaps better translated as "You shall celebrate" or "You shall have a party," depending on whether it was a state/cultic function (celebrate) or non-cultic feast (party).[24]

---

[21] Reflecting on problems of deciphering emotion terms in the Bible, Philip Michael Lasater writes: "Expecting to find the emotions before the modern period is anachronistic." Philip Michael Lasater, "'The Emotions' in Biblical Anthropology? A Genealogy and Case Study with ירא," *Harvard Theological Review* 110.4 (2017): 530. Paul A. Kruger contends: "A major problem in the study of emotions in a 'dead' language such as Biblical Hebrew, though, is that most of the emotion scenarios (mostly attested in the poetic books) are cast in highly figurative language." Paul A. Kruger, "Emotions in the Hebrew Bible: A Few Observations on Prospects and Challenges," *Old Testament Essays* 28.2 (2015): 396. For an analysis of how biblical understandings of emotion influenced later Jewish thought, see Michael Fishbane, "The Inwardness of Joy in Jewish Spirituality," *In Pursuit of Happiness* (ed. Leroy S. Rouner; Notre Dame: University of Notre Dame Press, 1995), 71–88.

[22] Françoise Mirguet, "What is an 'Emotion' in the Hebrew Bible? An Experience that Exceeds Most Contemporary Concepts," *Biblical Interpretation* 24 (2016): 442.

[23] David Hume, book 2 of the *Treatise of Human Nature* (1738), entitled "On the Passions," and Thomas Brown, *Lectures on the Philosophy of the Human Mind* (1820).

[24] See Gary A. Anderson, *A Time to Mourn, A Time to Dance: The Expression of Grief and Joy in Israelite Religion* (University Park: Pennsylvania State University Press, 1991). Although the thesis that biblical emotions were behavioral more than interior has gained adherents, it is not without its problems. Lowell Handy's review of Anderson's book cautions: "Nothing cited in this volume suggests that any of these activities were, in fact, ritualized into a certain set of movements rather than simply activities in which individual persons engaged when they were happy. This is not to say that they were neither commanded nor ritualized, only that there is a lack of data to support such a conclusion." Lowell K. Handy, "Review of *A Time to Mourn, a Time to Dance: The Expression of Grief and Joy in Israelite Religion* by Gary A. Anderson," *Journal of Near Eastern Studies* 55.3 (1996): 214. According to

This unity of emotion and action is common in musical experiences, where emotional responses are not only highly culture-bound but are also displayed through prescribed or semi-prescribed external behaviors, such as dancing, gesturing, and gesticulating. Like biblical emotions, musical emotions are best understood as "embodied," with different settings and different occasions calling for different types of responses and behaviors.[25] The same or similar sounds might elicit pleasurable emotions/behaviors in one context and ecstatic emotions/behaviors in another.

Given the above, it is worthwhile to catalog emotional qualities ascribed to the kinnor in the Hebrew Bible, recognizing that these qualities were tied to specific ritualized and/or customary behaviors. While these positive states can be placed under the generic heading of "joy," the forty-two occurrences suggest five specific "shades of joy."[26] Ranked from low to high intensity, these include tranquility, pleasure, gladness, excitement, and ecstasy. The definitions of these terms are not universally agreed upon across the literature.[27] Here, they roughly capture feelings and actions expressed or implied in biblical passages, rather than provide broadly applicable meanings. Any such categorization runs the risk of employing description as construction; unique features and outlying cases are inevitably smoothed over to preserve the categories. Acknowledging that this exercise is no

---

Yochanan Muffs, joy (שמחה) was essentially a volitional term, as it could be turned on and off as the situation required. This differs from the modern sense of joy as a strictly emotional response. See Yochanan Muffs, "Joy and Love as Metaphorical Expressions of Willingness and Spontaneity in Cuneiform, Ancient Hebrew, and Related Literature: Divine Investitures in the Midrash in the Light of Neo-Babylonian Royal Grants," *Judaism, Christianity, and Other Greco-Roman Cults: Studies for Morton Smith at Sixty* (ed. Jacob Neusner; Leiden: Brill, 1975), 1–36, and "Love and Joy as Metaphors for Volition in Hebrew and Related Literatures, Part II: The Joy of Giving," *The Journal of the Ancient Near Eastern Society of Columbia University* 11 (1979): 91–111.

[25] See Marc Leman and Pieter-Jan Maes, "Music Perception and Embodied Music Cognition," *The Routledge Handbook of Embodied Cognition* (ed. Lawrence Shapiro; New York: Routledge, 2014), 81–89.

[26] This phrase is borrowed from P. C. Ellsworth and C. A. Smith, "Shades of Joy: Patterns of Appraisal Differentiating Pleasant Emotions," *Cognition and Emotion* 2 (1988): 271–302.

[27] See Ute Frevert et al., *Emotional Lexicons: Continuity and Change in the Vocabulary of Feeling 1700–2000* (New York: Oxford University Press, 2014).

exception, it should nonetheless enrich our understanding of the character of the kinnor.

Biblical References

The kinnor is the most widely attested string instrument in the Hebrew Bible. Of all the biblical instruments, only the shofar occurs more frequently (seventy-two) — although some question the Bovidae horn's classification as a *musical* instrument because of its signal function and limited pitches. Most of the forty-two instances of the kinnor can be classified according to emotional qualities: tranquility, pleasure, gladness, excitement, or ecstasy. Other references tell us when, where, and by whom the instrument was played (or not played). The Bible portrays the kinnor as a companion to positive experiences and events, both sacred and profane. These passages, along with the absence of the kinnor in times of mourning and suffering, affirm the kinnor as a symbol of joy (or "shades of joy").

General References

A handful of biblical verses dryly mention the kinnor and its cultic use. The instrument is first attested in Genesis 4:21, where its invention is attributed to Jubal, "the father of all who play the lyre and *ugav* (pipe)." Jubal is a sixth-generation descendant of Cain who, along with his brother Jabal, "the father of those who dwell in tents and amidst herds" (Gen 4:20), and his half-brother Tubal-cain, "who forged all implements of copper and iron" (Gen 4:22), are portrayed as founders of human civilization. The placement of musical instruments with herding and toolmaking reflects the importance of music in oral societies, where stories, warnings, histories, and rituals are often delivered in song with string accompaniment. It is possible that Naamah, "the sister of Tubal-Cain" (Gen 4:22), was originally the singing companion of Jubal, although her role in the primeval sibling group is strangely absent from the text. Psalm 49 fills in the gap: "My mouth utters wisdom; the utterance of my heart is full of insight. I will turn my attention to a theme; set forth my lesson to the music of the lyre" (vv. 4–5). Several passages identify the kinnor as a Levitical instrument. King David reportedly singled out specific Levites "with lyres to lead on the *sheminit*" (1 Chr 15:21; also 1 Chr 16:5).[28] Hezekiah reestablished the Levitical singers and instrument players during his reign over Judah (c. 715–686 BCE) (2 Chr 29:25). Other passages list the kinnor with cymbals (מצילתים) and harps (נבלים) as instruments accompanying singing in divine services (1 Chr 25:6; 2 Chr 5:12). During the Solomonic period, the instrument was made from almug timber (עצי אלמוגים, possibly sandalwood) imported from Lebanon (1 Kgs 10:12; 2 Chr 9:11).

There are also passages highlighting the incompatibility of the kinnor with moods contrary to joy. Isaiah 24 imagines the end-time destruction of the social and natural orders. During that time of unimaginable devastation, the merriment of the kinnor will be silenced (Isa 24:8). Ezekiel 26 offers a similar message in an oracle concerning the demise of Tyre, an ally of Judah during the failed revolt against Babylonia: "the sound of your lyres shall be heard no more" (v. 13). Psalm 137 depicts the Levites hanging their *kinnorot* on the poplars instead of playing joyful music for their Babylonian captors (vv. 1–4). Job, in his lamentable state, continues the theme: "So my lyre is given to mourning" (Job 30:31). Isaiah 16:11 seems to contradict these references: "Like a lyre my heart mourns for Moab."[29] However, viewed in light of the other passages, the poetic verse could refer to the futility of playing the characteristically upbeat kinnor in the face of tragedy. As with Job, the joyful

---

[28] The meaning of *sheminit* (שמינית) is uncertain. Related to the Hebrew "eight" (שמונה), it might refer to an eight-stringed instrument (lyre), a particular melody, an octave lower than the normal register (bass or baritone), or a key/mode. Burgh, *Listening to the Artifacts*, 25; E. D. Dalglish, *Psalm Fifty-One in the Light of Ancient Near Eastern Patternism* (Leiden: Brill, 1962), 236; and H. Graetz, *Kritischer Commentar zu den Psalmen*, vol. 1 (Breslau: Schottlaender, 1882), 85. Obscurity also surrounds a similar musical term, *asor* (עשור), which is related to the Hebrew "ten" (עשר). It is unclear if *asor* refers to an independent ten-string instrument (distinct from a harp or lyre), or if the term was a modifier signifying a variation of another instrument. It occurs in just three verses (Pss 33:2; 92:3; 114:9), and each time is associated with the *nevel* (harp), suggesting it might have been a species of ten-stringed *nevel*, rather than a unique instrument. See Sachs, *The History of Musical Instruments*, 117–18; Jeremy Montagu, *Musical Instruments of the Bible* (Lanham, MD: Scarecrow, 2002), 44; and Yelena Kolyada, *A Compendium of Musical Instruments and Instrumental Terminology in the Bible* (New York: Routledge, 2014), 29–32.

[29] According to Genesis 19:36–37, the Moabites descended from Abraham's nephew Lot, making them relatives of the Israelites, although relations between the two nations were often strained. The oracle either predicts the defeat of Moab, or was composed after Moab's defeat by some invader.

instrument is turned to mourning—a metaphor for the severity of the situation.

Tranquility

David's rise to kingship includes interactions with King Saul that have been described as music therapy.[30] Concerned about the agitated mental state of their king, Saul's courtiers urge that he invite a musician "skilled at playing the kinnor" to his bedside (1 Sam 16:16).[31] This is the only such use of the kinnor in the Hebrew Bible, but it points to a wider prevalence of musical healing practices. The courtiers do not hesitate to recommend a musical treatment for Saul; their search for a musician is an automatic response to his condition. The kinnor is the only healing method proposed, and the author does not justify or elaborate upon its efficacy. The ancient Greeks were similarly aware of the lyre's soothing effect, leading one scholar to call it "the first musical instrument ever to be used in healing."[32] This function of the lyre, as well as the closely related harp, is recognized by modern music therapists, who play the instruments to help ease distress caused by numerous ailments.[33] David's playing brings temporary relief to Saul and earns him a place as Saul's musical soother-in-residence (1 Sam 16:21-23).

The effect of David's kinnor is closest to tranquility, defined

---

[30] For example, Jonathan Kirsch, *King David: The Real Life of the Man who Ruled Israel* (New York: Ballantine, 2000), 47–49.

[31] Saul is possessed by an "evil spirit of God" (רוח אלהים רעה), possibly a biblical term for the modern diagnosis of paranoid schizophrenia or bipolar disorder.

[32] Antonietta Provenza, "Soothing Lyres and *Epodai*: Music Therapy and the Cases of Orpheus, Empedocles and David," *Music in Antiquity: The Near Eastern and the Mediterranean* (eds. Joan Goodnick Westenholz, Yossi Maurey, and Edwin Seroussi; Berlin: Walter de Gruyter, 2014), 307. This claim is overstated, as drums have long been used in shamanic healing practices of indigenous people, some of which likely predate the ancient Greeks. According to Ted Gioia, Orpheus, the prophet, poet, and musician of Greek legend, reformed musical healing practices by replacing the shaman's drum with the soothing lyre. Ted Gioia, *Healing Songs* (Durham: Duke University Press, 2006), 75. David and Orpheus are sometimes conflated in artistic representations. See Rāḥēl Ḥaklîlî, *Ancient Jewish Art and Archaeology in the Diaspora* (Boston: Brill, 1998), 247–49.

[33] For example, L. Freeman et al., "Music Thanatology: Prescriptive Harp Music as Palliative Care for the Dying Patient," *American Journal of Hospital Palliative Care* 23.2 (2006): 100–04; Sarajane Williams, "Patients with Parkinson's Disease Find Relief with Harp Music," *The Harp Therapy Journal* 6.1 (2001): 6-7; and Karen A. Bock, "Harp Music Eases Pain from Lupus," *The Harp Therapy Journal* 4.1 (1999): 4.

here as a low arousal state of psychological equilibrium or homeostasis expressed by calmness and serenity. The kinnor helps Saul "find relief," "feel better," and causes anguish to "leave him" (1 Sam 23). The calming influence wears off as Saul's condition worsens and he begins to see David as a rival for his throne. On two occasions, Saul attempts to drive a spear through David during their daily "music therapy" session (1 Sam 18:10–12, 19:9–10). The relaxing sounds become a source of aggravation, vividly illustrating how far Saul's mental health has declined. The ineffectiveness of the kinnor in these later encounters also shows that the instrument's tranquilizing effect was not merely intrinsic, but depended on the mood and cooperation of the auditor.

Pleasure

The kinnor is also associated with pleasure in the hedonistic sense of seeking satisfaction or enjoyment and avoiding pain. This function resonates with portrayals of humans as pleasure-seekers, following Democritus and Epicurus, and contrasts with the Bible's prophetic tradition, which uncompromisingly demands moral and physical uprightness. Given its social-theological agenda, it is unsurprising that the Bible casts this use of the kinnor in a negative light.

The kinnor is first connected to "pleasure gatherings" in the story of Jacob and his uncle/father-in-law Laban (Gen 29–31). Jacob falls for Laban's daughter Rachel and agrees to tend his uncle's flocks for seven years as a bride price. However, when that period ends, Laban slyly substitutes his eldest daughter Leah for Rachel, thus compelling Jacob to work seven more years for Rachel. Eventually, Jacob escapes Haran with his wives and children, only to be overtaken by Laban and his kinsmen in the hill country of Gilead. Laban asks Jacob why he left without the proper musical send-off: "Why did you flee in secrecy and mislead and not tell me? I would have sent you off with festive music, with timbrel and lyre" (Gen 31:27).

This story depicts Laban as selfish, greedy, and duplicitous. Yet, at the same time, he is a man concerned with his family's welfare and the preservation of societal norms. He makes sure that his eldest daughter is married first, strives to keep his family close to home, and seeks to uphold ceremonial customs—values still held in traditional societies. This could explain Laban's anger at being deprived of the opportunity to bid Jacob and his family a dignified farewell. As a traditionalist, Laban objected to the group leaving without the customary "festive music, with timbrel and lyre."

The Bible typically views non-cultic festive music disapprovingly. It is no accident that Laban, a man of questionable morals, is the biblical character who introduces the practice. Isaiah goes a step further, complaining that those who indulge in such extravagances have chosen parties over piety, and will be punished accordingly: "They have harps and lyres at their banquets, pipes and timbrels and wine, but they have no regard for the deeds of the Lord, no respect for the work of His hands" (Isa 5:12). Instead of attending to the needy or fighting injustices, the privileged class feeds its insatiable appetites.[34]

Job 21:12 reiterates the theme of the wicked indulging in the kinnor. Isaiah 23:16 metaphorically ties the kinnor to prostitution, reinforcing the instrument as a companion to unholy pleasures. The Bible draws a line between these indulgent (mis)uses and the higher purpose of the kinnor in the hands of King David and the Levites. Again, this distinction reflects a textual bias rather than the social reality, in which the kinnor's joyful sounds were exploited in a variety of settings.

Gladness

The Bible equates divine praise with gladness, an emotion derived from a sense of awe, gratitude, and/or accomplishment. In a number of psalms, gladness is linked to the sound of the kinnor. These psalms were presumably sung in cultic settings, where singing joined string instruments to inspire, harness, and enhance feelings and ritualized behaviors of gladness. The term "psalm" derives from the Greek *psalmos*, "striking [of musical strings]," which is an adaptation of the Hebrew *mizmor*, meaning a song with string accompaniment.[35] The Hebrew title for the Psalter is *Sefer*

---

[34] The complaint continues: "Assuredly, my people will suffer exile," perhaps alluding to the fate of northern Israel.

[35] The root of *mizmor* (זמר) is of Akkadian origin, where it means both "to play an instrument" and "to sing." This differs from the Hebrew term *shir* (שיר), which in Psalms means only "song" or "poem." The two terms occasionally appear together, for instance in the superscription of Psalm 92: מזמור שיר ליום השבת ("A song with string accompaniment, a song for the Sabbath day").

Tehillim, which translates to Book of Praises (from תהלה, "song of praise"). These terms combine to define psalms as "songs of praise sung to string accompaniment."

Praise is a feature of psalms representing diverse genres, from exuberant hymns to dire complaints. Eight psalms reference praise and the kinnor together: "praise the Lord with the lyre" (הודו ליהוה בכנור, Ps 33:2); "praise you with the lyre" (אודך בכנור, Ps 43:4); "I will sing a hymn to You with a lyre" (אזמרה לך בכנור, Ps 71:22); "it is good to give thanks to the Lord and sing hymns to Your name, O Most High...with the lyre" (טוב להודות ליהוה ולזמר לשמך עליון...בכנור, Ps 92:1-4); "sing a hymn to the Lord with the lyre" (זמרו ליהוה בכנור, Ps 98:5); "sing a hymn to our God with the lyre" (זמרו לאלוהינו בכנור, Ps 147:7); "let them praise his name...[with] the lyre" (יהללו שמו... [ב]כנור, Ps 149:3); and "praise him with harp and lyre" (הללוהו בנבל וכנור, Ps 150:3).[36]

Additional psalms depict situations where the kinnor accompanied praise. Psalm 57 describes David waking at dawn to give praise with lyre and song (vv. 8-9). Psalm 81 includes the lyre among ceremonial instruments of praise (vv. 1-4). Outside of the Psalter, leaders of the Levites assign musicians from the Levitical class to play lyres, harps, and cymbals to "elevate with a voice of gladness" (להרים בקול לשמחה) (1 Chr 15:16). Lyres, harps, and cymbals were also heard at the celebratory dedication of the Second Jerusalem Temple (Neh 12:27).

Excitement

Excitement is a high arousal state of enthusiasm, eagerness, or jubilation. This meaning derives from Charles Darwin's measurement of "high spirits" in excited individuals, and Alexander Bain's understanding of excitement as "emotion in action," especially associated with hunting and fighting.[37] As with

---

[36] These verses appear in psalms from the three major genres, as categorized by Hermann Gunkel: thanksgiving (Pss 33; 92); complaint (Pss 43; 71); and hymn (Pss 98; 147; 150). Hermann Gunkel, *The Psalms: A Form-Critical Introduction* (Minneapolis: Fortress Press, 1967) [translation of *Die Religion in Geschichte und Gegenwart*, 2nd ed., 1930]; and Hermann Gunkel, *Introduction to Psalms: The Genres of the Religious Lyric of Israel* (comp. Joachim Begrich; Macon, GA: Mercer University Press, 1998) [translation of *Einleitung in die Psalmen: die Gattungen der religiösen Lyrik Israels*, 1933]. For a summary of Gunkel's findings, see Tyler F. Williams, "A Form-Critical Classification of the Psalms According to Hermann Gunkel," *Resources for Biblical, Theological, and Religious Studies* (Oct. 2006).

[37] Charles Darwin, *The Expression of Emotions in Man and Animal* (New York: D.

other shades of joy, excitement is aroused in response to an external event or stimulant. In biblical episodes linking excitement and the kinnor, the source of excitement is military victory.

After liberating Israel from Philistine domination, King David and his troops bring the Ark of God to Jerusalem, thereby establishing the city as an administrative and cultic center. The scene prompts celebrants to dance "before the Lord with all kinds of cypress wood [instruments], with lyres, harps, timbrels, sistrums, and cymbals" (2 Sam 6:5). Variations of this episode are portrayed in 1 Chronicles 13:8, with sistrums missing from the instrument list and trumpets taking their place, and 1 Chronicles 15:28, with the shofar added to lyres, harps, trumpets, and cymbals. In a similar scene, King Jehoshaphat, who ruled Judah from approximately 870 to 848 BCE, victoriously returns to Jerusalem with his men "to the accompaniment of harps, lyres, and cymbals" (2 Chr 20:28).

The Book of Isaiah also alludes to this customary celebration. During Hezekiah's reign (c. 714 or 701 BCE), Judah makes diplomatic overtures to Egypt in an attempt to mitigate the Assyrian threat. Isaiah opposes the strategy, insisting that Judah remain independent and rely solely on God's might in its struggle against Assyria. An oracle foretells the ultimate defeat of Judah's enemies in the end of days and compares God's punishing blows to the excited sounds of timrels and lyres (Isa 30:32).

Ecstasy

Prophets sometimes used musical ritual to propel them to a prophetic state. 1 Samuel 10:5 describes King Saul encountering a band of prophets "coming down from the shrine [of Gibeah], preceded by lyres, timbrels, flutes, and harps, and they will be speaking in ecstasy (מתנבאים)." 1 Chronicles 25:1 and 3 depict Levites prophesying to the accompaniment of lyres, harps, and cymbals, suggesting that musical performance—even when highly ritualized—opened lines of communication between humanity and God. These images recall the prophet Elisha, who requests a musician (possibly a lyrist) to transport him to a state suitable for prophesy (2 Kgs 3:15).[38]

Appleton, 1886), 212; Alexander Bain, *Emotions and the Will* (London: Longmans, Green, and Co., 1865), 68.

[38] Judah Moscato, a sixteenth-century Italian rabbi, poet, and philosopher, identified the instrument that aided Elisha as a kinnor, and compared its spiritual

Although examples of this sort are few, they suggest the wider use of music to encourage ecstasy in the classical sense of "standing outside of oneself or being enraptured."[39] From an anthropological perspective, prophecy is a type of spirit possession or "possession trance," coinciding with mediumistic communication or "possession divination."[40] The Bible rarely describes behaviors associated with these altered states, probably because the authors or editors were uncomfortable doing so. However, shamanic and mystical traditions across time and cultures confirm a natural union of music, dance, and prophetic ecstasy. Relevant to the Bible is Apollo's role as a god of both music and prophecy (among other things).[41] Several ancient Near Eastern texts indicate an interplay between music and prophecy, including the Ritual of Ištar, a Bronze-Age Mari text that presents music and prophecy in the same ritual act and describes musicians lifting prophetesses into prophetic states.[42] Similarly, the kinnor is conceived as a tool of divine inspiration due to its connection with David, the early prophets, and Levitical poet-musicians.[43] Its music

value to that of David's kinnor. The interpretation is analogous to rabbinic depictions of wind blowing across the strings of a lyre hung above David's bed, which caused him to wake at midnight (based on Psalm 119:62: "I arise at midnight to praise You for Your just rules"; BT *Berakhot* 3b–4a and BT *Sanhedrin* 161a–b). According to Don Harrán: "Like the kinnor, with its strings activated by *ruaḥ* (or wind, spiritus), so the prophet [Elisha] is 'an instrument,' played on by his 'spirit.'" Don Harrán, *Three Early Modern Hebrew Scholars on the Mysteries of Song* (Boston: Brill, 2014), 23, 91.

[39] Christophe Nihan, "Saul Among the Prophets (1 Sam 10:10–12 and 19:18–24): The Reworking of Saul's Figure in the Context of the Debate on 'Charismatic Prophecy' in the Persian Era," in *Saul in Story and Tradition* (eds. Carl S. Ehrlich and Marsha C. White; Tübingen: Mohr Siebeck, 2006), 98 n. 52.

[40] Nihan, "Saul Among the Prophets," 98.

[41] Other sources likewise deify the lyre and link it to prophecy. For example, John Curtis Franklin writes: "The exchange of oracular consultations with the king of Alashia is attested in texts from Ugarit. There the *knr* was probably associated with the craftsman-god Kothar-wa-Hasis, who seems to have presided over both music and prophecy. This at least is suggested by Philo of Byblos, who relates that Chusor, the Phoenician descendant of Kothar, 'cultivated poetry and spells and prophecy.' Here the local scribal equation of Kothar with Ea, Mesopotamian patron of both music and prophecy, has not been given sufficient weight." John Curtis Franklin, "Lyre Gods of the Bronze Age Musical Koine," *Journal of Ancient Near Eastern Religions* 6.1 (2006): 47.

[42] Ritual of Ištar, Text 3, Lines iii 1'–23'. Martti Nissinen, *Prophets and Prophecy in the Ancient Near East* (Atlanta: Society of Biblical Literature, 2003), 82–83.

[43] Johannes Botterweck, "Kinnor," *Theological Dictionary of the Old Testament*, (eds.

helped stimulate self-transcendence and an openness to mystical messages and visions.

Conclusion

Biblical instruments are difficult to identify or reconstruct. Even more remote is the potential of reacting to the instruments in the same manner as the original audience. The distance of time, space, and culture obscures that possibility. Still, context can provide clues about an instrument's character. This is particularly true of the kinnor, which occurs frequently enough and with enough supporting information to give a strong impression. Taken as a whole, the forty-two occurrences link the kinnor with positive arousals, typically grouped together as "joy." This is a fair generalization, as it implies a temporary state commonly associated with spiritual experiences (even as the instrument is also linked to hedonistic enjoyment). The foregoing does not challenge the conventional view of the kinnor as an instrument of joy but adds nuance to the longstanding conception by categorizing references into more precise emotional categories of tranquility, pleasure, gladness, excitement, and ecstasy.

G. Johannes Botterweck, Helmer Ringgren, and Heinz-Josef Fabry; Grand Rapids: Wm. B. Eerdmans, 1995), 7:203.

The Kinnor as a Symbol of Joy of the Past and the Future Messianic and Eternal Eras
Classical Rabbinic Traditions on the Kinnor

Joel Gereboff

Classical rabbinic documents, ranging in date from the tannaitic period (first to second centuries CE) through the late homiletical *midrashim*, redacted in the post-amoraic period between the sixth and ninth centuries CE, contain thirty traditions discussing the kinnor. Many of these traditions appear in multiple rabbinic documents, at times with some variation or additional commentary. Most of them cite and interpret various biblical verses. The majority of the traditions in tannaitic documents, Mishnah, Tosefta, and *halakhic midrashim*, clarify aspects of the use of the kinnor in the Temple by Levites, thereby expanding on details in biblical descriptions. They treat the kinnor as an instrument of joy and celebration. Two traditions address the question of the distinction among various string instruments mentioned in the Hebrew Bible, the *nevel* (harp) and the kinnor (lyre), each of which is a type of a lyre—a seven, an eight- and a ten-string version. One of these traditions introduces a connection between two types of *kinnorot* (the 8- and 10-string versions), the messianic age, and the heavenly realm of the future. It is only during those eras that these types of instruments will be played. Amoraic traditions, in turn, continue to associate the proper use of the kinnor with biblical times, and by contrast, citing Isaiah 5:12-14, connect the improper playing of the kinnor with the destruction of the Temple. Several traditions explicitly prohibit the use of music, including singing accompanied by the kinnor in the post-destruction era. Similarly, several traditions, by commenting upon Psalm 137, underscore the inappropriateness of playing the kinnor while the Temple is destroyed. In one tradition, appearing in a rabbinic document with a late date of redaction, Levites are described as having injured their thumbs so that they could not play for the Babylonian king. In contrast to this source, a tradition that appears in numerous rabbinic documents speaks of David hanging a kinnor over his bed that miraculously plays and wakes him at midnight to praise God and provoke others to do so. In some versions of this tradition, he and others began to study Torah at midnight. Finally, one late tradition connects David's lyre with the ram slaughtered in place of Isaac at the Akedah, thereby expressing a connection between that highly significant event and the music of David.

An overall pattern in the rabbinic comments on the kinnor emerges over the collection of rabbinic documents: during biblical times, especially while the Temple stood, the kinnor was a sign of joy. When the Temple was in ruins, the kinnor was not generally to be played, and if it was, it symbolized unacceptable celebration. Several traditions state explicitly that it is prayer, the words of the lips, and not the sounds of instruments, that are the appropriate manner of praising and celebrating the divine. In the future messianic era, and in the world to come, in the Garden of Eden, the righteous shall once again enjoy the sounds of the kinnor.

This chapter offers an analysis of the diverse traditions referring to the kinnor that appear in rabbinic documents composed from the early third through the ninth centuries. It draws connections, as well, to information available from non-rabbinic literary texts and to material evidence.

Tannaitic Documents

Eight of the ten traditions contained in Mishnah, Tosefta, or *halakhic midrashim* either directly connect the kinnor to the Temple in Jerusalem or comment on its construction. Only two traditions focus on symbolic messages associated with the playing of this musical instrument. The traditions containing details about the use of the kinnor in the Temple add information not contained in the Bible. m. *Arak.* 2:5 lists the minimum number of instruments that were in the Temple and indicates that "there were never less than two trumpets, but they may add to them infinitely, nor nine *kinnorot* (lyres), but they may add to them infinitely, and one cymbal." m. *Arak.* 2:6 goes on to indicate that "there was never less than twelve Levites standing on the platform, but they may add to them infinitely." It then continues with references to minor Levites and states that "they did not say [sing] with a *nevel* or a kinnor but by mouth [*a cappella*] in order to add flavor to the music." A dissenting opinion of R. Eleazar follows which indicates that the minor Levites did not stand on the platform. t. *Arak.* 2:1 provides a scriptural text,

1 Chronicles 25:9, to support the assertion that there were twelve Levites and twelve musical instruments. That verse indicates that the lottery used to determine who would be in charge of the musical instruments fell to a Levitical family numbering twelve. Information regarding the storage of the musical instruments appears in m. *Mid.* 2:6, which states: "Offices were located under the courtyard of the Israelites opening onto the women's courtyard, and there the Levites would put their *kinnorot*, their *nevalim*, and their cymbals, all the instruments of song." In an extended description of the ceremony for drawing water, a celebration observed during Sukkot and which builds on the reference in Isaiah 12:3 to "drawing water in happiness," m. *Suk.* 5:4 reports that "the Levites [playing] upon *kinnorot*, *nevalim*, cymbals, trumpets and other musical instruments beyond counting [stood] upon the fifteen steps that descend from the Israelites' court to the women's court, corresponding to the fifteen Song of Ascents in the Book of Psalms." t. *Suk.* 4:7 augments this *mishnah* by indicating they sang Psalm 134.

Two additional tannaitic traditions comment on the use of the kinnor in the Temple. m. *Yoma* 1:7 relates that to keep the High Priest awake on the night before the Day of Atonement, they would snap their "fall finger." t. *Kip.* 1:9 adds that they may not use a *nevel* or a kinnor for this purpose.[1] m. *Erub.* 10:3 and t. *Erub.* 8:19 provide several views on how to deal with a broken string of an instrument on the Sabbath. According to m. *Erub.* 10:3, "They tie a string of a musical instrument in the Temple [on the Sabbath], but not in the provinces." t. *Erub.* 8:19 focuses on the string of a kinnor. According to the anonymous law there, one may tie the string as many times as necessary. But R. Simeon b. Eleazar disagrees, indicating that doing so would change the sound. Instead, one "unwinds it [the string] from above [from the top cross piece] and ties it up below."[2]

---

[1] Amoraic comments in y. *Yoma* 1:7 and b. *Yoma* 19b indicate that, according to some views, while they did not use musical instruments, the finger tapping was accompanied by song (Psalm 127:2).

[2] y. *Erub.*10:12 26c cites the Tosefta and adds an additional remark by R. Simeon b. Eleazar that "Priests, Levites, musical instruments and the people are all necessary for the cult." The Babylonian Talmud (b. *Erub.* 102b–103a) introduces additional tannaitic sources about how to deal with broken strings, and also indicates that depending on how the string was tied, one may untie and retie it from either direction. Whether this text reflects the actual construction of *kinnorot*, such that the location of the excess string varied, is not clear.

Biblical and Second Temple sources leave two issues unclear regarding the kinnor: the distinction between and kinnor and a *nevel* in terms of their construction and the number of strings on each, and how they are played, whether by hand or with a plectrum. Biblical and later texts and artistic renditions are not fully aligned, and it is probable that there was a development in the construction of these two instruments, and also that the number of strings on each varied.[3]

What is clear is that these instruments are associated with joy and celebration. Two tannaitic traditions, m. *Kin.* 3:6 and t. *Arak.* 2:7, comment on these issues. The penultimate statement in tractate *Kinnim* is attributed to R. Joshua. He observes, "when it [a sheep or cow] is alive it has only one sound [voice], but after it dies its voice is sevenfold." The text then explains, "the two horns are [can be transformed into] two trumpets...its large intestine to *nevalim*, its small intestine to *kinnorot*." This would indicate that the *nevel* would have a lower pitch than the thin stringed kinnor. Josephus (*Ant.* 7.305–306) comments on the difference between the *kinyra* and the *nabla*. The former has ten strings and is struck with a plectrum; the latter, twelve strings and played by hand.[4] This would suggest that rabbinic texts see the two instruments in an opposite manner, as one would play a thicker stringed instrument with a plectrum. t. *Arak.* 2:7 also relates the number of strings in the kinnor and contains the following comment by R. Judah:[5]

---

[3] On biblical sources related to the kinnor, see the essays by Montagu, Friedmann, and Sweeney in this volume, as well as Sol Baruch Finesinger, "Musical Instruments in the OT," *Hebrew Union College Annual* 3 (1926): 21–76; Ovid R. Sellers, "Musical Instruments of Israel," *Biblical Archaeologist* 4.3 (1941): 33–47; and Yelena Kolyada, *Compendium of Musical Instruments and Instrumental Terminology in the Bible* (London: Taylor and Francis Group, 2014). Nahman Avigad, "The Kings Daughter and the Lyre," *Israel Exploration Journal* 28.3 (1978): 146–51, discusses a bulla found in Jerusalem from First Temple times and provides representations of numerous lyres from antiquity. A brief discussion of the material cultural evidence for the kinnor from the Greco-Roman period is in Daniel Sperber, *Material Culture in Eretz-Israel during the Talmudic Period* (Jerusalem: Yad Yitshak Ben Tsevi, 1993), 105–13 [Heb.].

[4] Emmanuel Friedheim, "Jewish Society in the Land of Israel and the Challenge of Music in the Roman Period," *Review of Rabbinic Judaism – Ancient, Medieval, and Modern* 15.1 (2012): 61–88, reviews a number of texts from the Second Temple period that comment on music and the kinnor in particular. A recurrent connection is between the kinnor and joy.

[5] Versions of this tradition also appear in *Num. Rab.* 15:11, *Pesiq. Rab.* 21:1, *Mid. Ps.* 81:3.

A. [There are] seven strings in the kinnor nowadays, as it is said, "In your presence is perfect joy (*sova semachot*)" (Ps 16:11);

B. In the days of the Messiah, [there will be] an eight stringed [kinnor], as it is said, "To the choirmaster, according to the *sheminit*" [Ps 12:1 — on the eight stringed one];

C. In the time to come (*le-atid she-yavo*) on a ten stringed [one], as it is said, "Praise the Lord with the kinnor, with a ten stringed *nevel* sing unto Him' (Ps 33:2)."

This statement seeks to sort out the various terms used for stringed instrument in the Bible that are all taken to be a kinnor. While in actual life there was probably some variation in the number of strings on a kinnor, this tradition assigns varying meanings to each of the instruments. In accordance with the view that the kinnor is an instrument of joy, the number of strings increases as the situation improves. Ultimately, in the days to come, generally taken as a reference to the "world to come," the afterlife, a more joyful instrument will be played. Also relevant here is the association of the kinnor with the days of the Messiah. As the kinnor is also connected to King David, and a descendant from the line of David will be the Messiah, it makes sense to see the kinnor as a symbol for the messianic era, the period when the people of Israel will regain political control and freedom in their land. We note here the use of the kinnor and *nevel* on one denomination of bronze coins minted during the Bar Kokhba revolt.[6] This underscores the use of the

---

[6] Hanan Eshel, "On Harps and Lyres: A Note on the Bronze Coins of the Bar Kokhba Administration," *Israel Numismatic Journal* 16 (2007–08): 118–30, catalogs and discusses all the known coins at the time of the article. With regard to the use of the image of string instruments, he notes that the coins from the first and second year use an instrument with a sound box on the bottom shaped like a goat skin, while those from the third year have an elegant wooden sound chest. He labels the former a *nevel* and the one from the third year a kinnor, and explains the change as an effort to make clearer the value of the coin. Those from year two were significantly lighter than those from the first year; yet, the same symbol appears on both. By the third year, to reduce confusion, a new musical instrument was used to correlate with the inscription on the other side: "For the freedom of Israel" (years one and two) and "For the Freedom of Jerusalem" (year three). Another iconographic connection between the kinnor and the battle at the end of days occurs in the War Scroll from Qumran. 1 QM 5.4 states, "Under the banner of the ten they shall write 'Rejoicings of God upon the ten stringed lyre (*asirit*).'"

instrument as a symbol for the restoration and freedom of Israel, events that in some Jewish views are related to the messianic era. As we will see below, additional rabbinic texts also make this connection between the kinnor and the messianic era.

The two remaining tannaitic traditions depict the kinnor as a symbol of joy. t. *Sot.* 3:6–8 (parallel versions in Mekhilta de Rabbi Ishmael *Shirata* 2 and *Sifre* Deut 43)[7] asserts that although the Generation of the Flood had experienced joy by divine blessing previous to their destruction, they became haughty and were then punished. Excerpts from Job 21:9–13 provide the description of their good life and joyful state. Evidence of their happiness is their having the luxury to play musical instruments. In these verses, Job complains about people whose "homes are secure, without fear….Their bulls breed and does not fail; Their cows calve and never miscarriage….They sing to the music of the timbrel and the kinnor, and revel to the tune of the pipe; They spend their days in happiness…" The passage goes on to note how they then told God they did not need Him nor His rain. Accordingly, they were punished with rain. While in this passage, playing the kinnor, an instrument of joy, in the end led to destruction, in *Sifre* Numbers 103 the reward for the righteous in the world to come is expressed through a commentary on Psalm 92:4.[8] The *midrash* contrasts the suffering of the righteous and the prosperity of the wicked in this world with their reverse fates in the world to come. Ezekiel 32:16 serves as the basis for the ultimate suffering of the wicked as it speaks of a *qinah*, a dirge or lamentation, to be recited over Egypt, a symbol of evil people. By contrast, Psalm 92:4 which speaks of singing praise to God and describes doing so "with a ten-stringed lyre (*asor*), with the *nevel*, with the voice (*higgayon*) and kinnor." The contrast between the *hegeh* (voice) of the joyous and the *qinah*, the dirge, for the evil allows the *midrash* to reinterpret Ezekiel 2:10, which tells of a scroll inscribed on front and back on which there is written *qinim vehegeh*. Although in its original context the verse refers to lamentations and dirges and woes, the *midrash* understands the verse in light of Ezekiel 32:16 and Psalm 92:4 to speak of opposing claims, in this case the ultimate joy of the righteous

---

[7] This *midrash* also appears in b. *Sanh.* 108a, *Pesiq. R. Kah.* 26:2, *Eccl. Rab.* 2:1, *Num. Rab.* 9:24, *Tan. Acharei Mot* 1, *Tan.* (Buber) *Acharei Mot* 1.

[8] Additional versions of the *midrash* appear in b. *Erub.* 21a and *Abot R. Natan* A 25.

symbolized by their use of musical instruments. Traditions first appearing in amoraic and post-amoraic documents continue to deploy the kinnor as a symbol of joy along with expressing some new themes.

Before concluding our examination of traditions in tannaitic documents, it is important to also take note of types of comments and reports not appearing in these works. Other than t. *Kip.* 1:9, which stipulates that one may not fix a broken string on Shabbat outside of the Temple by retying it, which of course deals with a period when the Temple still stood, there is no mention in these sources of rules pertaining to the playing of instruments, in particular of the kinnor, in the post-destruction period. Nor are there any anecdotal stories (*ma'asim*) relating to this topic. Mishnah and Tosefta do include at the end of tractate *Sotah* the statement, "After the Sanhedrin had ceased, song [singing] ceased from the house of feasting," with Isaiah 24:9, "They drink their wine without song," serving as a proof text. Emmanuel Friedheim's detailed discussion of the place of music in Roman Jewish Palestine speaks to this broader topic. After reviewing tannaitic and later amoraic traditions containing rabbinic statements about music, both vocal and instrumental, he concludes:

> It is commonly thought that following the destruction of the Second Temple the Rabbis sought to rid the Jewish people of any culture of instrumental music. It has been shown, however, that if there was an abrogation, which is highly doubtful, then it was limited to playing during weddings. Therefore the tannaim clearly did not issue a sweeping ban on all music....[They] viewed music, among other, no less destructive aspects of culture, as bearing idolatrous content that threatened the Jewish way of life, and they expressed their dissatisfaction in numerous expositions. Nonetheless, it seems they did not issue decrees against music, and the land of Israel sources do not contain sweeping prohibitions.[9]

---

[9] Friedheim, "Jewish Society," 78, 86. Don Harrán, "What Does *Halakhah* Say about Music: Two Early Rabbinic Writings on Music by Hai b. Sherira," *Hebrew Union College Annual* 84 (2014): 49–87, provides an extended analysis of two responsa of the tenth-century R. Hai Gaon on playing music. He also discusses in detail a broad range of tannaitic and amoraic rabbinic statements on playing music.

Friedheim's observations draw upon statements in a range of both early and later rabbinic texts, including remarks about the tannaitic period that are found only in later amoraic documents. Although, as we shall see, Talmudic traditions do speak more negatively about music, it is clear that tannaitic sources about the kinnor locate its use in the Temple. It is an instrument of the past as well as one that will be played again with joy in the days of the Messiah and in the afterlife.

Amoraic Documents and Midrashim from the Fifth and Sixth Centuries

Traditions appearing in the Palestinian and Babylonian Talmuds and in *midrashim* generally taken to be edited in the fifth and sixth centuries refer to the kinnor in relation to the Temple, define its character, and treat it as a symbol of joy. Several new topics, however, first appear in these texts. These include a connection between the kinnor and Torah study and observance of the commandments of the Torah. In addition, playing the kinnor under the wrong circumstances also serves as a symbol of unacceptable behavior.

Two traditions in the Babylonian Talmud and one in the Palestinian document, *Lamentations Rabbah*, speak of the kinnor in connection to the Temple. In a discussion (b. *Arak.* 11a) of whether the singing of Levites is essential for sacrifices to be valid, the third generation Palestinian *amora*, R. Isaac, cites Ps 81:3: "Raise up the song, sound the timbrel, the melodious kinnor and *nevel*." This indicates that playing those instruments accompanied the offering of sacrifices. A *baraita* (a tannaitic tradition not found in the Mishnah but cited by the Gemara) in b. *Shebu.* 15b states that when a valid physical addition was made to the Temple itself, they sang Psalm 100 accompanied by *kinnorot* and *nevalim* and cymbals. Finally, in the poignant proem 24 of *Lamentations Rabbah*, the *Shekhinah* (divine presence) mournfully reminds God that foxes now roam in the place where the seed of Abraham offered sacrifices, and the priests stood on the dais, and the Levites sang hymns of praise to the accompaniment of *kinnorot*.

Two traditions comment on the construction and sound of the kinnor. The second generation Palestinian *amora* R. Yohanan comments (b. *Meg.* 6a) that Kinneret is the same as Ginesor and was called Kinneret "because the smell of its fruits is as sweet as the sound of a kinnor." R. Chiyya bar Abba, a third generation Palestinian *amora*, in two comments in y. *Suk.* 5:4, 55c explains the difference between the kinnor and *nevel* and also the reasons for the name of the latter. He states the only difference between the two instruments is in their number of strings, which, based on the next statement he makes, is taken to mean the *nevel* has more strings. This aligns with Josephus' description of the two instruments. The reason it is called a *nevel* is because is "embarrasses" (*malbin*) all other instruments by virtue of its pleasant sound — its deep sound.[10]

Although the above sources in connecting the kinnor to the Temple associate it with joy, a number of traditions in the Babylonian Talmud treat the playing of the kinnor as a symbol of inappropriate or sinful behavior. In a litany of reasons for the destruction of the Jerusalem (b. *Shab.* 119b), R. Abbahu (third generation Palestinian *amora*) states: "Jerusalem was destroyed only because they neglected to recite the *Shema* morning and evening." A section from the Song of the Vineyard in Isaiah 5 (verses 11–13) then serves as proof for this claim. These verses lament that "those who chase liquor from early in the morning and till late in the evening inflamed with wine. Who at their banquets have kinnor and *nevel*...but who never give thought to the plea of God will suffer exile." This same verse is cited by R. Yohanan in his comment in b. *Sot.* 48a about the sinfulness and calamitous results of drinking wine while listening to music played on four instruments. These are the four instruments mentioned in Isaiah 5:12, the kinnor being one of them. Five calamities are enumerated based on interpretations of Isaiah 5:13, 15. One of the punishments, based on the interpretation of Isaiah 5:13, "And its masses parched with thirst," is that they caused the Torah to be forgotten from its students. This connection of the playing of the kinnor and the loss of Torah also finds expression in a b. *Sanh.* 101a. This *baraita* asserts that the recitation

---

[10] The *midrash* is based on a word play, as the *nevel* and *laban* share the same three letters. A version of this tradition in *Mid. Ps.* 81:3 contains three views on the differences between the two instruments. R. Chiyya says they are the same instrument. R. Simeon says they differ in the number of strings. R. Huna, in the name of R. Assi, says they also differed in the skin used for the sound box. The final comment explains that the *nevel* is so named as it shames (*menabel*) all other instruments. This collection of comments indicates that, by the time of the redaction of *Mid. Ps.*, a document whose date of redaction is disputed (with some scholars assigning it to the post-Geonic era), the nature of these instruments was not clear.

of verses from Shir ha-Shirim (Song of Songs) as a song, by singing it with a common melody, or the recitation of a verse in a wedding hall at an inappropriate time bring misfortune to the world. To underscore the negative effects, this tradition goes on to describe that "The Torah dons sackcloth and stands before the Holy One Blessed be He [and complains], 'Your children have treated me like a kinnor who scoffers play.'"[11] The text goes on to report that in response to the God's question, "What should they have done while eating and drinking?" the Torah states that they should have studied Torah at a level appropriate to their level of knowledge. Thus, some should study the Pentateuch while more advanced students should study rabbinic sources.

A final tradition (b. *Ber.* 63a) that connects playing music, the kinnor in particular, with the rejection of rabbinic authority is a report attributed to R. Abbahu about the objections of Chananiah, the son of the brother of R. Joshua, to Palestinian control of the intercalation of the year. Eventually, the Palestinian emissaries sent to Chananiah state that if the people in the diaspora choose to follow Chananiah, "Let them go up to a mountain, build an altar and let Chananiah play the kinnor. They have no portion in the God of Israel." In this instance, playing the kinnor symbolizes participating in the equivalent of idolatrous cultic activities.[12] All of these traditions in the Babylonian Talmud align with what appears to be a broader ambivalence among Babylonian rabbinic authorities

---

[11] In some manuscripts of this tradition foreigners (*goyim*) appears in *Kallah* 1:4 and in *Kallah Rabbati* 1:6.

[12] For a detailed analysis of this story, including a comparison with versions in the Palestinian Talmud, see Aharon Oppenheimer, "The Attempt of Hananiah, Son of Rabbi Joshua's Brother to Intercalate the Year in Babylonia: A Comparison of the Traditions in the Jerusalem and the Babylonian Talmuds," *Between Rome and Babylonia: Studies in the Leadership in Jewish Societies* (ed. Nili Oppenheimer; Tubingen: Mohr Siebeck, 2005), 255–64. One additional source in the Babylonian Talmud may also allude to negative consequences resulting from playing the kinnor after the destruction of the Second Temple. This source, b. *Moed Qat.* 26a, does not mention explicitly the word "kinnor," but speaks of the sounds of strings (*qal yeterei*). According to R. Ami, a third generation Palestinian *amora*, the Sassanian King Shapur attacked the Jews in Mezigat Caesarea in Cappadocia only after they had caused a great noise due to the sound of (musical) strings. Rashi and other commentaries take this to be an allusion to the sound of the strings of the kinnor. According to this interpretation, the playing of the kinnor was meant to celebrate rebellion, a joyous event. But in this instance as well, such a use of the kinnor resulted in destruction of the Jews. I thank Jonathan Friedmann for calling this source to my attention.

to the playing of music. Among statements expressing such views are the reported ban (*bitul*) of music (*zimra*) by R. Huna (which R. Hisda subsequently disparaged, b. *Sot.* 48a), and the response by Mar Uqba to an inquiry about the prohibition about music (*zimra*) at this time (after the destruction of the Temple). Uqba responds by citing Hosea 9:1: "Rejoice not, O Israel, to exultation, like the peoples." The *gemara* asks why did he not cite Isaiah 24:9, "They drink their wine without song"? The *gemara* responds by saying that the verse could have been understood as banning only instruments, while Hosea's statement applies to singing as well. In essence, these Babylonian traditions depict in a very negative manner playing instrumental music, including the kinnor.

In contrast to these traditions, a set of sayings about David's kinnor, which appear in multiple rabbinic documents, transform the instrument — at least as it was used in the past — into an agent for Torah study. One of the sayings, in fact, ascribes "magical" qualities to his kinnor. Both Talmuds discuss m. *Ber.* 1:1, which speaks of night watches. There is a dispute about how many watches there were. In the course of the discussion, appeal is made to the practices of King David as evidenced by certain verses from Psalms. Palestinian *amoraim* R. Zerikan and R. Ami, in the name of R. Simeon b. Laqish, cite Psalm 119:62: "I arise at midnight to praise You for Your just rules." After more discussion the *gemara* states, "In any event, morning never came and found David sleeping," citing Psalm 57:9: "Awake O my Soul. Awake, *ha-kinnor ve-ha-nevel*; I will wake the dawn." David always rose before dawn and called for the morning to awaken. Several statements follow which detail the connection between David's kinnor and midnight. According to R. Pinchas (fifth generation Palestinian *amora*) in the name of R. Eleazar b. Menachem (fourth generation Palestinian *amora*), David "would take a *nevel* and a kinnor and place them by his head (*mira'ashato*) and arise and play on them at midnight so that the Torah scholars should hear." The text then reports that the scholars would say, "If even King David is occupied with Torah, how much the more so should we be." There follows an alternate description of the connection of the kinnor and midnight. The third generation Palestinian *amora*, R. Levi said, "A kinnor was hung facing David's windows and when the north wind would blow at night, and it would play by itself." There follows an exegesis of 2 Kings 3:15, according to which a musical instrument can play by itself as did

David's kinnor.[13] In the versions of the story of the "magical" kinnor (*Pesiq. R. Kah.* 7:4, *Lam Rab.* 2:2, and *Pesiq. Rab.* 17:3), all of Israel engage in Torah study following the practice of King David.[14] These texts transform the kinnor into an agent to increase the study of Torah, and stand in contrast to traditions associating the improper playing of the kinnor with failure to properly observe the Torah and rabbinic directives.

Traditions in Rabbinic Documents from the Sixth to Ninth Centuries[15]

The small number of traditions that first appear in documents redacted in the second half of the first millennium carry forward the connection between the kinnor and joy, while also introducing several new themes. These include references to the construction of David's kinnor, statements about not playing the kinnor while in exile, and views underscoring the superiority of the words of prayers to the sounds of the kinnor and other musical instruments. A tradition about the experiences of Adam in the Garden of Eden in *Abot R. Natan* A 25 is a good example of the

---

[13] The version in the b. *Ber.* 3a (b. *Sanh.* 16b) differs slightly from the one in the Palestinian Talmud. The saying of R. Levi is attributed there to R. Aha bar Bizna in the name of R. Simeon Hasida, and here the harp hung over David's bed. David would then arise and engage in Torah study until the first rays of dawn. No mention is made of sages studying. They enter into his presence only at dawn to seek his advice. Moshe Benovitz, *Talmud Berakhot I* (Jerusalem: Haigud Lefarshanut Hatalmud, 2006), 112–16, provides a detailed comparison of the differing versions, as well as a source critical reconstruction of the entire *sugya* in the Babylonian Talmud. Additional citations of this story are in *Pesiq. R. Kah.* 7:4, *Num. Rab.* 15:16, *Ruth Rab.* 6:1, *Lam. Rab.* 2:22, *Pesiq. Rabi.* 49:2, *Mid. Ps.* 22:5; 57:4; 108:2. The versions in *Pesiq. R. Kah.*, *Lam. Rab.*, and *Pesiq. Rabi* include both sayings about the kinnor and report that all of Israel arose to study Torah.

[14] A number of scholars claim that the story of the magical harp expresses an assimilation of David to Orpheus. In turn, this text is connected to several material representations of the kinnor in Palestine at Sepphoris and at Gaza, and to the paintings in the synagogue in Dura Europus. Ephraim E. Halevi, "Kinoro shel David," *Moznayim* 22 (1966): 334–36 and Louis Ginzberg, *Legends of the Jews* (Philadelphia: Jewish Publication Society, 2003), 929, both identify parallels to the story of the magic harp in Greco-Roman sources. Benovitz (*Talmud Berakhot,* 123–24) demonstrates that these claims are unwarranted. Accordingly, there are no rabbinic texts that in any way ascribe Orphic attributes to King David.

[15] In what follows are traditions that first appear in these documents unless there are significant variations in traditions that already appear in documents with earlier dates of redaction.

association of the kinnor with joy. Adam became afraid when the sun was setting on Friday evening, his first day of existence, and was concerned that he was being punished. When the sun rose the next morning, he was exceedingly happy and built an altar and offered sacrifices to God. Thereupon "three bands of ministering angels came down with *kinnorot* and *nevalim* and joined with him in a song of praise" — a Psalm for the Sabbath day (Ps 92), which tells of singing God's praises in the morning.

Mid. Ps. 98:1 also connects the kinnor with celebration. Commenting on the opening verses of this psalm ("O Sing unto the Lord a new song"), the *midrash* remarks that this new song will be sung with a kinnor (Ps 98:5), but only when the deliverance of Israel from exile is complete. Here again we see the connection of the kinnor with messianic themes. *Mid. Ps.* 33:1 ends with a comment on Psalm 33:1–3 and states that the righteous should sing a new song to God with the kinnor and the ten-stringed *nevel* to celebrate that God left the heavens and made His presence dwell on earth. By contrast with these traditions connecting the kinnor with joy, a *midrash* in *Tanḥuma* (*Num. Balak* 22:1) cites Isaiah 16:11, "Like a kinnor my heart moans for Moab," to support the claim that the prophets of Israel expressed a merciful attitude both for Israel and the nations. This is the sole instance in all of the kinnor traditions that mentions its ability to express pain and not just joy.

Several late traditions also comment on David's lyre. Both *Mid. Ps.* 92:7 and *Pirqe R. Eliezer* 18, citing Psalm 92:4, state that David played upon a kinnor of ten strings. This statement is part of a unit indicating that, to be legally valid, all ceremonies require ten people. While describing the kinnor as having ten strings aligns with Josephus' description, this tradition disagrees with the more commonly stated view (t. *Arak.* 2:7 and parallels) that, prior to the messianic era, the kinnor has only seven strings. One tradition (*Pirqe R. El* 31) adds a mythological dimension to David's kinnor. Expanding on the tradition (m. *Abot* 5:6) that speaks of ten items having been created on the eve of the Sabbath at the time of creation, among which is the ram that would be substituted for Isaac by Abraham, R. Chanina b. Dosa said: "From that ram which was created at the twilight, nothing came forth which was useless....The sinews of the ram were the strings of the kinnor upon which David played." This comment ties together key events in the lives of the people of Israel with primordial occurrences.

As already mentioned, the full range of rabbinic traditions about the kinnor have a consistent temporal set of connections for this instrument. It is an instrument that was played in the past and will be played in the messianic era, but not in the present. Several traditions comment on Psalm 137, a psalm sung by the exiled community by the rivers of Babylon. R. Isaac in *Pesiq. Rab.* 28:3, commenting on the verse, "There on the poplars we hung our *kinnorot*" (Ps 137:2), observes that instead of singing joyous songs about Zion, the exiles longed for the soil of the Land of Israel and began to repent. *Mid. Ps.* 137:4–5 has a similar but more dramatic expanded version of the events in Babylonia.[16] In this account, Nebuchadnezzar tells the tribe of Levi to ready themselves to play before him, as he eats and drinks, the same way as they played before God. The Levites look at each other and say among themselves, "Is it not grievous enough that we brought about the destruction of the Temple? Must we now stand and strike up a song for the pleasure of this dwarf?" The story then continues, drawing upon the word choice of Psalm 137:4, "How can we sing?" (and not "We shall not sing"), to describe how the Levites put their thumbs in their mouths and mangled them. Having realized what the Levites had done, the enraged king slaughtered many of them. But "there was gladness among the Levites, because they had not sung for the pleasure of the alien god." In response to the Levites' actions with their hands, God promises that though for the moment he has restrained his right hand, allowing the punishment of Israel to be inflicted by the Babylonians, he will not forget Jerusalem. Here the *midrash* treats Psalm 137:5 as the words of God, asserting that should He forget Jerusalem, may his right hand forget its cunning. While this *midrash* speaks of the actions of the Levites in the past, its message for its audience may well be that, during this period of exile, playing the kinnor is not appropriate, even if refraining from playing might lead to martyrdom. Better to die than to play music among and for non-Jews.

---

16 *Midrash Psalms* consists of two distinct section, 1–118 and 119–150. The latter portion was not part of the manuscripts containing the first part of this work. The actual date of the second portion is not clear, with some scholars proposing that it is medieval as it draws upon the *Yalqut.* The traditions in the latter portion of *Mid. Ps.* may thus be from a much later date than other traditions discussed in this paper. On the composition of *Mid. Ps.*, see H. L. Strack and Gunter Stemberger, *Introduction to the Talmud and Midrash* (Minneapolis, MN: Fortress Press, 1996), 322–23.

This negative view of playing the kinnor in exile is underscored in several late traditions that highlight the superiority of prayer to music. Several of these statements appear in *Mid. Ps.*, a document that consistently highlights the value of prayer and sees King David as having originated the use of Psalms to serve God.[17] *Mid. Ps.* 92:4, ends the comment cited above about David playing a ten-stringed kinnor by interpreting the second part of Psalm 92:4, *aley higgayon be-khinnor*, as God saying: "For me (*ali*) are preferable the solemn sounds (*higgayon* — prayers) more than the kinnor. I desire from Israel not music of the kinnor, but the solemn utterances of their mouth."[18] Similarly, R. Shabbetai in *Mid. Ps.* 149:5 interprets Psalm 149:5–6, "Let the faithful (*hasidim*) exult in glory; let them shout for joy upon their couches," to mean that, after God Himself shall prepare couches for the faithful in the Garden of Eden, they will respond "with paeans to God in their throats, and the high praises of God will be in their mouths (*pipiyot*)." The *midrash* then observes: "The Holy One blessed be He, will say to them, 'Even though you praised me with *nevalim* and *kinnorot*, it [your music] is not as sweet to me as are your voice.'" The passage goes on to contrast God's not wanting, or accepting, praises from the wicked with His desire for the voices of the faithful, and ends by asserting: "The Holy One, blessed be He, will say, 'Because high praises of Me were in your mouths, therefore, for your sake I will fight the battles that will free you from exile and servitude. Thus, scripture declares that 'the mouth of Israel is like the sword (*herev pipiyot*).'" Prayers and not music protect Israel and lead to God defending them.

Conclusions

Although only a small number of traditions about the kinnor appear in rabbinic sources redacted over eight centuries, this musical instrument serves to distinguish several rabbinic views about the situation of the people of Israel after the loss of the Second Temple. The kinnor is consistently seen as an instrument of joy, though it can be misused and sound a sour note about Israel's situation when they fail to abide by the demands of Torah. The

---

[17] Esther M. Menn, "Praying King and Sanctuary of Prayer, Part II: David's Deferment and the Temple's Dedication in Rabbinic Psalms Commentary (Midrash Tehillim)," *Journal of Jewish Studies* 53 (2002): 299–323, foregrounds the repeated assertion of this claim in this rabbinic document.

[18] *Pirqe R. El.* 18 contains the same statement.

ambivalence of the rabbis toward music, including instrumental music, finds expression in the absence of traditions that discuss the playing of this instrument in the present lives of Israel. The kinnor was played by King David and also in the Temple, and the rabbis add details to its construction and use. The kinnor will also be sounded in the messianic era and in the world to come. But for the present, when in exile, it is seen only as an instrument played by those who may reject rabbinic authority. In the present it is the words that come from the mouths of the people of Israel, not the tones from instruments that were formerly central to expressing Israel's joy and praise of God, that maintain the connection of the divine to Israel. Praising with the words of the psalms will ultimately lead to God fulfilling promises made to Israel and result in their redemption. At that time, the kinnor will again be heard, and so too will an even larger kinnor with a full twelve strings be played in the world to come.

The Kinnor in Jewish Thought
Some Remarks

Dov Schwartz

Musical figures or instruments associated with music in the Bible (trumpet, lyre, timbrel, harp, pipe, horn, and drums) have been the object of extensive commentary. Batya Bayer, an expert in ancient musicology, notes: "How rich is Scripture in musical testimonies, that is, in descriptions of various sound experiences, each one and its special terms."[1] I will refer below to a few functions of the kinnor in Jewish thought.

Jubal

Scripture tells us that Jubal created the science of music, and was the father of all those who play the lyre and pipe (Gen 4:21).[2] In the Middle Ages and the Renaissance, Christian exegetes presented Pythagoras and Jubal as the forebears of music.[3] Various biblical exegetes, some of them rationalists and some mystics, have looked for the source of music around the biblical story and have themselves contributed to mythical interweavings in the tale of music's invention. R. Yitzhak Abrabanel (1437–1508), the Jewish statesman who, following the expulsion from Spain, was exiled to Italy and absorbed there the spirit of the Renaissance, added another dimension to the exegetical traditions on Jubal. He argued that the invention of music was inspired by rhythm and claimed that Jubal's brother, Tubal-Cain, "the forger of all implements of bronze and iron" (Gen 4:22), beat rhythmically on the anvil, leading Jubal to invent the science of sounds.[4] A similar explanation occurs

---

[1] Batya Bayer, "Including Religious Music in the Teaching of Jewish Subjects and the Humanities," *Dukhan* 2 (1961): 36 [Heb.].

[2] In the *midrash*, Naamah, Jubal's sister (on his father's side), was also linked to music (e.g., Genesis Rabba 23:3). See, for example, K. E. Grözinger, *Musik und Gesang in der Theologie der frühen jüdischen Literatur: Talmud Midrasch Mystik* (Tübingen: J. C. B. Mohr, 1982), 43–45.

[3] See Judith Cohen, "Jubal in the Middle Ages," *Yuval* 3 (1974): 83–99.

[4] Abrabanel on Genesis 4:21. Abrabanel claimed the source of this tradition was

in the opening of R. Judah Moscato's homily, *Higgayon BeKhinnor*.[5] Moscato also claimed that Jubal had preceded Pythagoras in the invention of music. Various kabbalists tied the two ancestral brothers to evil and revolt, claiming that Tubal-Cain forged weapons and Jubal composed songs of battle and evil, actions meant to awaken the negative divine powers and bring up the negative dimensions of the divine *sefirot* (emanations or inner divine forces). These kabbalists viewed singing as an expression of the *sefirah* of *Din*, or judgment,[6] thus tracing the origin of music to aggression and despicable instinctual drives.

Particularly during the Enlightenment, Jewish biblical commentary and *aggadic* exegesis began to rely on motifs from classical myths. Thinkers who usually turned away from radical positions also endorsed this new awareness.[7] Jubal is henceforth the god of music, with roots in Greek and Roman myths. R. Shmuel David Luzzatto (SHaDaL, 1800–1865) viewed the text in Genesis 4:20–22 as detailing the tasks whose performers people deified. In his view, this text shows that these performers are merely flesh and blood, and that is the purpose of pointing to their family origin. SHaDaL identified Jubal, "the father of all those who play the lyre and pipe," with Apollo.[8]

Talmudic Interpretation

Besides biblical literature, Talmudic and midrashic literature used music extensively as a metaphor, often describing divine revelation and its expressions in terms of song and melody.[9] Just as

---

Sefer Jossipon. On Abrabanel's classical sources, see, for example, Moshe Idel, "Kabbalah and Ancient Philosophy for Isaac and Judah Abravanel," *The Philosophy of Leone Ebreo: Four Lectures at the Colloquium of Haifa University, January 16, 1984* (eds. Menahem Dorman and Ze'ev Levy; Tel Aviv: Hakibbutz Hameuchad, 1985), 73–112 [Heb.].

[5] Yehuda Moscato, *Nefutsot Yehudah* (Bnei Berak/New York: Mishor, 2000), 1b.

[6] See Menachem Recanati, *Commentary on the Torah* (Lublin, 1595; offset, Jerusalem, 1961), 16d; *Sefer ha-Peli'ah*, vol. 2 (Przemyśl, 1883), 63a. The tradition in the Zohar usually ascribes other symbols to terms associated with music.

[7] See, for example, Peretz Sandler, *The Be'ur of Moses Mendelssohn: Origin and Influence* (Jerusalem: Rubin Mass, 1984), 101–03 [Heb.]; Noah Rosenblum, *ha-Malbim: Interpretation, Philosophy, Science and Mystery in the Writings of R. Meir Leibush Malbim* (Jerusalem: Mosad Harav Kook, 1988), 131–32 [Heb.].

[8] Samuel David Luzzatto, *Torah Commentary*, vol. 1, (tr. Eliyahu Munk; Jerusalem/New York: Lambda, 2012), 86.

[9] See, at length, Jacob Neusner, *Judaism's Theological Voice: The Melody of the*

many biblical sources were the basis for later commentaries, there are a series of Talmudic *aggadot* that became sources for commentary and for the development of the conceptual component. The philosophical and kabbalistic interpretation of Aggadah evoked great interest in Jewish thought over the generations. One example is the widespread series of *aggadot* relating to the lyre, the instrument most often mentioned in Scripture (aside from the shofar, whose musical qualities are debated). Symbolic meanings have long been pinned on musical instruments according to their sounds and shapes. I present now two well-known *aggadot* on the lyre and briefly illustrate the subsequent commentaries on them:

> A lyre [kinnor] hung [*talui*][10] over David's bed,[11] and as soon as midnight arrived [*ba*],[12] a northerly wind blew [*noshevet bo*][13] upon its strings and caused it to play of its own accord. David would immediately [*mi-yad hayiah*][14] stand <David sat>[15] and studied Torah until the break [*she-`alah*][16] of dawn.[17]

> R. Judah says, "The lyre in our time has seven strings,[18] as it is said, 'In thy presence there is fullness of joy' (Ps 16:11). In the time of the Messiah it will have eight,[19] as it is said, 'To the choirmaster: upon an eight-stringed lyre' (Ps 12:1). And in the future that will come,[20] [it will have] ten,[21] as it is said, 'Praise the Lord with the lyre, make melody to him

---

Talmud (Chicago: University of Chicago Press, 1995).

[10] In *Babylonian Talmud Manuscript Munich Codex Hebraicus 95* (henceforth, Munich MS), *talui lo*.

[11] In the parallel version in the Palestinian Talmud — "against his windows."

[12] Munich MS *bat*.

[13] In the parallel version in the Palestinian Talmud — *u-menafnefet bo*.

[14] "*hayiah*" is not in the Munich MS.

[15] According to Munich MS.

[16] In Munich MS, *she-ya`aleh*.

[17] BT *Berakhot* 3b; *Sanhedrin* 16a. See JT *Berakhot* 1:1, 2d.

[18] BT *Arakhin* 13b, "The harp of the Sanctuary had seven cords."

[19] An eight-stringed instrument appears in a fresco of the Egyptian period that is parallel to the era of the patriarchs. See Batya Bayer, "The Biblical Harp in Light of Archeological Findings," *Dukhan* 5 (1964): 115 [Heb.].

[20] The parallel version in the Babylonian Talmud reads: "of the world to come."

[21] *Flavius Josephus Online, Judean Antiquities*, (tr. William Whiston; Brill Online Reference Works), Book 7, 12.3, notes that harps have ten strings. See Abraham Z. Idelsohn, *Jewish Music: Its Historical Development* (New York: Dover, 1992 [1929]), 8 and J. Kuehn, *Die Musik in den Heiligen Schriften im Talmud und in der Kabbalah* (Wien: Kuehn, 1930), 53 [Heb.].

with the harp of ten strings' (Ps 33:2)."[22]

The first source, which has been extensively discussed in the exegetical and research literature, became a paradigm for an *aggadic* source shaping different conceptions of music. The Renaissance Italian thinker Yehuda Moscato (c. 1530–1590) devoted the first homily in *Nefutsot Yehuda* to an interpretation of this *aggadah*. This homily, which he called *Higgayon BeKhinor* (the melody of the lyre), is discussed below. The *aggadah* at times led some thinkers to compare the human body to a lyre, which is also empty and ruled by the spirit.[23] Thinkers found the *aggadah* in BT *Berakhot* intriguing on a number of issues:

1) The nature of the miracle in the self-playing lyre.
2) The relationship between the north motif and automatic playing.
3) The lyre's modes of functioning—noting the time, serving as a learning aid, and so forth.

Several kabbalists ascribed the lyre's self-produced melody to the harsh, negative forces in the world. They referred to these forces as *Din*, *Gevurah* (divine force of stern judgment), *Sitra Ahra* (the other or evil side), and so forth. In this reading, the sounds made by David's lyre dispelled these forces, meaning that a musical instrument acted to prevent the spread of the negative emanations or the depressing temperament of the powers of *Din*.[24] This *aggadah* is among the sources of the *tikkun hatsot* (midnight rectification) practice.[25]

---

[22] Tosefta, *Arakhin* 2:7, Zuckermandel ed., 544. See BT *Arakhin* 13b and parallel versions in the *midrashim*. See also the analysis of Karl E. Grözinger, *Musik und Gesang in der Theologie der frühen jüdischen Literatur: Talmud Midrasch Mystik* (Tübingen: J. C. B. Möhr, 1982), 222–23. For a discussion on Hasidic commentaries on this *aggadah*, see Adaya Hadar, *Music in the Thought of Rabbi Nahman of Braslav*, Ph.D. Diss., Bar Ilan University, Ramat Gan 2017, 28–44 [Heb.].

[23] Amnon Shiloah, *The Musical Legacy of Jewish Communities* (Tel Aviv: Open University, 1985–1987), Unit 8, 26 [Heb.].

[24] See, for example, the interpretation of Shalom Buzaglo, who was active in Morocco in the eighteenth century, on *Tikkunei Zohar*: "When the melody comes from the left side, David's harp plays to stir joy" (*Kise Melekh* [Amsterdam, 1769], 35b).

[25] See Samuel Stern, *Poetry and Melody in the Worship of God* (Jerusalem: Machon Leb Bratslav, 2006), 58–74 [Heb.], which includes sources on the harp in the philosophical literature. The book by Stern, a Bratslav Hasid, has three parts: *Shir Binah* (song of understanding) (1994), *Shirat ha-Lev* (song of the heart) (1997) and the booklet *va-Ani Rofe Otah* (and I heal her) (2003). Stern provides in this work an impressive collection of sources on music, but his approach is based mainly on the

An interesting attempt to grapple with some of the issues tied to this *aggadah* is the discussion of Abraham Dov Dubsewitz (1843–1900), a *maskil* from Pinsk, who argued that the Palestinian Talmud version, claiming that the sounds of the lyre had been meant to awaken King David, was preferable. The lyre, then, did not produce a melody and there was no miracle here. Dubsewitz used the Palestinian Talmud's version in accordance with the principle stating: "As for sayings and stories appearing in various forms, adopt the plain one, hold on to it and do not give up."[26] The symbolic-mystical interpretation on the one hand and the natural interpretation on the other reflect a range of possible interpretations of this *aggadic* text. Moreover, the issues considered above encouraged scholars to expose different views on the role of music in the surrounding cultures in connection with the *aggadah* about the self-playing lyre.[27]

The second source encouraged a numerological interpretation such as the one that presented the strings as hinting at the ten *sefirot*. The seven lower ones are seen in the present and, in the future, the *sefirot* of *Daat* ("the eighth string"), *Ḥokhmah,* and *Binah* ("ten strings") will be revealed.[28] In both sources, as noted, the lyre appears as a leitmotif, and would later be perceived as such in systematic Jewish thought as well; but the second source provides information about the physical shape of the instrument, that is, about the number of strings. The biblical instrument is probably an Egyptian lyre, a string instrument resembling a small harp (sytar).[29] Many exegetes, at various times, obviously identified a kinnor with musical instruments familiar to them. The *tanna* R. Judah, for

---

teachings of Nahman of Bratslav, and his conclusions often do not follow from the ancient sources he cites (rabbinic homilies, Zohar literature, and so forth). On his interpretation of the harp *aggadah*, see below.

[26] Abraham Dov Dubzevitz, *Sefer ha-Mitsraf* (Odessa: Beilinson, 1871), 2 [Heb.].

[27] Elimelech Halevi, *Aggadic Passages in Light of Greek Sources* (Tel Aviv: Armoni, 1973), 393–97 [Heb.].

[28] Stern, *Poetry and Melody, Shir Binah*, 98–99.

[29] For discussions relying on archeological evidence about the biblical harp, see Bayer, "The Biblical Harp," 109–121; Z. Meshel, "The Painting of the Harp Player in Kuntilat Adjaroud in Sinai," *Tatslil* 9 (1977), 109–10 [Heb.]; Joachim Braun, *Music in Ancient Israel/Palestine: Archeological, Written, and Comparative Sources* (tr. Douglas W. Stott; Grand Rapids, MI: Wm. B. Eerdmans, 2002), 16–19. For instruments in the Talmudic period (flute, symphonia, horn, and harp) see Daniel Sperber, *Material Culture in Eretz Israel During the Talmudic Period*, vol. 2 (Ramat-Gan: Bar-Ilan University, 2006), 87–113 [Heb.].

example, identified it with a seven-stringed instrument. Saadia Gaon (882–942) identified it with the sytar and the tambourine, both of which he understood as a four-stringed strumming instrument.[30] Medieval exegetes who adopted a literal approach identified the *sheminit* as an eight-stringed musical instrument.[31] R. Zvi Yehuda Berlin, (ha-Netsiv) of Volozhin (1816–1893), may have identified the kinnor with the modern strumming or bowed string instrument when he wrote: "As for both these instruments [lyre and pipe]— they are interchangeable. The lyre is better suited for rest and sleep, and the pipe is the opposite—it thunders."[32] Some thinkers have openly admitted that we cannot precisely identify the actual biblical instruments.[33] In any event, the symbolism that the *tannaim* ascribed to the number of strings in the biblical kinnor (seven, eight, and ten—respectively, the present, the messianic era, and the world to come) is interesting and intriguing. In the Islamic world, scholars ascribed vast significance to the four strings of the oud (for example, a parallel to the four elements and the four humors).[34] The symbolism of the number of kinnor strings has been extensively discussed among philosophers, mystics, and exegetes of Aggadah, and I address their interpretations below.

Renaissance

R. Judah Lowe of Prague (Maharal, c. 1520–1609), who dealt at length with the messianic question[35] and, as usual, built his claims around Talmudic *aggadot*, offers a theoretical formulation of this view. According to the Maharal, song and melody characterize

---

30 Yehuda Ratzaby, *A Dictionary of Judaeo-Arabic in R. Saadya's Tafsir* (Ramat-Gan: Bar-Ilan University, 1985), 96 (under tambourine), 112 (under sytar) [Heb.]. See also the comments of Yosef Kafih, trans., *R. Saadia Gaon's Commentary on the Torah* (Jerusalem: Mosad Harav Kook, 1963), 18 [Heb.].

31 See Simon, *Four Approaches*, 216–17.

32 Naphtali Zvi Yehuda Berlin (ha-Netziv), *Ha`amek Davar* (Vilnius, 1879), 20a, on Genesis 4:21. In the preface to his commentary on the Torah, ha-Netziv compared the Torah to poetry in the wake of rabbinic statements, and elaborated on the implications of this comparison.

33 Abraham Hayyun (fifteenth century) noted about the instruments mentioned in Psalms, "we cannot fully know their nature." Cited in Abraham Gross, *R. Yosef ben Abraham Hayyun: Leader of the Lisbon Community and His Literary Work* (Ramat-Gan: Bar-Ilan University, 1993), 176 [Heb.].

34 Shiloah, *Music in the World of Islam*, 51–52.

35 See Benjamin Gross, *L'Eternite d'Israel: La doctrine messianique de l'exil et de la redemption du Maharal de Prague (1512–1609)* (Strassbourg: n. p., 1968).

both perfection ("it is the way of perfection to sing and make music") and joy, which explains why, in the rabbinic period, the time of redemption was symbolized through lyrical and musical motifs. Maharal tended to focus on the meanings of specific numbers. He created a messianic orientation by alluding to the symbolism of the lyre's eight strings:[36] the present world is symbolized by seven strings, since the number seven represents the order and regularity of nature. The era of the days of the Messiah is symbolized by eight because it symbolizes a kind of perfection that does not exist in the present. Maharal presented two alternatives on the nature and the essence of the days of the Messiah:

> And on the days of the Messiah, [the lyre will have] eight strings, because perfection in the days of the Messiah will transcend nature. And even for one who says (BT *Berakhot* 34b) that the sole difference between this world and the days of the Messiah is delivery from bondage to foreign kingdoms,[37] perfection will still reach a higher rank than in this world, and the lyre in the days of the Messiah therefore has eight strings.[38]

Clearly, then, Maharal avoided a decision on the miracles and wonders of the days of the Messiah. Be it according to the apocalyptic view, which assumes a change in the natural order in the days of the Messiah, or according to the naturalistic view, which assumes that only social and political changes will occur at that time, the world in the days of the Messiah will be more perfect that the present one. In any event, the last stage according to the Maharal is apocalyptic. Ultimately, matter will disappear altogether, as symbolized by the ten-stringed lyre. The number ten conveys absolute perfection.

Maharal, as noted, could be viewed as offering a theoretical formulation of the kabbalistic symbolic interpretation. The motif of *niggun* (melody) as perfection and joy characterizes "sacred" history on the one hand — the Temple period — and the end of history and

---

36 Tosefta *Arakhin* 2:7, Zuckermandel ed., 544. See also BT *Arakhin* 13b and parallel versions in the *midrashim*. See the analysis of Karl-Erich Grözinger, *Musik und Gesang in der Theologie der frühen jüdischen Literatur: Talmud Midrasch Mystik* (Tübingen: J. C. B. Mohr, 1982), 222–23.

37 BT *Berakhot* 34b; BT *Sanhedrin* 99a.

38 R. Judah Lowe, *Netsah Israel* (Jerusalem, 1972), 102–03 [Heb.]. Maharal reformulates this interpretation in chapter 32.

the messianic era on the other. The increasing number of lyre strings conveys a view of history as developing from the past to the present.

R. Judah Moscato's musical approach is as an expression of the status of music among Italian rabbis in the Renaissance. Moscato opens the anthology of his sermons with a famous one on the importance of music,[39] and occasionally relies on it in his commentary on *The Kuzari* as well. This sermon—*Higgayon BeKhinnor* (Sounds for Contemplation on a Lyre)—is titled after David's lyre. In it, Moscato presents intervals and consonances as mirroring the whole of existence in both its material and spiritual dimensions when the substance of the soul, its "origin and beginning[40] lies in the soul itself, [is] ordered in every way[41] and preserved in harmonic ratios."[42]

The Age of Enlightenment changed the rules of the game. Aesthetics became a philosophical discipline. Moses Mendelssohn (1729–1786) discussed music in his aesthetic writings in connection with harmony and the sublime. In one article, he claimed that sensory perceptions are autonomous, and so is the musical experience. He described the loss of this autonomy through a metaphor of the soul as a violin, whose quality is evaluated without the virtuoso who yields a harmonious sound from it.[43] Playing reveals the substantial and independent powers of an instrument.

David's Lyre in Israeli Discourse

From the dawn of Jewish scholarship, researchers have been

---

[39] On Moscato's preaching, see Yosef Dan, "The *Tefilah u-Dim'ah* Sermon of R. Judah Moscato," *Sinai* 76 (1975), 209–32 [Heb.], and Moshe Idel, "Judah Moscato: A Late Renaissance Jewish Preacher," *Preachers of the Italian Ghetto* (ed. David B. Ruderman; Berkeley: University of California Press, 1992), 41–66. Both rabbinic writers and scholars—justifiably—liked this sermon. See, for example, Simon Jacob Glicksberg, *The Jewish Sermon* (Tel Aviv: n. p., 1940), 168–70 [Heb.], and Isaac E. Barzilay, *Between Reason and Faith: Anti-Rationalism in Italian Jewish Thought 1250–1650* (The Hague: Mouton, 1967), 168.

[40] "Beginning" (as a translation of *hathalah*) refers here to a principle or a foundation regulating the activity of the soul.

[41] A preferable variant reading is "according to the universe."

[42] Judah Moscato, *Sermons*, vol. 1 (eds. and trs. Gianfranco Miletto and Giuseppe Veltri; Leiden: Brill, 2011), 80.

[43] Alexander Altmann, "Moses Mendelssohn on Education and the Image of Man," *Studies in Jewish Thought: An Anthology of German Jewish Scholarship* (ed. Alfred Jospe; Detroit: Wayne State University Press, 1981), 398.

awed by the sacred poetry (*piyyutim*) of Judah Halevi.[44] Ezra Fleischer (1928-2006), among the most prominent scholars of medieval Hebrew poetry, described the dynamic of Halevi's religious poetry in distinctly musical terms:

> When you read the *piyyutim* of R. Judah Halevi you are at times captivated by this wondrous movement as if by magic. You forget the words and their meanings, the ideas they seek to represent, and you listen only to the sublime, intangible melody, to the sounds fusing into a harmony that, as it were, is not of this world.[45]

Fleischer obviously meant the flow and the brilliant use of language in Halevi's poems, but music enabled him a suitable formulation and he certainly relied on the fact that the musical dimension is built into the *piyyut*. The reading of poetry becomes music. Note, in this context, the comment of Ben-Zion Meir Hai Uzziel (1880-1953), who was the Chief Sephardi Rabbi. R. Uzziel divided poets who needed inspiration from those who did not, since their being was woven into poetry. Judah Halevi obviously belonged to the second kind, and R. Uzziel relied on the lyre image to convey this distinction:

> A special virtue singles out Judah Halevi from all the other Jewish poets who preceded him and from those who followed him. All engaged in poetry and song at set times, when the spirit of poetry descended upon them or the lyre of poetry hang above them and, when the spirit blew on its strings—awoke the poet and inspired his poetry. Not so Judah Halevi: he was a poetic soul—poetry never ceased in him and was his sole and constant amusement [...]. He, therefore, knew himself as if his body and soul were a lyre for the poetry of Israel, and the spirit of poetry bursts forth from him and voices its lament for the intensity of its pain and suffering, hankers for its God and demands retribution and justice, and yet never ceases in its praise and its song to the Rock of its strength and the God of its exaltation.[46]

---

[44] Aviva Doron, ed., *Yehuda Halevi: A Selection of Critical Essays on His Poetry* (Tel Aviv: Hakibbutz Hameuchad, 1988), 9–41 [Heb.].

[45] Ezra Fleischer, "The Sacred Poetry of Judah Halevi," *The Philosophical Teachings of Judah Halevi* (ed. Haya Schwarz; Jerusalem: Ministry of Education, 1978), 178 [Heb.].

[46] Ben-Zion Meir Hai Uzziel, *Hegiyonei Uzziel*, vol. 2 (Jerusalem: Va'ad le-

R. Uzziel's metaphor hints to the *aggadah* about the lyre that hung above King David's bed. The daring of his statements is astounding. King David had, as it were, needed a lyre, that is, inspiration, whereas Halevi had not since he himself was a kind of lyre. R. Uzziel transposed the distinction between Mosaic prophecy and that of other prophets to the realm of aesthetic inspiration. In any event, poetry and song are part of Halevi's sublime work, as is claimed at the end of the passage.

On December 17, 1997, at a concert celebrating the sixtieth anniversary of the Israeli Philharmonic Orchestra, Minister Zevulun Hammer (1936–1998) declared that "had not the candelabrum been set as the symbol of the State of Israel, we would surely have chosen the [King David's] harp as our symbol." Hammer referred to the combination of the valiant warrior and the musician in the figure of King David. He then added:

> No one has succeeded in taking away the harp from us. We hang up our lyres by the streams of Babylon,[47] we took them with us wherever we went. Our joys and our sorrows were expressed in song. A persecuted, devastated, and struggling people—never ceased singing. Music was for us a ladder of existence that we climbed in all of history's weathers when striving to ascend to universal beauty…. We have a people here that never ceased to love music, even in the storm of wars.[48]

Presenting King David as a musician became a national endeavor. The emphasis on the "national" preeminence of the Jewish people in connection with music (regarding both composition and performance) became a natural and self-evident motif in Jewish thought after Judah Halevi. Thus, the kinnor became one of the symbols of renewed Jewish nationalism.

These remarks presented only a few motifs and trends in the story of the kinnor in rabbinic consciousness and hermeneutics. However, I have traced the contours of the instrument in some of the main rabbinic literary genres. *Ve-idach zil gemor.*

Hotsa'at Kitvei ha-Rav, 1992), 185 [Heb.].

[47] According to Psalms 137:2.

[48] In David Alexander, "Faith, Truth and Art: Notes on the Relationship between the Tradition and the Theater," *Zevulun Hammer: In Memoriam* (ed. Yitzhak Heckelman; Jerusalem: Ministry of Education, 1999), 388 [Heb.].

Artistic Depictions of David and the Kinnor

Siobhán Dowling Long

Introduction

The *kinnôr* (Heb. lyre), which is the instrument that King David played for Saul in 1 Samuel 16:16 and 18:10, has been called a "harp" for well over a thousand years in literature, and in depictions of King David in medieval manuscripts, paintings, and sculpture.[1] Although the construction of the lyre (*kinnôr*) and the harp (*nevel*) are very different,[2] it wasn't until the later Middle Ages and in the Renaissance that artists began to depict David playing or tuning a ninth-century triangular harp.[3] Prior to this period, artists of mosaics and frescoes generally depicted David's kinnor as a type of lyre, similar to that found in translations of the term in the Septuagint (LXX), where *kinnôr* is translated into Greek as a *kithara* in twenty out of forty-two references, and as a *kinyra* in seventeen references; and into Latin by Jerome in the Latin Vulgate, as a "*cithara*" in thirty-seven instances. Sachs concludes that the Hebrew *kinnôr* was a lyre similar to that which the Greeks called a *kithara*.[4] The Latin Vulgate translated it mostly as *cithara* but also as *lyra* in 1

---

[1] I would like to acknowledge the support of the College of Arts, Social Studies and Celtic Studies Research Support Fund, University College Cork, for funding the procurement of two images (Fig. 1 and Fig. 9) used in this chapter. I would also like to express my thanks to the University of Glasgow Library, Archives & Special Collections, and to the Braginsky Collection, Zurich, for their generous permissions to enable me to use the images in Fig. 5 and Fig. 10 respectively.

[2] The lyre had a rectangular or trapezoidal sound box with two curved arms of unequal length joined by a crossbar, with a varying number of strings. Interestingly, the earliest form of lyres stemmed from primaeval arched harps. Dumbrill notes that the period at which the lyre distinguished itself from the harp is difficult to assess owing to the lack of iconographic evidence. In one example, however, in a graffito from Megiddo, the instrument depicted shows a possibility of a hybrid instrument, i.e., a lyre-form harp or a harp-form lyre. Richard Dumbrill, *The Musicology and Organology of the Ancient Near East* (London: Tadema, 1998), 245.

[3] Jeremy Montagu, *The World of Medieval & Renaissance Musical Instruments* (Woodstock, NY: Overlook, 1976), 14.

[4] Curt Sachs, *The History of Musical Instruments* (New York: W. W. Norton, 1940), 107.

Chronicles 15:16; 16:5. While we may never know with certainty the exact type of lyre that the shepherd-boy David played, we may speculate that it was portable and perhaps similar to those played by the Judean lyre-players among the prisoners from Lachish (modern-day Tell ed-Duweir, Israel) on an Assyrian relief depicting the conquests of Sennacherib in Israel (seventh century BCE). We may also speculate that David's lyre was not as elaborate or as big as those excavated by Leonard Woolley at Ur (modern-day Tell al-Muqayyar) in Southern Mesopotamia (1922–1934), from the graves Woolley named the Royal Cemetery. When viewing paintings and illuminated manuscripts it must be borne in mind that artists and illuminators who depicted David playing a harp instead of a lyre generally, although not always, based their illustrations on harps from the period in which the painting was executed.

David as a Type of Orpheus

In Greek mythology, the lyre was regarded as "a divine instrument,"[5] and associated with many notable Greek gods and heroes, among them, Hermes,[6] Apollo,[7] Achilles,[8] and Orpheus to name but a few. Indeed, music was understood to have the power to restore harmony and order to the soul, as noted here in Plato's *Timaeus* (c. 360 BCE):

> And all such composition as lends itself to making audible musical sound is given in order to express harmony, and so serves this purpose as well. And harmony whose movements are akin to the orbits within our souls, is a gift of the Muses, if our dealings with them are guided by

---

[5] Sachs, *The History of Musical Instruments*, 129.

[6] Hermes, the son of Zeus and Maia, is credited with the invention of the lyre shortly after his birth. He crafted his seven-stringed lyre from the shell of a tortoise, while on the way to steal his brother Apollo's oxen (*Homeric Hymns*, IV, 25–67). Later, when Apollo approached Hermes to retrieve the stolen animals, the mystical sound of the instrument so entranced him that he longed to possess it. Hermes accepted Apollo's offer of cattle in exchange for the lyre, along with the promise of dominion over flocks, herds, and wild animals. This story is available in a web edition of the book: H. G. Evelyn White, *Hesiod, Homeric, Hymns and Homerica* (Adelaide: University of Adelaide, 2014), https://ebooks.adelaide.edu.au/h/hesiod/white/complete.html#chapter3.4 (accessed July 16, 2019).

[7] Apollo is the god of music and master of the lyre.

[8] Achilles, a hero from the Trojan War, learned how to play the lyre from Chiron the centaur.

understanding, not for additional pleasure, for which people nowadays seem to make use of it, but to serve as an ally in the fight to bring order to any orbit in our souls that has become unharmonized, and make it concordant with itself. Rhythm, too, has likewise been given us by the Muses for the same purpose, to assist us. For with most of us our condition is such that we have lost all sense of measure and are lacking in grace (47 d–e).

It is well known that Apollonian music (i.e., stringed music) had a harmonizing effect on the soul, whereas Dionysian music (i.e., music from pipes and percussion) had the potential to incite it to frenzy, passion, and violence. The music from Orpheus' lyre, which had been gifted to him by Apollo, had special magical powers that could enchant not only the wild animals but also the trees and rocks. Following the loss of his beloved wife, Eurydice, Orpheus consoled himself with the music from his lyre, as he sang to the wild men of Thrace of the origin of the cosmos and the gods. The therapeutic benefits of music have been long attested in the ancient world, in literature that postdates the biblical story of King David's cure of Saul, for example in Pythagorean theory and practice as attested in two Neoplatonic sources, in Iamblichus' *De vita pythagorica* and Porphyry's *Vita Pythagorae*; in Plato's *Republic* and *The Laws*, where the influence of music on behavior is discussed along with the types of music that ought to be permitted in an enlightened civilization; in Aristotle's *Politics* (Book 7), on the influence of music on character; and in the mythological stories of the Greek gods. In legendary sources, the sound emitted from the lyre represented the harmony of the cosmos.

From the second century, Jewish and Christian writers and artists conflated the character of Orpheus[9] with King David and with Christ in second- and third-century catacomb frescoes, funerary art, and sarcophagi, in sixth century synagogue mosaics, and later, in illuminated manuscripts and paintings. For example, a discovery in 1965 of an early sixth-century CE Gaza synagogue

---

[9] The Hellenic poets Ovid in *Metamorphoses* and Virgil in *Georgics* told how Orpheus, who was regarded as the greatest of all musicians, descended into the underworld and seduced the gods Pluto and Persephone with his singing and music on the lyre in order to win back his wife Eurydice, who had been killed by a snake. Although he was subject to an agreement not to look back at his wife until he had brought her to the upperworld, such was his love that he looked back and she was lost forever.

pavement mosaic revealed a depiction of King David as a type of Orpheus. Dressed as a Byzantine emperor, David's name appears as an inscription in square Hebrew script above the thirteen-string lyre that he strikes with a plectrum in his right hand. Surrounded by a lion cub who is illustrated bowing, a giraffe and a snake, David, like Orpheus, charms the wild animals with his celestial music.[10]

Fig. 1. Figure of King David from the Synagogue at Gaza. (Used with permission from Shutterstock)

The Orpheus scene in the fifth-century Jerusalem floor mosaic from a funerary chapel in Jerusalem, which was discovered by P.H. Vincent in 1901 near the Damascus Gate in Jerusalem, and later transferred to the Archaeological Museum in Istanbul, also depicts Orpheus in a frontal scene, wearing a Phrygian cap and

---

[10] The mosaic dated from 508/509CE on a Greek inscription commemorates the names of its donors. It was part of a synagogue rather than a church, as confirmed by Prof. Asher Ovadiah (1969), who states that the image of King David is "most indicative for after 427 CE such figures were forbidden in Christian churches." Ovadiah contends that the synagogue seems to have belonged to Maiumas Neapolis, which was named Constantia from the fourth century CE onwards. Asher Ovadiah, "Excavations in the Area of the Ancient Synagogue at Gaza (Preliminary Report)," *Israel Exploration Journal* 19.4 (1969): 196.

playing a lyre. Although not named as David, he, too, is surrounded by animals—a marten and a snake, a lamb and a bear, a songbird and an eagle—while Pan and a centaur at the bottom of the panel listen attentively to Orpheus' music. It is thought that this mosaic was laid at the end of the fourth or the beginning of the fifth century, and that it belonged to a pagan family, after which time it was adopted by the Christians, who saw Orpheus as a type of Christ.[11]

Another similar depiction of Orpheus-as-David can be found in the central fresco above the prayer-niche at the synagogue of Dura-Europos. Here the character of Orpheus-David is depicted in a frontal scene, wearing Phrygian garments, and playing a lyre. Stern notes that the character of Orpheus had been taken over by the Jews of Alexandria in the second century BCE[12] when Orphic poems were current in Greek circles. One such Orphic poem, "The Testament," was referred to by numerous Christian apologists, among them Clement of Alexandria in his *Proptrepticus*. In it, Orpheus declares himself to have been "converted to the one true God of monotheism, and to have passed on the Hermetic teachings of monotheism to his son, Museus."[13] Given his adoption by Jewish and Christian writers and artists, it is therefore not surprising, as Stern notes, to find such a representation of a "Judaicized Orpheus" in a third-century synagogue mosaic. The image of Orpheus-David charming the beasts was the symbol *par excellence* of a state of heavenly peace and may have been used in conjunction with other mosaics in this synagogue to illustrate the Golden Age of the Messiah.[14] The image of Orpheus-David calming the animals calls to mind the "Peaceable Kingdom" prophesied by the Prophet Isaiah (11:6–9), in which it is proclaimed that all the animals will live peaceably together when the Messiah establishes his rule of peace and righteousness over the earth.[15]

---

[11] Rina Talgam, *Mosaics of Faith: Floors of Pagans, Jews, Samaritans, Christians, and Muslims in the Holy Land* (Jerusalem: Yad Ben-Zvi Press and University Park, PA: The Pennsylvania State University Press, 2014), 247.

[12] H. Stern, "The Orpheus in the Synagogue of Dura-Europos," *Journal of the Warburg and Courtauld Institutes*, 21.1/2 (1958): 3.

[13] Stern, "The Orpheus in the Synagogue of Dura-Europos," 4.

[14] Stern, "The Orpheus in the Synagogue of Dura-Europos," 4.

[15] This image has been popularized by Edward Hicks (1780–1849) in the painting "Peaceable Kingdom" (1830–32), The Met Fifth Avenue, New York. For details of painting, see https://www.metmuseum.org/art/collection/search/11081 (access-

The figure of Christ was also typified through the figure of Orpheus in early Christian writings. Talgam notes that Clement of Alexandria, in his *Proprepticus* (1.8) in particular, contrasted the pagan song of Orpheus with the song of Christ. Unlike Orpheus who "deceived humankind through his music and led them into idolatry by the enchantment of his music, the Logos was understood to free those who listened to his music, thus giving order to the cosmos."[16] This interpretation found its way into catacomb paintings of Christ, the Son of David, who was portrayed as the new Orpheus. Indeed, images of Orpheus-Christ playing the lyre feature in a number of third century Christian sarcophagi, and third- and fourth-century catacomb frescoes. Orpheus is depicted as a type of Christ, the Good Shepherd, in a seated frontal pose, and attired in Phrygian dress, surrounded by a group of animals. In the Catacomb fresco from the Cemetery of Callistus, Rome (c. third century), for example, the artist replaces the group of animals from the Orpheus synagogue mosaics with two lambs (to represent Christ as the Good Shepherd), two doves (representing peace), a peacock (symbolizing immortality), and sea monsters (to suggest the Jonah narrative). By the second century, Christ had come to be established among Christians and pagans alike as a psychopomp, i.e., as a leader of souls to an immortal home, in funerary art of the catacomb frescoes, sarcophagus carving, and mosaic pavement.[17]

While there have been many examples of King David as a type of Orpheus-Christ down through the centuries, a notable example is found in the tenth-century Paris Psalter (BnF, Ms.gr.139r).[18] Produced in Constantinople during the Macedonian Renaissance, it is lavishly decorated in the classical revival style. Seven of its fourteen full page illustrations depict events in the life of David. Given the prominence of David in this manuscript, it is thought that it may have been created either by or for a Macedonian emperor. From medieval times, images of David as a musician — who bestowed order on the cosmos — and David as a warrior — who

---

ed July 4, 2019).

[16] Talgam, *Mosaics of Faith*, 248.

[17] John B. Friedman, *Orpheus in the Middle Ages* (Cambridge, MA: Harvard University Press, 1970), 38.

[18] To see this image, visit the *Bibliothèque nationale de Paris* Gallica at: https://gallica.bnf.fr/ark:/12148/btv1b10515446x/f6.image (accessed August 1, 2019).

defeated the enemy Goliath and the Philistines—were used to represent David as a model of the ideal king and emperor.[19] This may well have been the intended outcome of the Paris Psalter. Here, David-Orpheus plays the lyre seated on a rock, surrounded by goats and sheep, a faithful dog, the personification of Melody, who sits beside her counterpart David, and Echo, who peers out from behind a pillar. A bronzed youth in the lower right-hand corner, who personifies Mount Bethlehem, has his left arm around a tree stump, which is a symbolic reference, no doubt, to the root of Jesse, who was the father of King David (Isa 11:1–3) and an ancestor of Christ as interpreted by Christian tradition. The illustration links the pagan past with the Christian future in the depiction of the mystical lyre players, David and Orpheus, as types of Christ.

The Son of Jesse

The genealogy of Christ, which is illustrated in artistic representations of the "Jesse Tree" in stained glass windows, illuminated manuscripts, and paintings, very often features an image of David playing his harp above the reclining, sleeping or seated body of his father Jesse. Based on Isaiah's prophecy (Isa 11:1–3):

> *Et egredietur virga de radice Iesse et flos de radice eius ascendet.*

The root or stump in the biblical passage represents Jesse's body, while the rod is the branch—sometimes depicted as a tree trunk—out of which other branches grow, such as the kings and royal ancestors of Christ—David, Solomon, etc.—all the way up to the top, to the flower—the fruit of the womb of the Virgin—the Christ-child. Below is a vivid depiction of the Jesse Tree by Geertgen tot Sint Jans (c. 1455/1465–1485/1495), hailed as the founder of Northern Netherlandish art. David is depicted in a prominent position above Jesse. To his right is his son King Solomon, while above him are other notable Old Testament Kings, Rehoboam,

---

[19] King Henry VIII of England is also represented as a type of King David who played the harp in his Psalter (f. 63v) (pub. 1530–47) illustrating Psalm 52. The other character in this illustration is the King's jester, William Sommers. For further details, see The British Library Digitized Manuscripts at: http://www.bl.uk/manuscripts/FullDisplay.aspx?ref=Royal_MS_2_A_XVI (accessed August 1, 2019).

Abijah, Asa, Jehoshaphat, Jehoram, Uzziah, Jotham, Ahaz, Hezekiah, and Manasseh. At the top the Virgin Mary is enthroned with the Christ-child flanked by angels.

Fig. 2. Geertgen tot Sint Jans, The Tree of Jesse (c. 1500), Rijks Museum. (Europeana Collections, Public Domain)

Other notable representations that feature David the harpist include: The Tree of Jesse window at the Cathedral of Our Lady of

Chartres (1145), which is famed for being the oldest complete Jesse Tree window; the Tree of Jesse window at the Cathedral of Notre Dame in Paris; and the High Altar of the Dominican Church in Frankfurt, painted by the artist Hans Holbein the Elder (1460–1524).[20] In the latter, the four panels on the left trace the royal genealogy of Christ with half-length figures inhabiting the vine that sprouts forth out of Jesse who is seated, awake, and surrounded by the Patriarchs Abraham, Isaac, and Jacob. King David is represented as a musician who plays a harp among other Old Testament kings and prophets. In the four panels to the right, the saints of the Dominican order also inhabit a vine that sprouts forth from its founder. On either side the two vines weave their way up to the top of each panel, to an image of the Virgin enthroned with the Christ-child on her lap. On the left-hand side the Virgin holds an apple before the Christ-child, whilst on the right she receives from one of the saints a white robe of the Dominican order.

David's ancestral link with Christ also features on Celtic High Crosses in Ireland and Scotland from as early as the sixth century. These crosses were intended to teach the foundational stories from the Old and New Testaments to a largely illiterate populace. While many scenes from the life of David are illustrated on Celtic Crosses, the most frequent image by far is that of David playing the lyre. Peter Harbison attributes this frequency to his ancestry with Christ and to his portrayal as a type of Christ.[21] Images of David playing his lyre would have evoked other stories about David such as his composition of the psalms and his encounter with King Saul at the Royal Court (1 Sam 16:21–23 and 18:10–11).

The Royal Court of Saul

It has been stated that David's lyre-playing in 1 Samuel 16:21–23 and 18:10–11 is a classic example of music therapy in action.[22] In these two biblical passages, the young shepherd-boy

---

[20] To view this image, see the Städel Museum Digital Collection at: https://sammlung.staedelmuseum.de/en/work/high-altar-of-the-dominican-church-in-frankfurt-1 (accessed August 1, 2019).

[21] Peter Harbison, *The High Crosses of Ireland: An Iconographical and Photographic*, vol. 1 (Bonn: Rudolph Habelt, 1992), 210.

[22] See Jonathan L. Friedmann, *Music in Biblical Life: The Roles of Song in Ancient Israel* (Jefferson, NC: McFarland, 2013), 58–82; Siobhán Dowling Long, "'Why Weepest Thou?... And Why Is Thy Heart Grieved?' (1 Sam 1:8): Grief and Loss in

David, like Orpheus, attempted to calm the evil spirit who was inhabiting and terrorizing Saul's body and mind. By playing the lyre with his hand, i.e., without a plectrum, David sought to alleviate Saul's pain and suffering through music therapy with a view to restoring harmony and order to Saul's life. The two biblical episodes as they are presented in 1 Samuel 16 and 18 also highlight the opposing effects of David's music on Saul, one positive (16:21–23) and the other negative (18:10–11). In the first, David's music caused the evil spirit to depart, and Saul loved David. In the second episode, David's music incited Saul into a frenzied rage, and he despised David, so much so that he cast his spear at David on two occasions without success (18:10–11). The cause of Saul's disquiet, however, was his growing realization that David was usurping his authority as King, and for this reason he eyed him with suspicion (18:11). Also, by succumbing to David's music on a daily basis, Saul was further relinquishing power to the one whose music not only controlled the evil spirit, but also his own emotional and psychological wellbeing. With each passing day, Saul was becoming more and more dependent on David until it finally dawned on him what was happening: God had departed and was now with David (18:12). This newfound knowledge made him afraid of David (18:12), and so he removed him and made him a commander of a thousand (18:13).

While David's victory over the giant Goliath is perhaps one of the most popular episodes in paintings and manuscript illuminations, David's cure of Saul is next in popularity. Artists such as Lucas van Leyden,[23] Jan van den Hoecke (early 1630s),[24] Giovanni Francesco Barbieri (1646), Aernt de Gelder (1682), Bernardo Cavallino (1645; three times), Ernst Josephson (1878), Julius Kronberg (1885), and Marc Chagall (1958), among others, painted these scenes, either with a harp, an Egyptian bow harp, or a lyre.

---

the Books of Samuel: A Musical Interpretation," *The Books of Samuel: Stories-History-Reception History* (ed. Walter Dietrich; Leuven: Peeters, 2016), 271–82.

[23] To view this image, see the Art Institute Chicago at: https://www.artic.edu/artworks/138156/david-playing-the-harp-before-saul (accessed August 1, 2019).

[24] To view this image, see the Museum of Fine Arts, Budapest at: https://www.mfab.hu/artworks/david-playing-the-harp-for-king-saul/ (accessed August 1, 2019).

Rembrandt (1606–1669) also painted the two biblical scenes (1 Sam 16:21–23 and 18:10–11), beginning with the second biblical account (Stadelsches Kunstinstitut, Frankfurt, 1629/30). Here, Saul holds his spear firmly in his right hand, as he eyes the harpist David with malevolence and contempt. Twenty-eight years later, Rembrandt painted this scene again (Mauritshuis, The Hague, c. 1651–1654 and 1655–1658), only this time illustrating King Saul weeping into the drapery that now symbolically separates him from David, who plays what appears to be a medieval harp. Unlike the earlier painting, here Rembrandt depicts a distraught Saul whose loose grip on his spear symbolizes his kingship slipping away to David. The biblical narrator recounts that David played the harp before Saul without a plectrum, and this is how Rembrandt and many other artists and illuminators have generally depicted David playing the instrument.

Fig. 3. Rembrandt van Rijn, Saul and David (c. 1651–1654 and 1655–1658). (Courtesy of Mauritshuis, The Hague)

Manuscript illuminators sometimes personified the demon as a creature who whispered into Saul's ear. A miniature by the Master of the Ingeborg Psalter, for example, sets this scene in Hell, with the gold paint in the background of the medallion representing its fiery flames. The demon, who represents Satan, climbs onto the back of Saul's chair and whispers into his right ear, while pointing at David. One could interpret this representation as exonerating Saul of any crime of his attempted murder of David, since it was the demon/Satan who told Saul to cast his spear. David, who is playing a portable green medieval harp, catches Saul's eye at the very moment before he darts out of the way to save his own life.

Fig. 4. Master of the Ingeborg Psalter (French, active about 1195 to about 1210), Initial Q: David Before Saul, after 1205, tempera colors and gold leaf on parchment. Leaf: 31 × 21.9 cm (12 3/16 × 8 5/8 in.), Ms. 66 (99.MK.48), fol. 55. (Courtesy of the Getty's Open Content Program)

So why did the biblical narrator state that David played the lyre without a plectrum when it was more usual to play this ancient lyre with a plectrum? The first possible answer concerns music therapy as a treatment for alleviating Saul's psychiatric disorder. In this case, the use of a plectrum would have created a brighter and therefore sharper sound, which would not have been effective in treating Saul's psychiatric condition. Therefore, it is reasonable to speculate that David left the plectrum aside and plucked the strings with his fingers in order to create a softer, meditative sound, which induced healing.

The second concerns the symbolism of this action and the attitude towards instrumental music in the ancient world. Sachs notes that in the second *Book of Laws*, Plato condemned instrumental music as subordinate to music used in the accompaniment of singing or in the recitation of poetry.[25] Solo playing without singing, known as *psilê kithárisis*, as opposed to the *kitharodía* or plectrum playing to accompany a song,[26] involved hand plucking with bare fingers, i.e., without a plectrum. Given that David played instrumental music in the presence of Saul, one might conclude that this method of playing reinforced Saul's subordinate status in the presence of the new king in waiting.

The Transportation of Ark to Jerusalem

The Ark of the Covenant makes its journey to Jerusalem in two stages, each with a procession and to the accompaniment of musical instruments (2 Sam 6:1-11; 12-15).[27] In paintings and illuminated manuscripts David is frequently depicted playing the harp ahead of a procession. In these representations, painters and illuminators have brought together elements of the two processions in 2 Samuel 6. To differentiate between stage 1 and stage 2 of the Ark's journey to Jerusalem, let us note some salient features of each stage. At stage 1 the Ark is taken from the house of Abinadab and mounted upon a cart driven by Abinadab's two sons, Uzzah and

---

[25] Sachs, *The History of Musical Instruments*, 129.

[26] Sachs, *The History of Musical Instruments*, 108.

[27] The translation of these instruments differs in various translations of the Hebrew text. For the purpose of this chapter, however, I have confined my translation to the Latin Vulgate, as this version was the source generally used by Medieval and Renaissance painters and illuminators.

Ahio (2 Sam 6:3). David appears to be among the crowd rather than ahead of the procession. He and the people of Israel are singing songs before the Lord and playing an array of instruments made of conifer wood, and harps and lyres and hand drums and rattles (sistrums) and cymbals (2 Sam 6:5):

> *David autem et omnis Israël ludebant coram Domino in omnibus lignis fabrefactis, et citharis et lyris et tympanis et sistris et cymbalis.*

After this event and following the death of Uzzah, who had been struck down by God for grasping the Ark to prevent it from falling after the oxen had stumbled, David brought the Ark to the house of Obed-edom the Gittite, where it remained for three months. Stage 2 of its journey began when David moved the Ark on its second trek to Jerusalem, where it was carried rather than mounted on a cart (2 Sam 6:13). After the Ark had gone six paces from the house of Obed-edom, David performed a ritual sacrifice of an ox and a ram (*immolabat bovem et atietem*; Vulgate 2 Sam 6:13). Unlike the first stage of Ark's journey, however, the biblical narrator recounts that David was girded with an ephod. There is a suggestion that he led the procession, as he danced with all his might before God (v. 14). David and all of Israel brought up the Ark with shouts of joy and blasts of the horn (vv. 13–15).

> *Et David saltabat totis viribus ante Dominum porro David erat accinctus ephod lineo.*
> *Et David et omnis domus Israhel ducebant arcam testamenti Domini in iubilo, et in clangore bucinae.*

Although the biblical narrator mentions only horns and ritual shouting at stage 2, artists also illustrated David playing the harp or lyre at this point. The second stage is identified by the people or Levites carrying the Ark on their shoulders. Jan de Bray (1627–1697) for example, brought the elements of the two stages together by illustrating this scene with David playing the harp ahead of the procession, together with two long trumpets amid the sound of singing by the people who read from books, most likely from seventeenth-century psalters. Three centuries later, Chagall also depicted the scene in a lithograph entitled *L'Arche d'alliance transportée à Jérusalem, précédée de David qui danse et joue de la harpe*

101

(1956).[28] Here, Chagall depicts David holding his lyre with one hand while his other is raised in the air, amid the people of Israel who play an array of musical instruments—the lyre, stringed instruments, drum, horn, flute, and cymbals. The scene depicted resembles the parade of the *Aron Kodesh* (holy cabinet or ark) at the joyous Simchat Torah celebration, which falls on the last day of Sukkot.

The two stages of the Ark's transportation to Jerusalem are also minutely detailed in MS M.638, fol. 39v from the Morgan library.[29] Of interest here are the upper panels in which David plays the harp and dances together with long trumpets. In the right panel, the illuminator depicted the ritual slaughter of two sheep to the sound of long trumpets, a stringed instrument, and a square *toph*. In this panel also, Michal looks out a window pointing her finger accusingly at David as an expression of her disapproval at his outrageous display (1 Sam 6: 16).

The scene from 2 Samuel 6 is also recounted by the narrator of 1 Chronicles 13 and 15. In the latter, the narrator recounts how the Levites brought the Ark of God up to Jerusalem upon their shoulders and with poles (1 Chr 15:15), and that the people brought up the Ark of God with shouting to the sound of the horn, trumpets, cymbals, and made loud music on harps and lyres. The illumination from the Morgan Library shows the influence of this passage from 1 Chronicles 15:28.

At this event also David organized the Temple musicians (1 Chr 15:16–24). Manuscript illuminators often depicted David surrounded by musicians, among them Ethan, Iduthin, Asaph, and Heman (cf. fn.16). The Vivian Bible (c. 845), a ninth-century Carolingian manuscript, which was presented to Charles the Bald in 846, contains a miniature of David, half-naked, playing a triangular frame with fifteen strings, surrounded by the four above named musicians, two bodyguards, and the four cardinal virtues of Prudence, Justice, Fortitude and Temperance (Bibliothèque

---

[28] To view this image, see the WIKIART Visual Art Encyclopaedia at: https://www.wikiart.org/en/marc-chagall/the-ark-of-the-covenant-transported-to-jerusalem-preceded-by-david-dancing-and-playing-the-harp (accessed August 1, 2019).

[29] To view this image, see the Morgan Library and Museum at: http://ica.themorgan.org/manuscript/page/78/158530 (accessed August 1, 2019).

Nationale, Paris, folio 215v).[30] It features as the frontispiece to the Book of Psalms. Amos 6:5 also points to David as the inventor of musical instruments.

Another notable depiction displaying David playing his harp, or in this case tuning his harp among the musicians, is found in the Hunterian manuscript (see Fig. 5). The act of tuning symbolizes the orderly effect of David's music, like Orpheus, on the cosmos. The medieval instruments depicted include handbells, which are stuck by two figures on either side of King David; a vielle or bowed lyra to the left below King David; a triple pipe played by two figures in the center; and a lyra da gamba played by a figure to the right. In the roundel on the lower left, two figures play a psaltery (see section 10 below) and handbells, and in the roundel on the lower right two figures play an organistrum. This full-page illustration (left side) is part of a double page opening. The page that follows on the right is a miniature of an historiated B(eatus Vir/Blessed is the Man)—the first psalm of the Psalter (see section 9) and a reference to King David, who is traditionally regarded as the author and composer of the psalms.

---

[30] To see this image, see the Bibliothèque nationale de Paris Gallica at: https://gallica.bnf.fr/ark:/12148/btv1b8455903b/f438.item (accessed August 1, 2019).

Fig. 5. Full Page Miniature depicting David Tuning his Harp, The Hunterian Psalter, Folio 21v. (Used with permission of University of Glasgow Library, Archives & Special Collections)

David in Prayer

In countless representations—in paintings, stained glass windows, illuminated manuscripts, and sculptures—artists have depicted King David, the harpist and "sweet singer of Israel" (2 Sam 23:2), at different stages of his adult life playing the lyre or more commonly the harp, which he plays or tunes either alone or in the company of other musicians (see Fig. 5). While David's age is open to speculation, Ginzberg notes one rabbinic tradition that states he was anointed by Samuel at the age of twenty-eight.[31] Whether or not Christian artists were aware of this tradition, they, too, illustrated David either as a young man or as an older man who played the harp as he composed and prayed the psalms.[32]

In Christian and Jewish illuminated manuscripts, a penitent King David is often depicted praying in solitude, enraptured, and with eyes raised upwards, as he plays his harp either outdoors on an area of grass, a desert or on stony ground amid mountains and buildings, or indoors before an altar or a prie-dieu. Other illustrations show him in prayer with his harp cast aside, either outdoors or indoors, pointing to his prayer focused wholly on God. Such depictions of David are found in abundance in thirteenth-, fourteenth-, and fifteenth-century Hora. One such example is the "Book of Hours for Use in Rome" (Bibliothèque de Genève, Ms. lat. 32a, f. 74v), which shows an older King David kneeling on his right leg in prayer as he plucks the strings of his harp to accompany his song of praise/petition before God, who is illustrated in the top right corner bestowing a blessing on David and holding a cross (see Fig. 6). Here, the illuminator depicted David without his crown but robed in a sumptuous fur-trimmed garment. The absence of a crown, turban, staff, and/or shoes in such miniatures symbolize David's heightened penitence. In the background, there are medieval buildings with turrets to represent David's palace (2 Sam 5:11), and a mountain that calls to mind biblical mountains such as

---

[31] Louis Ginzberg, *The Legends of the Jews*, vol. 4: *Bible Times and Characters from Joshua to Esther* (tr. Henrietta Szold; Philadelphia: Jewish Publication Society, 1987), 83.

[32] The view that David authored the entire Book of Psalms is found only in late rabbinic literature. The superscriptions of many psalms, which came later, indicate their authorship or attribution of authorship to the following: 73 to David, 2 to Solomon, Psalm 90 to Moses, 12 to Asaph, 11 to the Sons of Korah, Psalm 88 to Heman, and Psalm 89 to Ethan.

Calvary, where Christ was crucified, and Mount Moriah, the site of Abraham's near-sacrifice of Isaac (Gen 22).

Alluding to David's older age, Ginzberg, referencing Josephus'*Antiquities* (VII, 12.3), notes that:

> being freed from wars and dangers, David enjoyed for the remainder of his life a profound peace, composed songs and hymns to God in several sorts of meters: some of those which he made were trimeters, and other pentameters. He also made instruments of music, and taught the Levites to sing hymns to God, both on the Sabbath and on.[33]

---

[33] Louis Ginzberg, *The Legends of the Jews,* vol. 6: *Notes to Volumes III and IV: From Moses in the Wilderness to Esther* (tr. by Henrietta Szold; Philadelphia: Jewish Publication Society, 1987), 263.

Fig. 6. Bibliothèque de Genève, Ms. lat. 32a, f. 74v – Book of Hours for use in Rome. (Attribution-NonCommercial 4.0 International)

Commenting on David's great piety, Ginzberg also notes a tradition about David and his study of the Torah. Here, David contented himself with only sixty breadths of sleep, after which time, at midnight, the strings of his harp, which were made of the gut of the ram sacrificed by Abraham on Mount Moriah, began to vibrate and the sound emitted awakened him and caused him to arise and to devote himself to the study of the Torah.[34]

A miniature from the Master of the Lübeck Bible (c. 1485–1520) depicts David in prayer in an illustration of Psalm 37:2, the third of seven penitential psalms (*Domine ne in furore tuo arguas me, neque in ira tua corripias me*). David is dressed as a king in a fur-trimmed red ceremonial robe, while his harp, staff, and crown are cast aside. Other scenes from the life of David are included in the border, among them, a young David wrestling a bear, David the shepherd with a sheep, and the return of David in triumph with the decapitated head of Goliath on a pike, greeted by a band of women singers and musicians who are depicted playing the medieval harp, lute, and a woodwind instrument, possibly a douçaine.

---

[34] Ginzberg, *The Legends of the Jews*, vol. 4, 101.

Fig. 7. Master of the Lübeck Bible (Flemish, about 1485 to about 1520), DAVID IN PRAYER, about 1510–1520, tempera colors, gold, and ink on parchment. Leaf: 23.2 × 16.7 cm (9 1/8 × 6 9/16 in.), Ms. Ludwig IX 18 (83.ML.114), fol. 166. (Digital image courtesy of the Getty's Open Content Program)

Other representations show David praying indoors at an altar or a prie-dieu. In one such example in the BL Harley manuscript 2935, a miniature illuminating Psalm 37:2, David kneels before an altar upon which rests an open book, most likely the Book of Psalms. In regal robes and crowned, he plays the harp, as a dog, symbolizing fidelity, sits obediently in upright position to his left, while above in the left-hand corner God bestows a blessing with his right hand.

Fig. 8. Miniature of King David playing harp, decorated initial D(omine) and foliate borders, at the beginning of the Penitential Psalms. Image taken from BL Harley 2935, f. 88 of Book of Hours, Use of Chatres. (Europeana Collections, Public Domain)

King David in the Company of Angels

King David is often represented playing various types of harps, surrounded by angels, with eyes raised heavenwards in rapture, praying supplications and praises to God. For example, the seventeenth-century painter Domenichino, who served as papal architect during the pontificate of Gregory XV (1621–1623), depicted him playing a tall triple-strung harp (invented in Bologna in mid-sixteenth century), with a decorated sound-box and a golden angel. Dressed in sumptuous regal attire, David, who wears a golden crown reminiscent of a crown of thorns, is oblivious to the putti, one to the left who holds a book (perhaps representing a psalter) and the other to the right, placed behind King David who writes or copies the psalms using a feathered stylus in imitation of David.

The Jewish Illuminated manuscript Tradition

Of the surviving illustrated medieval Hebrew manuscript Psalters (*Tehillim*), Jacob Leveen notes that the number, of which descriptions have been published, is relatively small.[35] While this still holds true today, one of the earliest and extant manuscripts is the Ms. Parma. 1870 (Cod. De Rossi 510) from the Palatina Library in Parma, Italy, which contains a text and commentary by Abraham Ibn Ezra (b. 1089), as well as miniatures of David playing his harp, Saul in flight, and the weeping exiles in Babylon who hung up their harps (Ps 137).

Within this illuminated manuscript tradition, Cohen points out that a rich custom of decorating Hebrew manuscripts flourished in Europe from the thirteenth century through to the Renaissance in the regions of Spain and Portugal (Sephardic) and Germany and France (Ashkenazic).[36] The decoration of Hebrew codices from Italy also occurred during this period and reached a peak in the fifteenth century, where members of wealthy Jewish banking families commissioned elaborate illuminations. Many of these show the influence of the Christian illuminated manuscript tradition in their depiction of David playing a harp rather than a lyre (*kinnôr*). One such manuscript is the Rothschild Miscellany, which is now housed

---

[35] Jacob Leveen, *The Hebrew Bible in Art*, The Schweich Lectures of the British Academy 1939 (reprint ed.; New York: Hermon, 1974), 93.

[36] Evelyn M. Cohen, "Isaac Norsa's Hebrew Miscellany of 1523," *The Princeton University Library Chronicle* 64.1 (2002): 87.

in the Israel Museum, Jerusalem, and which represents the highpoint of Hebrew illumination. Of interest is a miniature of Psalm 1 in which an older, bearded King David plays his harp among the animals (deer and a rabbit), like and yet unlike the young, clean-shaven Orpheus who played his lyre (fol. 1b). Whether it was influenced by the Orphic story in Jewish exegetical tradition or not, what it shows is a certain affinity with the subject matter of Orpheus. Although David is not surrounded by any type of vicious animal, the presence of deer and rabbits symbolizes the gentle yet powerful effect of his divinely inspired words and music on creation.

Berakhot 10a states that every psalm chapter that was particularly pleasing to David began and ended with the word "happy." From his reading of this passage, Ginzberg notes that King David's favorite psalms were those beginning with *Ashre*, "Happy is he."[37] The illuminated scene accompanying Psalm 1 certainly reflects the contentment of David as he played his harp, which was an activity that would have brought great happiness not only to David, but to everyone in his company. The level of happiness would have been even greater given that David's music-making activity was directed not only inwards but outwards, in praise and honor of God.

---

[37] Ginzberg, *The Legends of the Jews*, vol. 6, 262.

Fig. 9. Fol.1v from The Rothschild Miscellany, Northern Italy, c.1450–80 (pen, ink, tempera & gold leaf on paper), Italian School (fifteenth century). Gift of James A. de Rothschild, London. (Used with permission from The Israel Museum, Jerusalem, Israel)

Similarly, a Book of Psalms (parchment, 129ff) copied and decorated by Moses Judah Leib ben Wolf Broda of Trebitsch (1723), who was also responsible for the "most famous decorated Hebrew manuscript of the eighteenth century, the Von Geldern Haggadah of 1723," has a depiction of King David on folio 6v at the beginning of Psalm 1, under the word "*Ashre*." Here David plays a harp rather than a lyre (*kinnôr*) on a palatial terrace, before an open book — most likely the Book of Psalms.

Fig. 10. Zürich, Braginsky Collection, B222. Parchment: 129 ff. 12 × 8.1 cm [Vienna/Amsterdam?], copied and decorated by Moses Judah Leib ben Wolf Broda of Trebitsch, 1723 Tehillim (Psalms). (Used with permission of the Braginsky Collection, Zurich; photography by Ardon Bar-Hama, Ra'anana, Israel)

The Haggadah, the ritual script of the Eve of Passover in the home, came to be associated *par excellence* with biblical illustrations.[38] A notable example is the Charlotte Rothschild Haggadah, with German translation, copied by Eliezer Sussman Mezeritsch and illustrated by Charlotte Rothschild (1807-1859).[39] Inspired by illuminations from Christian and Jewish manuscripts — the biblical cycle painted in the Vatican loggias by the workshop of Raphael, and the copperplate engravings of the printed Amsterdam Haggadah of 1695 — this Haggadah is known as the only Hebrew manuscript to have been illuminated by a woman.[40] Rothschild produced this work for her uncle, Amschel Mayer Rothschild (1773-1855), on the occasion of his seventieth birthday. Her illustration of King David playing the harp (f. 62), one of seven illustrations, shows him crowned and robed in kingly attire as he plays the harp with raised eyes before an angel, who holds the music in the same manner as Joseph holds a manuscript of music for an angel musician in Caravaggio's "Rest on the Flight into Egypt" (Matt 2:12-13) (c. 1597, Galleria Doria-Pamphili, Rome).

Historiated Initials in Christian Illuminated Manuscripts

In Christian illuminated manuscripts, David is frequently depicted in the historiated initials of many the psalms of the Vulgate Bible, most popularly in the historiated initial B(eatus) at the beginning of Psalm 1, where he is depicted visually as a model of the Blessed Man praying the psalms to the accompaniment of the harp (or another instrument such as a psaltery or a carillon of bells), either alone or in the company of other instrumentalists or surrounded by various musical instruments. One such example is the Fieschi Psalter (Walters Ms. W.45), a thirteenth-century north-eastern French Psalter with an additional Office of the Dead. In fol. 16r,[41] the artist illustrates David playing his harp in the upper part

---

[38] Leveen, *The Hebrew Bible in Art*, 96.

[39] To view this image, see e-codices (Virtual Manuscript of Switzerland) at: https://www.e-codices.unifr.ch/en/bc/b-0314/62/0/Sequence-2809 (accessed August 1, 2019).

[40] To view this image, see the Braginsky Collection at: http://braginskycollection.com/ajaxzoom/single.php?zoomDir=/pic/BCB/BCB_314&zoomFile=BCB_314_001.jpg (accessed August 1, 2019).

[41] To view this image, see the Digital Walters Manuscript at: http://www.thedigitalwalters.org/Data/WaltersManuscripts/W45/data/W.45/s

of the historiated initial B, whilst decapitating the head of the enemy Goliath in its lower part. Details in the bottom margin below the text (from left to right) have illustrated scenes from 1 Samuel 17: Saul playing a bagpipe (a non-biblical detail), David aiming a slingshot at Goliath and a shepherd's staff (vv. 40, 49, 50), Goliath holding a spear and shield (vv. 41, 45), and a lone flock of sheep (v. 15). Given the bagpipe's[42] association with the music of lowly peasants in Renaissance art, the depiction in the hands of Saul in this illumination is negative, contrasting Saul's lowly status with that of David's, who would soon succeed him as King. Although there are many illustrations of sheep in illuminated manuscripts, depictions of the young shepherd boy who plays his harp whilst caring for his sheep are sparse, and tend to exist more often in children's Bibles or story books about King David. Some examples of other historiated initials of David playing the harp or other musical instruments include the initial D(omine) of Penitential Psalm No. 6, the initial E(xsulte) of Psalm 80, the initial C of Psalm 97, which in some illuminations has an illustration of King David striking a carillon of bells with hammers, surrounded by other musicians (See Fig. 11), and the historiated initial S(alvum) at the beginning of Psalm 68, which shows scenes of David bringing the Ark to Jerusalem (see section 5 above).

---

ap/W45_000034_sap.jpg (accessed August 1, 2019).

[42] See Siobhán Dowling Long, "Musical Instruments in Biblical Art," *Bible, Art, Gallery* (ed. Martin O'Kane; Sheffield: Sheffield Phoenix Press, 2011), 104–07.

Letamini iusti in domino: et confitemini
in memorie sanctificationis eius. ps
dauid:
canticum nouum: quia mirabi
lia fecit.
Saluauit sibi dexteram eius: et bra
chium sanctum eius.
Notum fecit dominus salutare suu:

Fig. 11. Master of the Ingeborg Psalter (French, active about 1195 to about 1210), INITIAL C: DAVID PLAYING BELLS, after 1205, tempera colors and gold leaf on parchment. Leaf: 31 × 21.9 cm (12 3/16 × 8 5/8 in.), Ms. 66 (99.MK.48), fol. 105v. (Digital image courtesy of the Getty's Open Content Program)

King David Playing the Psaltery

While Renaissance artists continued to depict King David playing the harp, they also illustrated him playing many other instruments, most notably the psaltery, the second most common instrument played by David in medieval manuscripts. Deltoid in shape, this stringed instrument was also played with a plectrum. The ancient Greek version was called a psalterion and bore similarities to the triangular harp, while the medieval psaltery was held against the chest, as can be seen in the following full-page miniature from BL Harley 2953 (f. 20) at the beginning of the Psalms (Fig. 12). Echoing 1 Samuel 16:23, David is depicted playing the psaltery without a plectrum.

Fig. 12. Full-page miniature of King David Playing the Psaltery (probably added) at the beginning of the Psalms, BL Harley 2953, f. 20v. (The British Library, Europeana Collections, Public Domain)

In the third century, the *nevel* (harp) was translated as a psalterion in the Septuagint (LXX), which may explain the psaltery's association with King David in medieval illuminated manuscripts. In addition, this instrument had a symbolic association with Christ going back to the time of the church fathers and early medieval theologians. Hilarius of Potiers and Augustine, for example, both likened its deltoid shape to the body of Christ crucified. Augustine also regarded it as a heavenly instrument in contrast to the earthly cithara. In addition to its association with Christ, its ten strings, according to Basil, Augustine, and Aquinas, also signified the Ten Commandments. Robert Boenig points out that Joachim of Fiore (twelfth century) associated the psaltery with the Trinity in his work, the *Psalterium decem chordanum* (Ten-Stringed Psaltery). For Joachim, the psaltery of Psalm 33 was also "an image of the moral universe, analogous to the beatific vision."[43]

While there are many fine examples of King David playing the psaltery in Christian medieval manuscripts, there is also a miniature of King David playing the psaltery in folio 167b of the lavish Garret Hebrew MS. 6. Measuring just 8.8cm x 7cm x 3.5cm, and containing the Pentateuch, the Psalms, miscellaneous anti-Christian polemical writings from the Prophets, and a prayer book according to the Roman rite, it was copied in 1523 for a wealthy Jewish banker Isaac Norsa,[44] who lived in Ferrara from c. 1485 to 1560.[45] Cohen points out that although illuminations in Hebrew manuscripts had been lavishly decorated in fifteenth-century Italy,

---

[43] Robert Boenig and Kathleen Davis, eds. *Manuscript, Narrative, Lexicon Essays on Literary and Cultural Transmission in Honor of Whitney F. Bolton* (Lewisburg and London: Bucknell University Press and Associated University Presses, 2000), 103.

[44] According to Evelyn Cohen, Isaac's father, Emmanuel Norsa, who married into the illustrious Pisa family of bankers, was thought to have been the second wealthiest Jew during the fifteenth and early sixteenth century. He commissioned a number of Hebrew manuscripts, three of which were copied by the notable scribe, Abraham Farissol. The first, a prayer book with psalms copied in 1496; the second completed in 1496, a diminutive Pentateuch with *haftarot* and *megillot*; and the third completed in 1502, a Hagiographia containing the Psalms, Job, Proverbs, the Five Scrolls and *Sefer Shimushei Tehillim* (Parma, Biblioteca Palatina 3503). Cohen notes that Emanuel's daughter also appears to have possessed what is known today as the *Rothschild Mahzor* (JTS MS 8892), a beautiful illuminated prayer book, scribed by Abraham Judah of Camerino. Cohen, "Isaac Norsa's Hebrew Miscellany of 1523," 92–93.

[45] Cohen, "Isaac Norsa's Hebrew Miscellany of 1523," 96.

Hebrew illuminated manuscripts from sixteenth-century Italy are rare. Bearing this in mind, the Garret MS contains only one illustration, that of King David (folio 167b). In a similar fashion to other similar Christian illuminated miniatures, David is depicted in the foreground as an old man with white hair, a crown, and a bifurcated beard, playing a gold psaltery. An unfurled scroll, which winds its way out of the psaltery, contains the Hebrew words taken from Psalm 67:2: "May God be gracious to us and bless us." The margins are decorated with an elaborate floral border on three sides, and an image of a lion on the bottom margin represents, most likely, the tribe of Judah from whom David was descended.[46] Given the similarities to other Christian illuminations, folio 167b might well have been completed by a professional Christian illuminator.

Conclusion

This chapter explored the depiction of David's *kinnôr* in paintings and medieval manuscripts. It highlighted the ways in which Jewish and Christian writers and artists conflated the character of Orpheus, known by Pindar as the "minstrel of songs," with King David, "the sweet singer of Israel," in the early centuries (CE). Christian artists and writers also conflated the Orpheus-David figures with Christ in catacomb frescoes, funerary art, and sarcophagi from the second and third centuries. On Irish and Scottish Celtic Crosses from the sixth to tenth centuries, sculptors, too, represented David as a musician who played a triangular-shaped *kinnôr*. This portrayal called to mind for a largely illiterate populace David's ability as a music therapist from 1 Samuel 16:16 and 18:10, and the power of his mystical music, like the music of Orpheus, in bringing about harmony and order to Saul's life (1 Sam 16:16). As in numerous medieval manuscripts, the image of David as a musician highlighted his connection with the Book of Psalms. From the later Middle Ages and Renaissance period, artists and illuminators often represented David playing or tuning a harp, the latter a symbol of the order brought about by David's music. Miniatures in illuminated manuscripts also depicted David in the historiated initials of certain psalms, at prayer as a middle-aged and as an older man, and also surrounded by musicians to recall his organization of the First Temple musicians and music, and his

---

[46] Cohen, "Isaac Norsa's Hebrew Miscellany of 1523," 100.

invention of musical instruments (Amos 6:5). In addition to the lyre and harp, David is also depicted playing other musical instruments, among them bells and other stringed instruments, such as the psaltery, which would have been popular during the lifetimes of artists and illuminators. The psaltery, in particular, was symbolic of Christ crucified, the Trinity, and the Ten Commandments. David's involvement in the Transportation of the Ark of the Covenant to Jerusalem (2 Sam 6:1–11; 12–15) also enjoyed depictions in paintings and illuminated manuscripts, although not as many as those of David's cure of Saul (1 Sam 16:16) and Saul's attempted murder of David (1 Sam 18:10). In the twentieth century, Jewish artist Marc Chagall restored to David his original instrument, the *kinnôr*. It now remains to be seen what instrument(s) artists and sculptors of the twenty-first century will ascribe to King David, and to see if they, too, will represent the *kinnôr* as a harp instead of a lyre.

Handel's Harpists and the Morals of Music

Ruth Smith

George Frideric Handel (1685–1759) wrote mainly in the style of his time and with extensions of that style, not in a consciously historicizing fashion. But his musical mimesis of instruments named in his verbal texts occasionally included imitation and even employment of obsolete and archaic instruments. Several of his English librettos mention the lyre and/or harp.[1] In some of their texts, lyre/harp and lute are synonymous, allowing standard orchestral plucked or pluckable instruments— theorbo, archlute, strings—to provide the imitation, as for example in "Tune your harps" in *Esther*. The harp (unlike the lyre) was extant, but was not a regular instrument of the London orchestra.[2] However, Handel's desire for verisimilitude led him to introduce the harp in an opera (*Giulio Cesare*, 1724), an ode (*Alexander's Feast*, 1736), and three oratorios (*Esther*, 1720, *Saul*, 1739, and *Alexander Balus*, 1748), to represent variously the ancient Jewish harp and "pagan" lyre. He used the harp for "oriental" flavor in *Alexander Balus* (set in Egypt; story from 1 Macc 11–12) and in the famous Parnassus scene of *Giulio Cesare* (also set in Egypt), in which Cleopatra beguiles Caesar with "V'adoro, pupille," accompanied by an on-stage orchestra. This chapter considers Handel's use of the harp in *Saul* and *Alexander's Feast*.

Handel wrote his harp music for the *arpa doppia*, a chromatically tuned instrument with two or three ranks of strings, in ranges of about three or four octaves.[3] There is no certain record

---

[1] *Esther, Athalia, Alexander's Feast, Samson, An Occasional Oratorio, Judas Maccabeus, Alexander Balus, Joshua, Solomon, Theodora,* and *Jephtha.*

[2] For definitions from Handel's time of contemporary harp vs ancient lyre see, for example, Sébastian de Brossard, *A Musical Dictionary* (tr. James Grassineau; London: printed for J. Wilcox, 1740), 98–99, 123–25.

[3] Dagmar Glüxam, "Instrumentation, 9: Harp," *The Cambridge Handel Encyclopedia* (ed. David Vickers and Annette Landgraf; Cambridge: Cambridge University Press, 2009), 341–42.

of his composing for specific harpists. It seems likely that the harp part in *Esther* was for the Welsh virtuoso William Powell (died 1750) when he was employed by Handel's and *Esther's* patron James Brydges (the future Duke of Chandos). According to *Grove's Dictionary*, Sir John Hawkins stated that the harp part in *Alexander's Feast* was likewise premiered by Powell; and independent performances during 1739–1742 of what was probably or certainly the *Alexander's Feast* harp concerto were advertised as being performed by another famous Welsh player, John Parry, harpist (1734–1782) to the family of Handel enthusiast Sir Watkin Williams Wynn II.[4] A "Mr. Jones" is advertised as performing "a concerto of Mr. Handel's on the Welsh Harp" at Lincoln's Inn Fields theatre in 1737,[5] and Winton Dean states in connection with Handel's performance of *Esther* at Oxford in 1733 that "Chandos is known to have sent a harpist, one Thomas Jones, to Oxford at the time of the Public Act; he may have played the harp part in *Esther*."[6]

Handel's most extended diegetic demonstrations of a musician's attempt to sway the hearer through instrumental music alone, in *Saul* and *Alexander's Feast*, foreground a discrete solo movement for the harp/lyre, directed — with life-changing results — at rulers who have the power to benefit or to destroy their own nation and others'.[7] In *Saul* and *Alexander's Feast* the harp/lyre is

---

[4] Cheryl Ann Fulton, "Harp, V, Europe and the Americas, 5, Multi-rank harps in Europe outside Spain, i, The Instruments, iii, Wales and England," *The New Grove Dictionary of Music and Musicians*, 2nd ed. (ed. Stanley Sadie and John Tyrrell; London: Oxford University Press, 2001), https://doi-org.ezp.lib.cam.ac.uk/10.1093/gmo/9781561592630.article.45738 (accessed 7/21/19); Donald Burrows, Helen Coffey, Anthony Hicks and John Greenacombe, eds., *George Frideric Handel: Collected Documents (3), 1734-1742* (Cambridge: Cambridge University Press, 2019), 489, 504, 670–71, 683, 687, 689; and Owain Edwards and Phyllis Kinney, "Parry, John (i)," *The New Grove Dictionary of Music and Musicians*, 2nd ed. (ed. Stanley Sadie and John Tyrrell; London: Oxford University Press, 2001) https://doi-org.ezp.lib.cam.ac.uk/10.1093/gmo/9781561592630.article.20950 (accessed 7/21/19).

[5] Burrows et al., *Handel: Collected Documents (3)*, 270.

[6] Winton Dean, *Handel's Dramatic Oratorios and Masques* (London: Oxford University Press, 1959), 211.

[7] The other occasion in Handel's oratorios on which diegetic music and monarchy combine affectively is the concert put on by the king for the Queen of Sheba in Part 3 of *Solomon*, but its music does not affect behavior beyond arousing admiration, and there is no mention of a harp, though there is elsewhere in the libretto. The other occasions in the oratorios on which diegetic music has life-changing results are the fall of Jericho in *Joshua* and the welcome of Jephtha by his

played by two morally contrasting musicians: the virtuous David and the irresponsible Timotheus.

Handel the Lyre Player

Fig. 1. George Frideric Handel by Louis-François Roubiliac (1702-1762), marble statue signed and dated 1738. Victoria and Albert Museum, London (Courtesy of Wikipedia Foundation)

---

daughter Iphis in *Jephtha*; neither score includes a harp and neither occasion specifically calls for one, though Iphis refers to the harp in her preparatory air, "Tune the soft melodious lute, pleasant harp and warbling flute."

On May 1, 1738 a statue of Handel by Louis-François Roubiliac (1702–1762) was unveiled in London's Vauxhall Gardens.[8] It was unprecedented and remarkable, not least in that it was the first ever statue of a living composer, it was full length, it was highly detailed and realistic, and it combined informal modernity with archaic allusion. It showed Handel at his ease, improvising. The instruments on which he did this in real life, to admiring audiences, were the organ and the harpsichord, but Roubiliac showed him playing the lyre. The relatively small and simple lyre was not only more amenable to composition in marble, it invited identification of Handel with classical lyre-players, hallowed by antiquity and reputation.

Like Purcell before him, Handel had often been hailed as the Orpheus of the age, and here he was playing Orpheus' instrument. The lyre was also the instrument of the classical god of music, Apollo, and Roubiliac gave Handel's lyre the god's sun-burst emblem.[9] Many of the commendatory verses that greeted, and continued to celebrate, the statue reinforced these classical parallels.[10] But at least one poem, in *The Gentleman's Magazine*, has Handel playing not the lyre but the harp:

> As still, amaz'd, I'm straying,
>   O'er this inchanted-grove,
> I spy a HARPER playing
>   All in his proud alcove...

("HARPER" is annotated: "Mr Handel's statue.")[11] The speaker is

---

[8] For the statue, now at London's Victoria and Albert Museum, in its original context, see in particular David Bindman, "Roubiliac's Statue of Handel and the Keeping of Order in Vauxhall Gardens in the Early Eighteenth Century," *Sculpture Journal* 1 (1997): 22–31; Suzanne Aspden, "'Fam'd Handel Breathing, tho' Transformed to Stone': The Composer as Monument," *Journal of the American Musicological Society* 55.1 (2002): 39–90; David Coke, "Roubiliac's Handel for Vauxhall Gardens: A Sculpture in Context," *Sculpture Journal* 16.2 (2007): 5–22; and David Coke and Alan Borg, *Vauxhall Gardens: A History* (New Haven and London: Yale University Press, 2011), 89–96.

[9] On the origin of the sculpture in a proposal for an image of Apollo see Burrows et al., *Handel: Collected Documents (3)*, 386.

[10] Verses: e.g., Burrows et al., *Handel: Collected Documents (3)*, 398 [Orpheus], 405 [Orpheus], 406 [Apollo], 413–14, 540 [Orpheus], 651, 673. See also Bindman, "Roubiliac's Statue," 29–30.

[11] "Green-Wood Hall: or Colin's Description (to his Wife) of the Pleasures of Spring Gardens," *The Gentleman's Magazine for August 1742*, in Burrows et al., *Handel: Collected Documents (3)*, 846–47.

figured as a simple rustic, "Colin," to whom the lyre, by now an archaic instrument, would be unknown, but its nearest equivalent, the harp, was sufficiently similar for the statue's instrument to be identified as such, with particular resonances for the cultivated readers of *The Gentleman's Magazine* (see further below).

Music, especially Handel's, was a major attraction of Vauxhall Gardens. Like Orpheus, Handel was admired for his ability, seemingly almost uncanny, to affect the passions, and hence, behavior. In the gardens — open to all on payment of a shilling, and notoriously frequented on equal terms by all — his music was credited with a power to *order* the emotions and civilize the hearers: so claimed the entry (probably a puff) in *The London Daily Post, and General Advertiser* of 18 April 1738, noting the statue's erection at the expense of the gardens' proprietor, Jonathan Tyers, "who in Consideration of the real merit of that inimitable Master [Handel], thought it proper, that his Effigies should preside there, where his Harmony has so often charm'd even the greatest Crouds into the profoundest Calm and most decent behaviour."[12]

The power of the artist to direct the emotions, and hence the behavior, of individuals and of whole communities was a lively topic of concern to writers, thinkers and politicians of Handel's age. Music, in particular, was regarded as having enormous social potential. Capable not only of rallying communities, but of shaping and expressing their identity, music could unite them and prompt their success, and it could do so more powerfully than the other arts because it could stir the emotions unrestrained by any engagement of the intellect.[13] This theme was so commonplace that it could be treated jocularly. A full-page article on musical affectiveness in the weekly journal *Common Sense* for October 14, 1738 wishes for a national anthem which would strike a chord in British hearts, and cites as an example the Swiss equivalent, which is never played to the Swiss militia on foreign service, as it rouses such patriotic longing in them that they all rush back home.[14] A continual charge in early-eighteenth-century England against the Italian opera, fashionable among the nation's leaders, is that it sounds so contrary

---

[12] Bindman, "Roubiliac's Statue," 28, and Burrows et al., *Handel: Collected Documents (3)*, 385.

[13] Ruth Smith, *Handel's Oratorios and Eighteenth-Century Thought* (Cambridge: Cambridge University Press, 1995), 52–170.

[14] Smith, *Oratorios*, 77.

to the native temperament, which is manly, plain, and direct. Instrumental music in particular, lacking the definition of words, was hazardous: it could be soothing, refreshing, and uplifting, but it could be insidious, unmanning, and subverting. "Musick is almost as Dangerous as 'tis Useful, it has the Force of Gunpowder, and should be as carefully look'd after, that no unhallow'd Fire give it the power of Destroying."[15] The musician had great power and great responsibility.

Saul
The Words

Charles Jennens' libretto for Handel's oratorio *Saul*, which Handel began to compose three months after the unveiling of the Vauxhall Gardens statue, is a masterly dramatization and compression of the diffuse, repetitive narratives about Saul, David, and Jonathan in 1 Samuel. For Jennens, Handel, and their well-educated Protestant audience, David was a principal forebear of several fundamental aspects of British identity: he was an ancestor of Christ; the most exemplary of biblical monarchs; the author of the psalms, integral to the Book of Common Prayer (1662) and prescribed for reading in services twice daily; and a sanctified instrumental musician. His playing of what early modern Europe regarded as a harp (not lyre) justified the use of instrumental music in church worship, still in eighteenth-century Britain a contested issue.[16]

Handel had himself been invoked as David's true successor, uniquely able with his inspiring sacred music to restore the errant nation to the right path. In 1733 in the *Gentleman's Magazine*, Aaron Hill had responded to Handel's *Utrecht Te Deum* at the Feast of the Sons of the Clergy with a six-stanza ode to the composer, beginning:

> So *David*, to the GOD, who touch'd his Lyre,
>> The God, who did, at once, inspire
> The *Poet*'s Numbers, and the *Prophet*'s Fire,
>> Taught the wing'd Anthems to aspire! [...]
> Ah! give thy *Passport* to the Nation's Prayer!
>> Ne'er did Religion's languid Fire

---

[15] William Dingley, *Cathedral Service Decent and Useful, A Sermon Preach'd before the University of Oxford at St Mary's on Cecilia's Day, 1713* (Oxford: printed for Anthony Pelsley, 1713), 14.

[16] Smith, *Oratorios*, 83–85.

> Burn fainter – never more require
> The Aid of such a fam'd Enliv'ner's Care:
> Thy Pow'r can *force* the stubborn Heart to feel,
>   And rouze the Lucke-warm Doubter into *Zeal*.
>   Teach us to pray, as David pray'd before... [17]

Actual circumstances validated the analogy: Handel, like David, was musician to the king, and, like David, Handel composed anthems. Perhaps the recognition of the Vauxhall statue's instrument as a harp by "Colin" in the verse quoted above reflects this identification and was not meant simply to suggest rustic ignorance.

In the oratorio, David is first introduced to Saul as the savior of the nation, after his dispatch of Goliath (1 Sam 17:55–58). Then "the daughters of the land" come to greet the returning army, with the song that fatally rouses Saul's jealousy (as in 1 Sam 18:6–8). Saul exits enraged (this being an oratorio, the action is to be imagined). Notwithstanding the sequence of events so far, Saul's younger daughter Michal now recalls that David has in the past frequently cured Saul's distemper:

> *Michal: Recit [to David]*
> 'Tis but his old Disease, which thou canst cure.
> O take thy Harp, and as thou oft hast done,
> From the King's breast expel the raging Fiend,
> And sooth his tortur'd soul with Sounds Divine.
>
> *Michal: Air*
> Fell Rage and black Despair possest
> With horrid Sway the Monarch's Breast;
> When *David* with Celestial Fire
> Struck the sweet persuasive Lyre:
> Soft gliding down his ravish'd Ears,
> The healing Sounds dispel his Cares;
> Despair and Rage at once are gone,
> And Peace and Hope resume the Throne.

---

[17] Aaron Hill, "An Ode, on the Occasion of Mr. Handel's Great Te Deum, at the Feast of the Sons of the Clergy, Feb. 1, 1732-3," *The Gentleman's Magazine*, 1733, in Donald Burrows, Helen Coffey, Anthony Hicks, and John Greenacombe, eds., *George Frideric Handel: Collected Documents (2), 1725-1734* (Cambridge: Cambridge University Press, 2015), 587–89.

(It will be noticed that for Jennens, Handel, and their audience, "harp" and "lyre" are synonymous, as they are in others of Handel's oratorio librettos.)

David having gone, we assume, to fetch his harp during Michal's air, returns to face the still enraged Saul (1 Sam 18:10–11):

> *Abner: Recit*
> Rack'd with Infernal Pains, ev'n now the King
> Comes forth, and mutters horrid Words, which Hell,
> No human Tongue, has taught him.
>
> *David: Air*
> O Lord, whose Mercies numberless
>   O'er all thy Works prevail,
> Though daily Man thy law transgress,
>   Thy Patience cannot fail:
> If yet his Sin be not too great,
>   The busy Fiend control,
> Yet longer for Repentance wait,
>   And heal his wounded Soul.
>
> *Jonathan: Recit*
> 'Tis all in vain, his Fury still continues:
> With wild Distraction on my Friend he stares,
> Stamps on the Ground, and seems intent on Mischief.
>
> *Saul: Air*
> A Serpent in my Bosom warm'd,
>   Would sting me to the Heart:
> But of his Venom soon disarm'd,
>   Himself shall feel the Smart.
> Ambitious Boy! Now learn, what Danger
> It is to rouse a Monarch's Anger!
>   [*Throws his javelin. Exit* David]

This was the text as performed in *Saul*'s first season, after extensive revisions.[18] With his revisions — deleting the High Priest's rapt disquisition on the divine power of harmony (included in some recordings), reassigning "O Lord whose mercies numberless" from Michal (via the High Priest) to David, and omitting David's following air "Fly, malicious Spirit" — Handel brought the account

---

[18] On the textual history of this scene, see Natassa Varka, "Charles Jennens's Collection of Handel's Sacred Oratorios from *Saul* to *Jephtha*: Sources, Contexts, and Revisions" (Ph.D. diss., University of Cambridge, 2017), 1:34–35, 2:123.

of David's successful harp-playing much closer than it was in Jennens' original text to a real-time account of its failure (and after this disaster there is no more harp-playing in the oratorio). The new sequence seems to highlight problems which occupied contemporary biblical commentators and which Jennens' dramatization never really answers: what is the source of Saul's malady, and why does David's music cure it sometimes but not always.[19] But the devout Jennens would not stray from the biblical narrative so far as to omit or amend either the success or the failure of David's playing. Moreover, both of the oratorio's authors had an acute appreciation of dramatic possibilities. Having so recently been led by Michal's air to expect Saul (like the Vauxhall crowds!) to be calmed into decent behavior by David-Handel's music, the audience is doubly shocked by his unjustified savagery.

The Music

In December 1738 one of Handel's warmest supporters, the philosopher James Harris, received in Salisbury a letter from his brother Thomas in London about Handel's plans for *Saul*:

> Mr Handell, as I am informed, intends to introduce into his performance several old instruments used in the time of K[ing] David, when, as old Ashe [fellow amateur musician] says, musick was in its greatest perfection. I mean sackbutts, timbrells and tubal cain's. How they will succeed in these degenerate days I won't determine, but you will in Lent have an opportunity of judging yourself.[20]

Two elements in Harris' letter illuminate Handel's ambitions for *Saul*. One is the idea that at the time of David music was "in its greatest perfection." However unverifiable, this was a commonly stated belief among antiquarians and defenders of sacred music. And so, in taking upon himself the re-creation of David's music,

---

[19] See, for example, over 1500 words devoted to the topic in the composite biblical commentary by Handel's previous oratorio librettist and literary assistant, Samuel Humphreys, *The Sacred Books of the Old and New Testament, Recited at large: and Illustrated with Critical and Explanatory Annotations, Carefully Compiled from the Commentaries and other Writings of Grotius, Lightfoot, Pool, Calmet, Patrick, Le Clerc, Lock, Burkitt, Henry, Pearse, and a Variety of other Eminent Authors, Ancient and Modern* (London: printed by R. Penny, 1735), 1: 801–02.

[20] Donald Burrows and Rosemary Dunhill, eds., *Music and Theatre in Handel's World: The Family Papers of James Harris 1732–1780* (Oxford: Oxford University Press, 2002), 65, quoting Hampshire Record Office 9M73/G306/18.

Handel was making a bid for the artistic high ground. Secondly, Harris suggests that Handel aimed to evoke the music of the Old Testament in his oratorio.

Saul is everywhere marked by its authors' ambition to bring the Old Testament to life, without the visual aids of stage presentation and through sound alone. While apparently recognizing that musical archaism or pastiche would come between his audience and their engagement with the action, Handel employed an unprecedented array of orchestral instruments — including one obsolete in England (trombone) and one specially built ("tubal cain" = carillon, keyed glockenspiel) — to make the Old Testament present in his listeners' imagination.[21]

In Handel's time, as for centuries in the Christian West, David was portrayed playing what contemporaries termed a harp. Music and Bible historians contemporary with Handel variously thought that the kinnor was like a harp; identical with the classical lyre; an instrument of few strings (or many); plucked or bowed or both; that defining it was possible; that it was impossible to know what it was. Charles Burney, in his chapter on ancient Hebrew music in his *General History of Music*, notes that, "according to Eusebius, David carried his harp, or, as this prelate calls it his lyre, with him, wherever he went."[22] He gives more space to an account of David's playing to Saul than to any other aspect of "The History of Hebrew Music," annotating it: "The harp that David used upon the occasion, is called in the Hebrew *Kinor*."[23]

---

[21] See further Ruth Smith, "Early Music's Dramatic Significance in Handel's *Saul*," *Early Music* 35 (2007):173–89.

[22] Charles Burney, "The History of Hebrew Music," *A General History of Music, from the Earliest Ages to the Present Period. To which is Prefixed, A Dissertation on the Music of the Ancients* (London: printed for the author, 1776), 1:217.

[23] Burney, "History of Hebrew Music," 224–26.

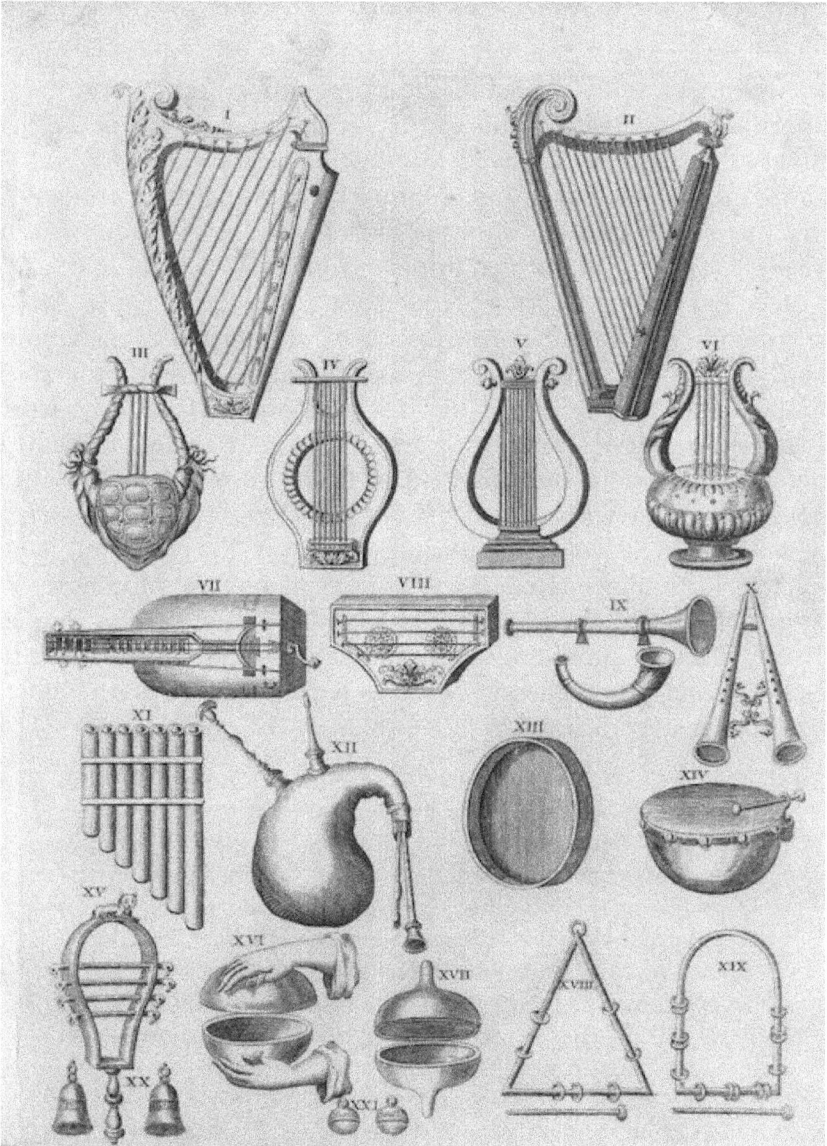

Fig. 2. Augustin Calmet, *Dissertation concerning the Musical Instruments of the Hebrews* (1724); extensive captions on the facing page identify the instruments as (I) "The *Nebel*, or *Nable*, or ancient *Psalterion*"; (II) "The antient *Cythara*, or the *Hazur*…much the same with our Harp"; (III) "The antient *Lyra*, or *Kinnor*"; (IV) "An antient *Lyra*"; (V) "The *Lyra* of *Timotheus* with nine Strings"; (VI) "A *Lyra*, as represented upon the Medals struck in the time of *Simon Maccabæus*." (Courtesy of Cambridge University Library)

133

The most detailed account of biblical instruments contemporary with Handel, and the most often quoted as authoritative by eighteenth-century historians, is Dom Augustin Calmet's *Dissertation sur les instruments de musique des Hébreux*, first included in the second of his volumes concerning the psalms (1713) in his *Commentaire littéral sur tous les livres de l'Ancien et du Nouveau Testament* (1707–1716), which appeared in English in 1724.[24] Calmet devoted ten pages of his "Dissertation concerning the Musical Instruments of the [ancient] Hebrews" to stringed instruments, identifying six variants, which he illustrates. Notwithstanding popular belief and imagery, he identifies one of the two harp-like instruments as the "*Nebel*, or *Nable*, or antient *Psalterion*" and the other as the "antient *Cythara*, or the *Hazur*" (both played "with the Fingers, or rather with sort of a Bow"), designating a three-stringed lyre with a tortoise-shell sounding board as the "ancient *Lyra* or *Kinnor*." He thus anticipated the verdict of Jeremy Montagu: "it is very probable that the kinnor was a lyre of some form, rather than an harp."[25] But Calmet allowed for great freedom of interpretation, which may be one reason why his work was so often cited by contemporaries in Britain:

> The Stringed Instruments of the Antients are very often confounded, and do differ but very little from one another, except in Name only. As they are exceeding ancient, many Alterations have happened to them, which has been the Occasion of their having new Names given them, tho' in the main they have still remain'd the same. Accordingly when we find that some give them three Strings, some seven, some ten, some twelve, some twenty four, and that these tell us, they were play'd upon with a Quill or Bow, and those again with the Fingers; or that some inform us, that the Strings were frequently stretch'd from the Top to the Bottom, and others, that they went Cross-ways from

---

[24] Augustin Calmet, "A Critical Dissertation on the Musical Instruments of the Hebrews," *Antiquities Sacred and Profane: or, A Collection of Curious and Critical Dissertations on the Old and New Testament* (tr. and ed. Nicholas Tindal; London: printed for J. Roberts, 1724), 61–97. From John Hawkins' *A General History of the Science and Practice of Music* (London: printed for T. Payne and Son, 1776) it is evident that the works of Mersenne, Kircher and Walther were also familiar to eighteenth-century English music historians.

[25] Jeremy Montagu, *Musical Instruments of the Bible* (London: Scarecrow, 2002), 12.

one Side to t'other; we must not for this Reason immediately conclude that the Instruments are different, and that it is impossible things so unlike shou'd be called by the same Name....We know the *Seventy* have rendred Hebrew *Kinnor*, by *Kynnara, Cythara* and *Psalterion.* The same Instrument is called by the Greeks, *Kinnyra, Lyra, Phorminx, Cythara, Chelys, Pectis, Barbitos.*[26]

Such latitude allowed a composer aiming at verisimilitude to represent the kinnor of 1 Samuel with the extant harp.

The score of *Saul* is interspersed with instrumental movements, some foregrounding dramatically appropriate instruments, such as the "tubal cain" introduction to the women's welcoming chorus. In the performing (fair copy) score David's air "O Lord, whose mercies numberless" is followed by the oratorio's only movement for a single instrument, a solo for unaccompanied harp, which we are to imagine being played by David.[27] Had Handel accompanied David's air with a harp, its sound might have gone unnoticed among the plucked instruments of the continuo section, and been further overlaid by the bowed string sections, not to mention David's voice. Handel may have derived that perception from experience. The Handel scholar John Roberts writes of "Praise the Lord" in Handel's *Esther*, scored in the autograph for harp, unison violins, and viola doubled by cello, that it has "indications for an added flute part largely doubling the treble part of the harp....Handel may have decided to add the flute after discovering that the harp—an instrument he had probably not encountered previously in an ensemble setting—could not hold its own against the violins."[28]

As mentioned above, initially the air that David sang to calm Saul was "Fly, malicious spirit," which was never performed, being replaced by "O Lord, whose mercies numberless" (initially for Michal). In "Fly, malicious spirit," Handel had illustrated David's harp-playing by scoring the air for accompaniment with harp,

[26] Calmet, "Dissertation," 76.

[27] Score: Autograph: London, British Library, R.M.20.g.3, ed. Percy M. Young, Hallische Händel Ausgabe 1.13 (Kassel: Bärenreiter, 1962), harp movement = no. 33, p. 114; for the harp movement in the performing (fair copy) score see Hamburg, Staats- und Universitätsbibliothek M C/267, f. 42v.

[28] John H. Roberts, "The Composition of Handel's *Esther*, 1718–1720," *Händel Jahrbuch* 55 (2009): 376.

theorbo, and pizzicato strings.[29] Here again, perhaps, though harp-like sounds would have been evident, the individual sound of the actual harp would probably have been absorbed into the whole aural texture. In adding a harp solo after "O Lord, whose mercies numberless" to compensate for the loss of the harp in "Fly, malicious spirit," Handel was giving David's harp the particular distinction of contributing the only entirely solo instrumental movement in the whole oratorio. David's harp solo is the more readily assimilable by the audience because it uses the melody already heard twice in his preceding air, and it is lightly scored, allowing the player to choose either to decorate it (perhaps still more elaborately than the singer has decorated the second stanza of "O Lord whose mercies numberless") or to deliver a mood of pellucid serenity on which Saul's violence then breaks with maximum horror.

Oratorio is often called opera of the mind. Staged performance of *Saul* obliges Saul to be seen reacting not only after but *during* David's song and his harp solo, not only distracting from them, but both imposing a reading of Saul's response and abolishing the suspense-and-shock that the audience which only listens will experience.

Alexander's Feast
The Words

The figure of Handel in Roubiliac's Vauxhall Gardens sculpture leans his left elbow on a pile of four books. Three are titled respectively "LESSONS," "OPERAS," and "ORA[torio]S," but the fourth, at the top of the pile, has the title of a specific work: "ALEX[ander's] FEAST."[30] When the statue of Handel playing a lyre was installed in Vauxhall Gardens, his setting (1736) of Dryden's admired ode *Alexander's Feast; or the Power of Musique. An Ode, in honour of St Cecilia's Day* (1697) was not only one of his most recent and already one of his most celebrated works, but a happily apt reference for the statue, because it recounts and evokes a lyre-

---

[29] British Library, R.M.20.g.3, f. 50v, and Percy M. Young, *Saul: Kritischer Bericht, Hallische Händel Ausgabe, Kritische Gesamtausgabe 1:13* (Kassel: Bärenreiter, 1964), 89–92, 146–48.

[30] On *Alexander's Feast* and the Vauxhall statue, at greater length than is possible here, see Aspden, "'Fam'd Handel,'" 54–67.

playing composer's mastery of his art and his audience.[31] The musician in question was Timotheus, whose skill was so familiar a paradigm of musical persuasiveness that a few years earlier it could be compared, without explanation, to that of Handel himself, in a verse oration in praise of Handel's oratorios by Henry Baynbrigg Buckeridge (gentleman commoner of St John's College), during the "Oxford Act," to which Handel contributed performances of his English theatre works.[32]

Handel's music, says Buckeridge in his oration, is no less persuasive than Timotheus' (and Orpheus'), and it is better, because it is sacred. That is the underlying theme, magnificently developed, of Dryden's poem, honoring St. Cecilia, patron saint of music, on the occasion of her annual feast. Cecilia's music, to which Dryden turns in his final stanza, is religious, aiming only to stir the hearer to holiness. Timotheus' music, which occupies the previous six stanzas, is culpable: not only does it arouse in his hearer — the conqueror of the world — an involuntary uncoordinated series of extreme emotions, reducing him to a ridiculous puppet; it provokes him to destroy a great city, in one of ancient history's most unforgiveable acts of hooliganism.[33] Dryden was not simply illustrating the conventional view of his (and Handel's) time that sacred music was better than secular music. He was providing a witty, colorful, rhetorically splendid argument about the responsibility of the artist, who has the potential to "raise a mortal to the skies" in two very different ways, for good or for ill. The intention of the artist is crucial. This too is a given of conventional conservative music theory, in Dryden's time and Handel's.

The story of Alexander's susceptibility to his musician's rhetoric was familiar to Handel's audience in accounts prior to Dryden's version of it. One of the best known was that of conservative churchman and literary critic Jeremy Collier, in an

---

[31] Dryden's poem was (lightly) arranged and adapted for Handel by Newburgh Hamilton. Handel's setting was published (unusually) in full score in 1738.

[32] *Musica sacra dramatica, sive oratoriium (Carmine lyrico)*: with translation, Burrows et al., *Handel Collected Documents (2)*, 656–58.

[33] Ruth Smith, "The Argument and Contexts of Dryden's *Alexander's Feast*," *SEL: Studies in English Literature* 18 (1978): 465–90. By the time Buckeridge invoked Timotheus, that musician's mastery of Alexander would also have been familiar to literate English audiences from Alexander Pope's *An Essay on Criticism* (1711), lines 374–83, praising Dryden's ode (subsequently the epigraph to the 1736 wordbook of Handel's *Alexander's Feast*).

essay originally published in 1695 and in its seventh edition by 1732:

> *Timotheus*, a *Grecian*, was so great a *Master*, that he could make a Man storm and swagger like a Tempest. And then, by altering the *Notes*, and the *Time*, he would take him down again, and sweeten his Humour in a trice. One time, when *Alexander* was at dinner, this Man play'd him a *Phrygian* Air: The Prince immediately rises, snatches up his Lance, and puts himself into a Posture of Fighting. And the Retreat was no sooner sounded by the Change of the Harmony, but his Arms were Grounded, and his Fire extinct; and he sat down as orderly as if he had come from one of *Aristotle's Lectures*. I warrant you *Demosthenes* would have been flourishing about such a Business a long Hour, and may not have done it neither. But *Timotheus* had a nearer Cut to the Soul; he could Neck a Passion at a Stroke, and lay it asleep.[34]

Collier's account derives from the tradition that Alexander's court musician was a player of the aulos. But two musicians called Timotheus were known to Dryden, Handel, and their educated audiences, and Dryden fuses them. An earlier and better attested musician of that name was a lyre-player of Miletus (c. 450–c. 360 BCE) who had a reputation from antiquity onwards as a daring musical innovator. He himself declared, "I sing not the old songs, for my new songs are better; a young Zeus reigns, and Cronos' rule was long ago; away with the ancient Muse!" Most notoriously and illegally, he extended musical expressiveness. The ruling Spartans so objected to his addition of four strings to the traditional seven that they hung his lyre in the meeting house of the Assembly to express their disapproval of his rejection of the simplicity and grandeur of the ancient style in favor of complexity and virtuosity.[35]

---

[34] Jeremy Collier, "Of Musick," *Essays upon Several Moral Subjects. Part II. The Seventh Edition Corrected* (London: printed for J. and J. Knapton, G. Strahan, F. Clay, D. Brown, B. Motte, and R. Williamson, 1731), 27–28. Thomas Creech, *T. Lucretius Carus, Of the Nature of Things* (London: printed by J. Matthews for G. Sawbridge, 1714), 1:142, annotates his translation of Lucretius' line 585 "The Pipe with Phyrgian Airs disturbs their Souls" with the lines in Dryden's Ode ("Pleas'd with the sound...check'd his pride") that describe the same sequence as Collier's. Venerable prior sources included St Basil, *Ad adolescentes* VIII and Dio Chrysostom, *Discourse* I.

[35] For sources, see Warren Anderson and Thomas J. Mathiesen, "Timotheus," *The*

According to Boethius, a state trial followed with a sentence requiring Timotheus to dismantle his lyre and banishing him from Sparta.[36] By the time Handel set *Alexander's Feast,* the supposed decree was available to the English reading public who had no Latin, for it was included in Calmet's "Dissertation."[37]

The Music

The criminal reputation of the lyre-playing Miletian Timotheus enables Dryden to darken the narrative of Alexander's susceptibility and create an object-lesson in the power and devastating potential of the irresponsible musician. Dryden's Timotheus goads Alexander into actual and appalling destructiveness. Handel does not choose to follow Dryden by writing progressively darker and more disturbing music, dramatizing Timotheus' criminality; to do so would be to bring in question his own integrity, if only in a fiction.

Dryden is writing about a musician of antiquity who in his day was at the forefront of musical innovation and expressiveness. This gave Handel a conundrum: how far to write music that evokes the antique and—in necessary contrast—how far to write in his own expressive styles, proving his reputation as Timotheus' equal with his power to move his audience of 1736. He privileges the latter, demonstrating his skill in wielding "the Power of Music" by including every kind of music that unacted theatrical entertainment would permit: concerted instrumental music, solo instrumental concertos, settings of English words and of Italian words (the inserted cantata "Cecilia, volgi un sguardo") including recitative, arioso, arias, duets, and choruses, and employing Italian, French, German, and English styles, with a dazzling variety of orchestral scoring, up to six-part chorus and an orchestra including drums and

---

New Grove Dictionary of Music and Musicians, 2nd ed. (ed. Stanley Sadie and John Tyrrell; London: Oxford University Press, 2001), https://doi-org.ezp.lib.cam.ac.uk/10.1093/gmo/9781561592630.article.27983 (accessed 7/21/19), who give an excellent account of Timotheus' musical innovations, expressive style, position in Greek music and reputation.

[36] *De Musica,* Book 1, chapter 1.

[37] Calmet, "Dissertation," 78–9; for text see Ruth Smith, "Timotheus, Alexander, Semele and Handel," *Handel Institute Newsletter* 14.1 (Spring 2003): unnumbered 1–4; also referred to e.g., Benjamin Stillingfleet, *Principles and Power of Harmony* (London: printed by J. and H. Hughs, 1771), 136–37, and Hawkins, *History,* 1: ii: 217–18, 316.

trumpets. But in two places, towards the start and towards the end of the poem, where Dryden specifies the instruments of his fused Timotheus, Handel writes music suggesting them, carefully and deliberately.

Dryden's Timotheus is both flute-player and lyre-player. A lyre-player in stanzas 2 and 6, in stanza 7 he is explicitly both:

> Thus, long ago,
> Ere heaving bellows learned to blow,
> While organs yet were mute,
> Timotheus, to his breathing flute,
> And sounding lyre,
> Could swell the soul to rage, or kindle soft desire.

Handel follows Dryden, making his Timotheus both a lyre-and-flute player and a musician from ancient history, while also deploying all that modern music can do. Handel sets the stanza 7 lines, which put Timotheus back into the archaic past, as a little sinfonia of 47 bars for two recorders, suggesting the two pipes of the aulos by their simple figuration and their movement together and mostly in thirds, accompanying them only with viola, and making minimal vocal interjections. The score for the first performances, in 1736, does not imitate the "sounding lyre" (though it could have been suggested ad lib by the continuo instruments during the vocal statements).[38] But that initial performing version of "Thus, long ago" has a hinterland of variants, and at a previous point in composition Handel aimed to be more explicitly faithful to Dryden's text. As Donald Burrows elucidated, in the autograph score the version with recorders (a second thought) included a stave for a harp part which was never filled in.[39]

But Handel had already given Timotheus' lyre centre stage. Dryden first associates Timotheus with an instrument in stanza 2:

> Timotheus, placed on high
> Amid the tuneful quire,
> With flying fingers touched the lyre:

---

[38] Donald Burrows, ed., *Alexander's Feast* (Sevenoaks: Novello, 1982): 125–26.

[39] Autograph MS: London, British Library, R.M. 20.d.4, and see Donald Burrows, "The Composition and First Performance of Handel's *Alexander's Feast,*" *Music & Letters* 64.3/4 (Jul.–Oct. 1983): 206–8. For a survey of all Handel's revisions and performances see Donald Burrows, "Handel and *Alexander's Feast,*" *The Musical Times*, 123:1670 (Apr. 1982): 252–55.

The trembling notes ascend the sky,
And heavenly joys inspire.

Between these lines and the following one, "The song began from Jove," the wordbook indicates an entire concerto "for the Harp, Lute, Lyricord, and other instruments."[40] This is cued in the autograph score as "Concerto per la Harpa ex B"[41] and its music survives in another Handel autograph. It is a three-movement work lasting over ten minutes.[42] As Burrows points out, the emendation of the key sequence of the material either side of the cue in the autograph score indicates that this too was the outcome of reconsideration.[43] The concerto's autograph has no individual parts for lute or lyrichord (but the lute, more probably theorbo, would be one of the continuo instruments). Possibly Handel was hoping to multiply the plucked solo instruments to ensure the audibility of "Timotheus' lyre" over the necessary accompanying instruments. The autograph contains an instruction for the latter that suggests a concern for balance to favor the harp: at the outset the violins are marked to play with mutes ("con sordini," an instruction that is never cancelled). We have noted a similar concern for the harp's audibility in *Saul*, and the same concern and the same way of meeting it is evident in *Esther*, for John Roberts reports a copy in which the violin line of "Praise the Lord" is marked "con sordini."[44] To increase the "harp" effect, in the outer movements of the concerto the lower strings are marked pizzicato.[45]

---

[40] *Alexander's Feast; or, The Power of Musick. An Ode wrote in honour of St. Cecilia, by Mr. Dryden. Set to Musick by Mr. Handel* (London: printed for J. and R. Tonson, 1736), 9.

[41] London, British Library, R.M. 20.d.4 f. 11r.

[42] London, British Library, R.M. 20.g.12, ff 8-13, = HWV 294, published in 1738 as the organ concerto op. 4 no. 6; a version for harp is included on the recording of *Alexander's Feast* by Harry Christophers and The Sixteen, 1991, COR16028 (Andrew Lawrence-King, harp).

[43] Burrows, "Composition," 207: "The addition of the harp concerto involved a realignment in the key sequence of the surrounding movements. The recitative 'Timotheus plac'd on high' (No. 4), as composed, ended with a cadence on to F sharp minor introducing 'The song began from Jove' (No. 6) in B minor; since the concerto was in F [*recte* B Flat] major, the music on either side had to be adapted."

[44] Roberts, "Composition," 376.

[45] The frontispiece to the full score shows Timotheus "on high" playing the lyre to Alexander and Thais, surrounded by three other instrumentalists, playing, respectively, aulos, harp and triangle. London, British Library R.M. 7.g.22, reproduced in Coke, "Roubiliac's Handel," 11, and Aspden, "'Fam'd Handel,'" 56.

If Handel was really hoping for a lyrichord, he was (like Timotheus) at the forefront of musical innovation. According to Margaret Debenham and Michael Cole, a lyrichord—a new instrument—was being planned in London by early 1736. That was when Handel was completing *Alexander's Feast*, and he may have heard of it earlier, as the inventor had visited London in 1735. However, it did not materialize until 1745, which may account for the lack of a part for it in Handel's score, the wordbook notwithstanding. The first half of the name of the lyrichord rather than its form may have been the reason for its proposed participation; when it eventually reached production, it was more of a bowed harpsichord than a plucked lyre.[46]

The decree against Timotheus would have had particular meaning for conservative church music composers and writers, amongst whom the contrast of modern "airy" and old "grave" music was a staple lament.[47] But the application was wider than church music. The terms of the decree parallel more general preoccupations with "right" and "wrong" kinds of music in early eighteenth-century England. Calmet's account was soon taken up by a more popular publication. The *Plain Dealer* magazine of February 12, 1725 called for truly dramatic music in place of "our emasculating present Taste, of the *Italian* Luxury, and *Wantonness* of *Musick*." Praising "Spartan Plainness and Austerity" and "that Wise People's Rigour, against *Innovation*," the author approvingly quotes the order against Timotheus. Music as a shaper and an index of national character was a recurrent topic, and the article about it in the journal *Common Sense* (October 14, 1738, referred to above), brought together the story of Timotheus' effect on Alexander, Handel's account of the story in his *Alexander's Feast*, and Handel's

[46] Margaret Debenham and Michael Cole, "Pioneer Piano Makers in London, 1737-74: Newly Discovered Documentary Sources," *Royal Musical Association Research Chronicle* 44.1 (2013): 58–59, 60; Eric Halfpenny, "The Lyrichord," *The Galpin Journal* 3 (1950): 46–49; and Benjamin Martin, *The General Magazine of Arts and Sciences, Philosophical, Philological, Mathematical, and Mechanical* (London: printed for W. Owen, 1755-65): 2:381–2.

[47] See e.g., Christopher Hogwood, "Thomas Tudway's History of Music," *Music in Eighteenth-Century England: Essays in Memory of Charles Cudworth* (ed. Christopher Hogwood and Richard Luckett; Cambridge: Cambridge University Press, 1983), 26, 42 ("yᵉ corruption of that solemn, & grave style" in church music by "Levity, & wantonness of style"); John Wilson ed., *Roger North on Music* (London: Novello, 1959), 266–28 ("The Ecclesiaticall Style, as all agree, makes the best musick"); and Smith, *Handel's Oratorios*, 70–88.

possible shaping of British character with his music, stressing the need for musicians to identify with the nation state's best interests.

Coda: Handel in Westminster Abbey

One further connection of Handel and the kinnor should be mentioned. In a codicil to his will made three days before his death, Handel requested a funeral and, at the discretion of his executor, a monument (for which he left £600), in Westminster Abbey. He did not specify the form, or maker, of the monument, but, with pleasant completeness, Roubiliac was commissioned and it was his last work (1762).[48] Images of the monument are famous, but it is not easy to see whether Handel's raised finger is pointing at something, rather than just aloft (the finger is now missing from the sculpture; see model, Ashmolean Museum, Oxford). It is. Above Handel floats an angel, playing a harp. At the time, Suzanne Aspden notes, some viewers read the angel, despite its wings, as the harp player with whom Handel had so often been associated: David.[49]

---

[48] Ellen T. Harris, "Handel and his Will," *Handel's Will: Facsimile and Commentary* (ed. Donald Burrows; London: The Gerald Coke Handel Foundation, 2009), 18; facsimile, 43.

[49] Aspden, "'Fam'd Handel,'" 74.

Studies on the Kinnor and Ancient Lyres
An Annotated Bibliography

Jonathan L. Friedmann and Joel Gereboff

This annotated bibliography offers a representative list of books, articles, and chapters addressing the kinnor and related lyres of the ancient world. The varied publications demonstrate wide-ranging and multidisciplinary approaches to the subject, including history, musicology, anthropology, linguistics, philosophy, mythology, theology, archeology, art history, acoustics, comparative literature, musical practices, and more.

Adler, Israel. *Hebrew Writings Concerning Music in Manuscripts and Printed Books from Geonic Times up to 1800.* Munich: G. Henle Verlag, 1975.

Discusses aspects of Jewish thought on music from Geonic to early modern times, including comments on the nature and function of the kinnor.

Ayres, Larry M. "Problems of Sources for the Iconography of the Lyre Drawings." *Speculum: A Journal of Medieval Studies* 49.11 (1974): 61–68.

Examines lyre drawings included in the sketchbooks of medieval artists, and how those images functioned as motifs and "iconographic guides" for psalter illustrations.

Bakarezos, Efthimios et al. "Acoustics of the Chelys: An ancient Greek Tortoise-Shell Lyre." *Applied Acoustics* 73.5 (2012): 478–83.

Analyzes the acoustics of a reconstructed Greek tortoise-shell lyre using modern experimental methods, such as electronic speckle pattern laser interferometry and impulse response, to extract vibrational behaviors of the instrument and its main parts.

Barasch, Moshe. "The David Mosaic of Gaza." *Assaph* 1 (1988): 1–41

Discusses the David Mosaic from Gaza, which includes possible Orphic imagery of David playing the lyre to charm animals.

Ben-Horin, Michal. "Musical Discourse and Historical Narratives in Hebrew Literature: Senaz's *Musical Moment* and Shaham's *Rosendoft Quartet.*" *Israel Studies Forum* 21.2 (2006): 85–101.

Includes discussion of violinists and the violin (kinnor in Modern Hebrew) in some modern Hebrew literature.

Benovitz, Moshe. *Talmud Berakhot I.* Jerusalem: Haigud Lefarshanut Hatalmud, 2006.

Comments on a passage in the Babylonian Talmud containing the story of David's lyre playing at midnight, and disputes earlier claims of classical Greek influences on the account.

Braun, Joachim. *Music in Ancient Israel/Palestine: Archaeological, Written, and Comparative Sources.* Translated by Douglas W. Stott. Grand Rapids, MI: William B. Eerdmans, 2002.

Surveys written and archeological evidence from the Stone Age through the Hellenistic-Roman period for instruments mentioned in the Bible, including the kinnor.

Brown, John Pairman. "Kothar, Kinyras, and Kythereia." *Journal of Semitic Studies* 10.2 (1965): 197–219.

Proposes a connection between the minor Ugaritic deity Kinaru(m), the god of the lyre, and Kinyras, a hero-king of Cyprus in Greek mythology, as well as their connection to the Hebrew term "kinnor."

Burgh, Theodore W. *Listening to the Artifacts: Music Culture in Ancient Palestine.* New York: T & T Clark, 2006.

Includes analyses of various instrument types, including lyres, from an archaeomusicological perspective.

Cardona, Ana Borg. "The lyre player in Roman Malta." *Malta Archaeological Review* 6 (2005): 47–49.

Proposes the possibility of dramatic and musical performances in the Mediterranean archipelago of Malta during the period of Roman rule (218 BCE to 535 CE), based on remains and iconographic evidence of various types of wind, percussion, and string instruments, including lyres.

Concetta, Pennuto. "Andrea Torelli and His Orphic Lyre." *Sing Aloud Harmonious Spheres: Renaissance Conceptions of Cosmic Harmony*, 185–201. Edited by Jacomien Prins and Maude Vanhaelen. New York: Routledge, 2018.

Explores the literary approach of Andrea Torelli, a jurist and philosopher of the first half of the seventeenth century, focusing on how his understanding of the harmony of the spheres was influenced by his predilection for eloquence, which he felt comprised the truest form of music and the true harmony of the world, and his appraisal of the medicinal quality of the Orphic lyre, which was believed to create harmony between the heavenly and inferior realms.

Cross, Frank Moore. "David, Orpheus and Psalm 151:3–4." *Bulletin of the American Schools of Oriental Research* 231 (1978): 69–71.

Rejects the interpretation of Psalm 151, found in most copies of the Septuagint but not in the Masoretic text of the Hebrew Bible, as containing Orphic imagery (i.e., David playing the lyre to soothe animals).

Dimant, Devorah. "David's Youth in the Qumran Context (11 QPs 28:3–12)." *Prayer and Poetry in the Dead Sea Scrolls and Related Literature: Essays in Honor of Eileen Schuller on the Occasion of her 65th Birthday*, 97–114. Edited by Jeremy Pener et al. Leiden: Brill, 2012.

Challenges claims of Orphic imagery in this Qumran text, which includes the line, "My hands have made a harp [*ugav*], my fingers a lyre [kinnor]."

Dîrţu, Cătălin. "Pythagoras, Plato, and the Lyre-Soul." *Agathos* 9:1 (2018): 127–33.

Relates the concept of the "singing soul" who delights in playing music, as Pythagoras and Plato understood it, to the metaphor of the "lyre-soul."

Dowling Long, Siobhán. "Musical Instruments in Biblical Art." *Bible, Art, Gallery*, 97–121. Edited by Martin O'Kane. Sheffield: Sheffield Phoenix, 2011.

Explores various depictions of musical instruments, including the kinnor, in Bible-themed visual arts.

Eshel, Hanan. "On Harps and Lyres: A Note on the Bronze Coins of the Bar Kokhba Administration." *Israel Numismatic Journal* 16 (2007–08): 118–30.

Analyzes the iconography of Bar Kokhba coins, including those with depictions of harps and lyres.

Feldman, Louis H. *Studies in Hellenistic Judaism.* Leiden, Brill, 1996.

Chapter 20, "Philo's Views on Music," presents a detailed analysis of Philo's interpretation of music and musical instruments, tracing connections to classical Greek notions.

Fernandez-Marcos, Natalio. "David the Adolescent: On Psalm 151." *The Old Greek Psalter: Studies in Honour of Albert Pietersman*, 205–17. Edited by Robert J. V. Hiebert. London: Bloomsbury, 2001.

Disagrees with the Orphic interpretation of Psalm 151, noting that Hellenistic Jewish writers viewed Orpheus as a teacher of esoteric traditions and that only later iconography depicts him as a musician with control over animals.

Finesinger, Sol Baruch. "Musical Instruments in the OT." *Hebrew Union College Annual* 3 (1926): 21–76.

Comments on various musical instruments in the Bible, drawing upon information from the Septuagint and rabbinic sources.

Finney, Paul Corby. "Orpheus-David: A Connection in Iconography Between Greco-Roman Judaism and Early Christianity." *Journal of Jewish Art* 5 (1978): 6–15.

Traces the development of the tradition of depicting David with Orphic imagery in Jewish and Christian iconographic and written sources and argues for a later connection of the two figures.

Flesher, Paul V. M. "Reading the Reredos: David, Orpheus, and Messianism in the Dura Europos Synagogue." *Ancient Synagogues: Historical, Analysis and Archaeological Discovery, Vol. 2*, 346–66. Edited by Dan Urman et al. Leiden: Brill, 1995.

Contests the Orphic and messianic interpretations of Dura frescos depicting David.

Fraiman, Susan Nashman. "Of Provenance and Providence: On the Reappearance of *David Playing the Harp for Saul* by Moritz Oppenheim." *Ars Judaica* 7 (2011): 123–36.

Analyzes *David Playing the Harp for Saul*, a rediscovered painting by modern German-Jewish painter Moritz Oppenheim (1800–1882).

Franklin, John Curtis. "Ethnicity and Musical Identity in the Lyric Landscape of Early Cyprus." *Greek and Roman Musical Studies* 2 (2014): 146–76.

Re-examines assumptions about the lyre-types of early Iron Age Cyprus and their place in Cypriot musical identity.

Franklin, John Curtis. *Kinyras: The Divine Lyre*. Cambridge, MA: Harvard University Press, 2016.

Seeks to connect the hero-king Kinyras as a mythological symbol of pre-Greek Cyprus with the ritual music and deified instruments in the Bronze Age Near East, using evidence dating to early Mesopotamia.

Franklin, John Curtis. "Lyre Gods of the Bronze Age Musical Koine." *Journal of Ancient Near Eastern Religions* 6.1 (2006): 39–70.

Discusses evidence for the deification and sanctification of lyres/harps, which originated in late-third millennium Mesopotamia and spread abroad, including musical prophecy as depicted in the Hebrew Bible.

Franklin, John Curtis. "'Sweet Psalmist of Israel': The Kinnor and Royal Ideology in the United Monarchy." *Strings and Threads: A Celebration of the Work of Anne Draffkorn Kilmer*, 99–114. Edited by Wolfgang Heimpel. Winona Lake, IN: Eisenbrauns, 2011.

Compares references to the musical organization of the First Jerusalem Temple with that of other Late Bronze Age temple complexes, and the role of David's kinnor in narratives concerning the rise of the United Monarchy.

Franklin, John Curtis "Theios Aoidos: A New Reading of the Lyre-Player Group of Seals." *Gaia: Revue Interdisciplinaire sur la Grèce ancienne* 18 (2015): 405–18.

Contrasts the winged lyre-player on the lyre-player group of seals (Cilicia) with other representations of the divine lyre, including Kinnaru of Ugarit and Kinyras of Cyprus.

Franklin, John Curtis. "The Wisdom of the Lyre: Soundings in Ancient Greece, Cyprus and the Near East." *Musikarchäologie im Kontext: Archäologische Befunde, historische Zusammenhänge, soziokulturelle Beziehungen*, 379–98. Edited by Ellen Hickmann and Ricardo Eichmann. Leidorf: Rahden, 2006.

Examines the use of the lyre/harp as a divine instrument and ritual object in antiquity, drawing on evidence from Mesopotamia, Ugarit, Cyprus, ancient Israel, and elsewhere.

Friedmann, Jonathan L. *Music in Biblical Life: The Role of Song in Ancient Israel*. Jefferson, NC: McFarland, 2013.

Includes the chapter: "Therapeutic Functions of David's Lyre: 1 Samuel 16:14–23."

Friedmann, Jonathan L. *Music in the Hebrew Bible: Understanding References in the Torah, Nevi'im and Ketuvim*. Jefferson, NC: McFarland, 2014.

Includes an essay, "Instrument of Joy," linking the kinnor, joy, and Psalm 92.

Gillingham, Susan. "'I will solve my riddle to the music of the lyre' (Psalm 49:4): How 'Lyrical' is Hebrew Psalmody?" *Journal of Literary Theory* 11.1 (2017): 40–50.

Compares biblical poetry to the ancient Greek-Latin tradition of lyric poetry, both of which suggest poetry performed with musical instruments (such as the lyre) and singing.

Hägg, Thomas. "Hermes and the Invention of the Lyre: An Unorthodox Version." *Symbolae Osloenses: Norwegian Journal of Greek and Latin Studies* 64 (1989): 36–73.

Attempts to reconstruct a shared origin myth of the lyre from the Homeric *Hymn to Hermes*, wherein Hermes, on the day of his birth, meets a tortoise, kills it, and constructs the lyre from its shell, and an eleventh-century Persian verse-romance, where Hermes, as an adult, finds a tortoise-shell sounding in the wind and builds the lyre to imitate its sound.

Halevi, Ephraim E. "Kinor shel David." *Moznaim* 22 (1966): 334–36.

Proposes classical Greek influences on the story of David's kinnor in BT *Berakhot*.

Harrán, Don. "An Early Modern Hebrew Poem on Music in Its Beginnings and at the End of Time." *Journal of the American Musicological Society* 64.1 (2011): 3–50.

Analyzes a seventeenth-century poem by Paduan rabbi Samuel Archivolti that traces the history of music from the harmony of the planets, to the musician-inventor Jubal, to Pythagoras after the great flood, to David and his kinnor, to messianic times when David's seven-string kinnor will be expanded to eight strings.

Harrán, Don. "David's Lyre, Kabbalah, and the Power of Music." *Psalms in the Early Modern World*, 257–97. Edited by Linda Phyllis Austern, Kari Boyd McBride, and David L. Orvis. Burlington, VT: Ashgate, 2016.

Relates the therapeutic function of David's lyre to the curative effect of the biblical psalms, which are traditionally attributed to David.

Harrán, Don. "'Keḥi kinnor' by Samuel Archivolti (d. 1611): A Wedding Ode with Hidden Messages." *AJS Review* 35.2 (2011): 253–91.

Discusses Samuel Archivolti's Hebrew wedding ode "Keḥi kinnor" ("Take a lyre"), tracing its references to biblical and rabbinical literature, and exploring the few recorded examples of its melodies.

Harrán, Don. "The Levi Dynasty: Three Generations of Jewish Musicians in Sixteenth-Century Mantua." *Rabbi Judah Moscato and the Jewish Intellectual World of Mantua in the 16th–17th Centuries*, 186–95. Edited by Giuseppe Veltri, and Gianfranco Miletto. Boston: Brill, 2012.

Includes a discussion of a sermon, *Higgayon BeKhinnor*, by Italian rabbi Judah Moscato (c. 1530–1593) based on the rabbi's sermon about a self-playing harp that was hung above David's bed (BT *Berakhot*, 3b–4a), and situates Moscato's views on music within the history and thought of his family.

Harrán, Don. *Three Early Modern Hebrew Scholars on the Mysteries of Song*. Boston: Brill, 2014.

Chapter 2, "Sounds for Contemplation on a Lyre," provides a phrase-by-phrase exegesis of the sermon, *Higgayon BeKhinnor*, by Italian rabbi Judah Moscato (c. 1530–1593) concerning David's self-playing lyre (based on BT *Berakhot*, 3b–4a).

Herrero de Jauregi, Miguel. *Orphism and Christianity in Late Antiquity*. Berlin: De Gruyter, 2010.

Analyzes literary and artistic evidence related to Orphism in late antiquity and Christian uses of those beliefs.

Idel, Moshe. "The Magical and Theurgical Interpretations of Music from the Renaissance to Hasidism." *Yuval: Studies of the Jewish Music Research Center* 4 (1982): 33–62. [Heb.]

Discusses the views of various Jewish writers, primarily from the sixteenth and seventeenth centuries, on the magical or theurgical functions of vocal and instrumental music, situates those writers in the context of the Italian Renaissance, and concludes with brief comments on early Hasidic views on music.

Idel, Moshe. "Music and Prophetic Kabbalah." *Yuval: Studies of the Jewish Music Research Center* 4 (1982): 150–69.

Assesses the views of R. Abraham Abulafia and his disciples on the connection between vocal and instrumental music and prophetic experience.

Ivanov, Vyacheslav V. "An Ancient Name of the Lyre." *Archiv Orientdlni* 67 (1999): 585–600.

Investigates the appearance of the Western Semitic term *kinnârum* in a cuneiform tablet from 2340–2300 BCE and its relationship to similar terms in Hebrew, Hittite, Aramaic, Syriac, Egyptian, Greek, and other languages.

Jinbachian, Manuel. "Music and Musical Instruments in the Septuagint, the Peshitta and the Armenian Psalms." *Text Theology & Translation: Essays in Honour of Jan de Waard*, 53–77. Edited by Simon Crisp and Manuel Jinbachian. London: United Bible Societies, 2004.

Compares translations of instrument names as preserved in psalm texts in the Greek Septuagint, Syriac Peshitta, and Armenian Bible.

Kebede, Ashenafi. "The Bowl-Lyre of Northeast Africa: Krar the Devil's Instrument." *Ethnomusicology* 21.3 (1977): 379–95.

Compares the two main lyre-types in North Eastern Africa to lyres found in the Mediterranean, Middle East, and neighboring African regions.

Koitabasi, Matahisa. "The Deification of the 'Lyre' in Ancient Ugarit." *Orient* 28 (1992): 106–110.

Suggests possible reasons for the deification of the lyre in two Ugaritic texts.

Kollveit, Gjermund. "The Early Lyre in Scandinavia: A Survey." *Tiltai* 3.12 (2000): 19–25.

Presents archeological and written sources for the early Scandinavian lyre dating to c. 500–1400 CE.

Kolyada, Yelena. *A Compendium of Musical Instruments and Instrumental Terminology in the Bible*. New York: Routledge, 2014.

Surveys the kinnor in the chapter on plucked stringed instruments, drawing on historical research, comparative linguistic analysis, and musical study.

Koumartzis, N., D. Tzetzis, P. Kyratsis, and R. G. Kotsakis. "A New Music Instrument from Ancient Times: Modern Reconstruction of the Greek Lyre of Hermes using 3D Laser Scanning, Advanced Computer Aided Design and Audio Analysis." *Journal of New Music Research* 44.4 (2015): 324–46.

Describes the reconstruction of a playable Greek lyre made from materials available in antiquity, such as specific woods, tortoise shells, and sheep strings, and forged with modern 3D technology and carpentry tools.

Kurfürst, Pavel. "The Ancient Greek Kithara." *Archiv für Musikwissenschaft* 41 (1984): 295–308.

Summarizes conclusions about the construction and functions of the ancient Greek kithara.

Landels, John G. *Music in Ancient Greece and Rome*. London: Routledge, 1999.

Includes a discussion of Greco-Roman instruments, including lyres.

Lawergren, Bo. "A Lyre Common to Etruria, Greece, and Anatolia: The Cylinder Kithara."*Acta Musicologica* 57.1 (1985): 25–33.

Examines the shape and possible purposes of the cylinder kithara, or round-bottom lyre, depicted in parts of ancient Etruria, Anatolia, and Greece.

Lawergren, Bo. "The Cylinder Kithara in Etruria, Greece, and Anatolia." *Imago Musicae 1984: International Yearbook of Musical Iconography*, 147–74. Edited by Tilman Seebass. Durham, NC: Duke University Press, 1985.

Evaluates three-dimensional examples of lyres that existed in Greece and some neighboring regions, mainly between 600 and 400 BCE.

Lawergren, Bo. "Distinctions among Canaanite, Philistine, and Israelite Lyres, and Their Global Lyrical Contexts." *Bulletin of the American Schools of Oriental Research* 309 (1998): 41–68.

Proposes that the lyres of Palestine, such as depicted at Kuntillet Cajurd in the Negev (c. 800 BCE) and on the Bar Kokhba coins (133 CE), were not unique to the region, but demonstrate the spread of lyre types from the East (Fertile Crescent) and West (Aegean), and suggests that the biblical kinnor was likely an Eastern-style "thin lyre," known as *kinnirum*.

Lawergren, Bo, and O. R. Gurney. "Sound Holes and Geometrical Figures: Clues to the Terminology of Ancient Mesopotamian Harps." *Iraq* 49 (1987): 37–57.

Considers the names, geometrical shapes, and sound holes of Mesopotamian harps and lyres.

Lebaka, Morakeng E. K. "Music, Singing and Dancing in Relation to the Use of the Harp and the Ram's Horn or *Shofar* in the Bible: What Do We Know About This?" *HTS Teologieses Studies* 70.3 (2014): 1–7.

Explores cultic and non-cultic contexts for harp and shofar playing in the Bible, especially during celebrations, military operations, mourning, and lamentation, and how these performances helped the populace cope with the demands of everyday life.

Levarie, Siegmund. "Philo on Music." *Journal of Musicology* 9 (1991): 124–30.

Brief commentary on Philo's views on music, including his metaphorical comments on the kinnor and how its harmonious nature is analogous to the body and soul.

Maas, Martha. "Back Views of the Ancient Greek Kithara." *The Journal of Hellenistic Studies* 95 (1975): 175.

Explains that front-view paintings of the instrument do not reveal the types of sound box bulges, which may have affected the playing techniques.

Maas, Martha. "On the Shape of the Ancient Greek Lyre." *The Galpin Society Journal* 27 (1974): 113–17.

Presents pictographic evidence for a Greek lyre possessing a curved outer arm and a straight inner arm nearest to the player.

Maas, Martha. "Polychordia and the Fourth-Century Greek Lyre." *The Journal of Musicology* 10.1 (1992): 74–88.

Examines whether or not the number of strings of certain Greek lyres expanded from seven to eleven to twelve by the late classical period, as some contemporaneous sources suggest.

Mathiesen, Thomas J. *Apollo's Lyre: Greek Music and Music Theory in Antiquity and the Middle Ages.* Lincoln: University of Nebraska Press, 1999.

Includes a section on the constructions, tunings, performance practices, and social functions of various chordophones.

McKinnon, James W. *Music in Early Christian Literature.* Cambridge: Cambridge University Press, 1989.

Collects literary comments by church fathers who wrote in Latin and Greek on the nature of music, including allegorical interpretations of references in the Hebrew Bible to the playing of instruments, such as the kinnor.

Michael, Abbot David. *Making, Playing and Composing on the 10 Stringed Lyre Harp: Ancient Hebrew Diatonic 10-Stringed Lyre-Harp is Easy to Play!* Bowie, AZ: Glentivar Village, 2014.

Provides step-by-step instruction in making, playing, and composing on a reconstructed ten-stringed lyre-harp.

Miletto, Gianfranco. "The Human Body as a Muscial Instrument in the Sermons of Judah Moscato." *The Jewish Body: Corporality, Society and Identity in the Renaissance and Early Modern Period*, 277–94. Edited by Maria Diemling and Giuseppe Veltri. Leiden: Brill, 2009.

Analyzes Moscato's sermon, *Higgayon BaKinnor*, focusing on its notions of the relationship between the human body, music, and the kinnor, and situates Moscato in his broader Renaissance context.

Mistretta, Marco Romani. "Hermes the Craftsman: The Invention of the Lyre." *Gaia: Revue Interdisciplinaire sur la Grèce ancienne* 20 (2017): 5–22.

Explores Greek legends identifying Hermes, the god of commerce, rhetoric, and cunning intelligence, as the creator of the "fine arts," and lyre-playing in particular.

Molina Moreno, Francisco. "The Pleiades or the First Cosmic Lyre." *Hyperboreus* 14.1 (2008): 28–38.

Presents the association of Pleiades with the lyre as the first instance of a celestial body being linked with music in Greek thought.

Montagu, Jeremy. *Musical Instruments of the Bible*. Lanham, MD: Scarecrow, 2002.

Surveys references to numerous musical instruments, including the kinnor, in the Tanakh, Apocrypha, and New Testament.

Mucznik, Sonia. "Musicians and Musical Instruments in Roman and Early Byzantine Mosaics of Israel: Sources, Precursors and Significance." *Gerion* 29.1 (2011): 265–86.

Analyzes various iconographic depictions of musical instruments, including the lyre, in Jewish and Christian works from Roman and Byzantine eras, and traces ancient Near Eastern and Greek parallels and potential influences, such as Orpheus.

Olszewski, Marek-Titien. "The Orpheus Funerary Mosaic from Jerusalem in the Archaeological Museum at Istanbul." *11th International Colloquium on Ancient* Mosaics, 655–64. Edited by Mustafa Sahin. Istanbul: Uludag University Press, 2011.

Situates a late antique Christian funerary mosaic in Jerusalem, containing a depiction of Orpheus and a lyre, in the context of Christian understandings of this figure.

Ovadiah, Asher. "The Symbolic Meaning of the David-Orpheus Images in the Gaza Synagogue Mosaic." *Liber Annuus* 59 (2009): 301–07.

Argues for a messianic understanding of the David-Orpheus mosaic from Gaza.

Petersen, David L. "Portraits of David: Canonical and Otherwise." *Interpretation* 40.2 (1986):130–42.

Compares symbols found in Marc Chagall's portrait of David, including the kinnor, to the corresponding dimensions in the biblical portrait.

Provenza, Antonietta. "Soothing Lyres and *epôidai*: Music Therapy and the Cases of Orpheus, Empedocles and David." *Music in Antiquity: The Near East and the Mediterranean,* 300–41. Edited by Joan Goodnick-Westenholz, Yossi Maurey, and Edwin Seroussi. Berlin: De Gruyter, 2014.

Examines references to the lyre's healing powers in antiquity, as well as the wider perception and implementation of music's beneficial effects in the ancient world.

Psaroudakes, Stelios. "The Arm-Crossbar Junction of the Classical Hellenic Kithara." *Music Archaeology of Early Metal Ages*, 263–78. Edited by E. Hickmann, I. Laufs, and R. Eichmann. Rahden: Leidorf, 2000.

Examines the junction of the crossbar and arms in the construction of the large classical kithara of the ancient Greeks.

Rabinowitz, Isaac. "The Alleged Orphism of 11QPss 28:8–12." *Zeitschrift fur die Alttestamentliche Wissenschaft* 76 (1964): 193–200.

Challenges the Orphic interpretation of this text from Qumran.

Roberts, Helen. "Reconstructing the Greek Tortoise-Shell Lyre." *World Archaeology* 12 (1981): 303–12.

Describes the reconstruction of a Greek tortoise-shell lyre and its relationship to similar modern and ancient lyre-types.

Rowan, Diana. "The Universal Lyre: Three Perspectives." *The American Harp Journal* (Summer 2013): 55–63.

Profiles three contemporary scholar-artists involved in ancient lyre reconstruction: Temesgen Hussein of Ethiopia; Michalis Georgiou of Cyprus; and Michael Levy of the United Kingdom.

Rupeikaitė, Kamilė. "From the Kinnor to the Guitar: Historical Transformations of the Biblical Musical Instruments in Lithuanian Translations of the Bible Since the 16th Century." *Journal of Comparative Studies/Komparatovistikas Almanahs* 31.3 (2013): 193–201.

Explores instrument names and types in Lithuanian translations of the Bible from German, Latin, and Hebrew sources since the sixteenth century.

Russell, James R. "The Lyre of King David and the Greeks." *Judaica Petropolitana* 8 (2017): 12–33.

Suggests that the Talmud's depictions of David as a lyre player and "sweet singer" refuted Greek divisions between the divinity of the harmony of the spheres and the "demonic" nature of human music.

Sachs, Curt. *The History of Musical Instruments.* New York: W. W. Norton, 1940.

Surveys a variety of biblical instruments, including the kinnor, as well as the lyres of Greece, Rome, and Etruria.

Safiullinna, Liliya Garifullovna, and Gulnara Ibragimovna Batyrshina. "Musical Images as a Reflection of the Artistic Universalism of Marc Chagall." *Terra Sebus: Acta Musei Sabesiensis* (2014): 67–104.

Examines the symbolism of various musical contexts and instruments featured in Chagall paintings, including the biblical kinnor.

Schwartz, Dov. *Kinor Nishmati: HaMusika BeHagut HaYehudit.* Ramat Gan: Bar Ilan University Press, 2012. [Heb.]

Discusses rabbinic and modern understandings of the kinnor, such as in the poetry of Mikha Yosef Lebensohn.

Sellers, Ovid R. "Musical Instruments of Israel." *Biblical Archaeologist* 4.3 (1941): 33–47.

Explores biblical instruments, including the lyre and harp, based on textual and iconographic evidence.

Sendrey, Alfred. *Music in Ancient Israel.* New York: Philosophical Library, 1969.

Includes literary, archaeological, and comparative overviews of the kinnor and other biblical instruments.

Sendrey, Alfred, and Mildred Norton. *David's Harp: The Story of Music in Biblical Times.* New York: New American Library, 1964.

Presents a chapter on musical instruments of ancient Israel and images of several ancient Near Eastern lyres.

Seroussi, Edwin. "Music in Medieval Iberian Jewish Society." *Hispania Judaic* 5 (2007): 5–67.

Explores numerous aspects of music in pre-expulsion Iberian Jewish life, including perceptions of music, the use of instruments to accompany secular strophic Hebrew poetry, and Jewish minstrels who played stringed instruments in Christian Spain.

Shir, Yael. *Musical Instruments in the Illuminations of the Barcelona Haggadah.* MA thesis, Tel Aviv University, 1978.

Commentary on the representation of various musical instruments in the Barcelona Haggadah, including the kinnor.

Shirt, David John. "'Sing Psalms to the Lord with the Harp': Attitudes toward Musical Instruments in Early Christianity - 680 AD." *Journal of Early Christian History* 6 (2016): 97–115.

Examines a range of Christian writings, including those from the Mediterranean world, and argues that musical instruments, such as the lyre, were used in some Christian rituals.

Smith, John Arthur. *Music in Ancient Judaism and Early Christianity*. Burlington, VT: Ashgate, 2013.

Describes music among the ancient Israelites, ancient Jews, and early Christians in Mediterranean lands from 1000 BCE to 400 CE, including the use of the lyre and other instruments.

Smith, Morton. "Psalm 151, David, Jesus and Orpheus." *Zeitschrift fur die Alttestamentliche Wissenschaft* 93.2 (1981): 247–53.

Argues against Orphic allusions in the Qumran text of Psalm 151 (11QPs).

Sperber, Daniel. *Material Culture in Eretz-Israel during the Talmudic Period*. Jerusalem: Yad Yitshak Ben Tsevi, 1993.

Analyzes musical instruments during the Talmudic era, such as the kinnor, based on literary, artistic, and numismatic evidence.

Steiner, Deborah. "Sounding of the Lyre: Performing Homer in Archaic Greece." *Performing Homer: The Voyage of Ulysses from Epic to Opera*, 3–17. Edited by Wendy Heller and Eleonora Stoppino. New York: Routledge, 2020.

Explores the performance of Homeric epics in ancient Greece, during which the reciter played a lyre and incorporated a number of song types, such as funerary laments, wedding songs, harvest songs, shepherds' pan-pipe tunes, and more.

Theodosopoulou, Irene, L. Chartofylakas, M. Bakarezos, I. Orfanos, and N. A. Papadogiannis. "The Cretan Lyre: An Ethnomusicological and Music Acoustics Approach." *Proceeding of the CIM09* (Oct. 2009): 172–74.

Presents an ethnographic survey of traditional Cretan music and an analysis of the acoustic properties of Cretan "lyra."

Tobi, Yosef. *Between Hebrew and Arabic Poetry: Studies in Spanish Medieval Hebrew Poetry*. Boston: Brill, 2010.

Chapter 6, "Music and Musical Instruments in Spanish Medieval Hebrew Poetry: Poem of Yosef Ibn Ṣaddīq (Justo) in Praise of Yiṣḥaq Ibn Barun," discusses how the lyre was reinterpreted as an oud in Hebrew poems from medieval Spain.

Wacks, Mel. "Music to Sooth a Troubled King: David's Harp on Coins Old & New." *Shekel: The Journal of Israel and Jewish History and Numismatics* 47.2/3 (2014): 47–50.

Describes "David Playing for Saul," a commemorative coin produced by the Biblical Art Series in 2013 featuring an image of David playing the lyre taken from a sixth-century synagogue mosaic in Gaza.

Warner, Mira. "Aspects of Music Culture in the Land of Israel during the Hellenistic, Roman and Byzantine Periods: Sepphoris as a Case Study." *Music in Antiquity: The Near East and Mediterranean*, 273–97. Edited by Joan Goodnick Westenholz et al. Berlin: De Gruyter, 2014.

Examines artistic and numismatic renderings of musical instruments in mosaics from Sepphoris, noting the similarity of one of the lyres to the Orphic version.

Weiss, Zeev. "'The House of Orpheus': Another Villa from the Late Roman Period in Sepphoris." *Qadmoniot: A Journal for the Antiquities of Eretz-Israel and Bible Lands* 126 (2003): 94 –101.

Discusses the Orphic imagery of the lyre in the Sepphoris mosaic.

Weisser, Stéphanie. "Emotion and Music: The Ethiopian Lyre *Bagana*." *Musicae Scientiae* 16.1 (2012): 3–18.

Examines the *bagana*, a para-liturgical lyre played by the Christian Amhara of Ethiopia, which is believed to have spiritual origins connected to God, King David, and King Menelik I.

West, M. L. *Ancient Greek Music*. Oxford: Clarendon, 1992.

Includes a chapter on string instruments of ancient Greece.

Winnington-Ingram, R. P. "The Pentatonic Tuning of the Greek Lyre: A Theory Examined." *The Classical Quarterly* 6.3/4 (1956): 169–86.

Challenges the conventional view that strings of ancient Greek lyres could only produce one note each.

Xeravits, Geza. "The Reception of the Figure of David in Late Antique Synagogue Art." *Figures who Shaped Scriptures, Scriptures that Shaped Figures: Essays in Honour of Benjamin G. Wright III*, 71–90. Edited by Geza Xeravits et al. Berlin: De Gruyter, 2018.

Analyzes the figure of David, including depictions of his lyre, in late antique synagogue art, and argues against Orphic connections for most of the remains.

Zenger, Eric. "David as Musician and Poet: Plotted and Painted." *Biblical Studies, Cultural Studies: The Third Sheffield Colloquium*, 263–98. Edited by J. Cheryl Exum et al. Sheffield: Sheffield Academic, 1998.

Discusses literary and artistic renderings of David as a musician and poet from the biblical period through the Christian Middle Ages.

List of Contributors

Jonathan L. Friedmann is Professor of Jewish Music History and Associate Dean of the Master of Jewish Studies Program at the Academy for Jewish Religion California, President of the Western States Jewish History Association, Director of the Jewish Museum of the American West, and the author or editor of twenty-five books on Judaism, music, and religion.

Joel Gereboff is Associate Professor of Religious Studies at Arizona State University and Professor of Bible at the Academy for Jewish Religion California. His research focuses on Judaism in late antiquity and American Judaism. Recent publications include the essay, "Hate in Early Rabbinic Judaism," and the co-edited collections, *Qol Tamid: The Shofar in Ritual, History and Culture* (2017) and *Nondenominational Judaism: Perspectives on Pluralism and Inclusion in 21st-Century Jewish Professional Education* (2020).

Siobhán Dowling Long is an Irish biblical scholar, theologian, and musicologist, known primarily for her work on the reception of the Bible in music and art. She is a Lecturer at the School of Education, University College Cork, Ireland. A contributor to scholarly journals and edited collections, she is the author of *The Sacrifice of Isaac: The Reception of a Biblical Story in Music* (2013), with John F.A. Sawyer, *The Bible in Music: A Dictionary of Songs, Works and More* (2015), and with Fiachra Long (ed.), *Reading the Sacred Scriptures: From Oral Tradition to Written Documents and their Reception* (2018).

Jeremy Montagu was retired Lecturer/Curator of the Bate Collection in Faculty of Music, University of Oxford, and was Emeritus-Fellow of Wadham College, University of Oxford, Fellow of the Society of Antiquaries of London, Fellow of the Royal Anthropological Institute, and President of the Galpin Society. He was the author of many books and articles on musical instruments of all sorts and periods.

Dov Schwartz, former Dean of Humanities at Bar Ilan University and head of the Department of Music, is currently the head of the Department of Philosophy. He is also a senior researcher at the Shalom Hartman Institute in Jerusalem.

Ruth Smith writes, lectures and broadcasts on Handel's oratorios and operas. Her monograph *Handel's Oratorios and Eighteenth-Century Thought* (1995) was awarded a British Academy Prize. Other publications include *Charles Jennens: The Man behind Handel's Messiah*, written to accompany the exhibition she curated at the Handel House Museum, over 20 entries in the *Cambridge Handel Encyclopedia*, and numerous articles in academic journals. She is a Council member and trustee of the Handel Institute and an Ambassador for the Cambridge Handel Opera Company.

Marvin A. Sweeney is Professor of Hebrew Bible at the Claremont School of Theology, now located at Willamette University, Salem, Oregon. He is the author of some sixteen volumes in Hebrew Bible and Jewish Studies, most recently, *The Pentateuch* (2017) and *Jewish Mysticism: From Ancient Times Through Today* (2020). He is currently writing commentaries on Jeremiah (Illuminations; Eerdmans) and Samuel (New Cambridge Bible Commentary).

Bibliography

Abart, Christine. "Moments of Joy and Lasting Happiness: Examples from the Psalms." *Ancient Jewish Prayers and Emotions: Emotions Associated with Jewish Prayer in and Around the Second Temple Period*, 19–40. Edited by Stefan C. Reif and Renate Egger-Wentzel. Berlin: de Gruyter, 2015.

Alcalay, Reuben. *The Complete Hebrew-English Dictionary*. Ramat-Gan and Jerusalem: Massada, n.d.

Alexander, David. "Faith, Truth and Art: Notes on the Relationship between the Tradition and the Theater." *Zevulun Hammer: In Memoriam*. Edited by Yitzhak Heckelman. Jerusalem: Ministry of Education, 1999. [Heb.]

Altmann, Alexander. "Moses Mendelssohn on Education and the Image of Man." *Studies in Jewish Thought: An Anthology of German Jewish Scholarship*, 387–403. Edited by Alfred Jospe. Detroit: Wayne State University Press, 1981.

Anderson, Gary A. *A Time to Mourn, A Time to Dance: The Expression of Grief and Joy in Israelite Religion*. University Park: Pennsylvania State University Press, 1991.

Anderson, Warren, and Thomas J. Mathiesen. "Timotheus." *The New Grove Dictionary of Music and Musicians*, 2nd ed. Edited by Stanley Sadie and John Tyrrell. London: Oxford University Press, 2001.

Aspden, Suzanne. "'Fam'd Handel Breathing, tho' Transformed to Stone': The Composer as Monument." *Journal of the American Musicological Society* 55.1 (2002): 39–90.

Avenary, Hanoch. "Jüdische Musik." *Die Musik in Geschichte und Gegenwart: allgemeine Enzyklopädie der Musik*, vol. 7, 224–32. Kassel: Bärenreiter-Verlag, 1958.

Avigad, Nahman. "The King's Daughter and the Lyre." *Israel Exploration Journal* 28.3 (1978): 146–51.

Bagozzi, R. P. "Happiness." *Encyclopedia of Human Emotions*, 317–24. Edited by D. Levinson, J. J. Ponzetti, and P. F. Jorgenson. New York: Macmillan, 1999.

Bain, Alexander. *Emotions and the Will*. London: Longmans, Green, and Co., 1865.

Baker, Kyle. *Kind David*. New York: DC Comics, 2002.

Barnes, Albert. *Notes, Critical, Explanatory, and Practical on the Book of the Prophet Isaiah, vol. 1*. New York: Levitt & Allen, 1860.

Barnett, R. D. "New Facts About Instruments from Ur." *Iraq* 31.2 (Autumn 1969): 96–103.

Barnett, R. D., and D. J. Wiseman. *Fifty Masterpieces of Ancient Near Eastern Art in the Department of Western Asiatic Antiquities. The British Museum*. Reprint ed. London: The Trustees of the British Museum, 1969.

Barzilay, Isaac E. *Between Reason and Faith: Anti-Rationalism in Italian Jewish Thought 1250–1650*. The Hague: Mouton, 1967.

Bayer, Batya. "The Biblical Harp in Light of Archeological Findings." *Dukhan* 5 (1964): 109–121. [Heb.]

———. "Including Religious Music in the Teaching of Jewish Subjects and the Humanities." *Dukhan* 2 (1961). [Heb.]

Ben-Horin, Michal. "Musical Discourse and Historical Narratives in Hebrew Literature: Senaz's *Musical Moment* and Shaham's *Rosendoft Quartet*." *Israel Studies Forum* 21.2 (2006): 85–101.

Benovitz, Moshe. *Talmud Berakhot I*. Jerusalem: Haigud Lefarshanut Hatalmud, 2006.

Beuken, Willem A. M. *Isaiah II: Isaiah 28–39*. Historical Commentary on the Old Testament. Leuven: Peeters, 2000.

Bindman, David. "Roubiliac's Statue of Handel and the Keeping of Order in Vauxhall Gardens in the Early Eighteenth Century." *Sculpture Journal* 1 (1997): 22–31.

Blenkinsopp, Joseph. *Ezra-Nehemiah: A Commentary*. Old Testament Library. Philadelphia: Westminster, 1988.

Bock, Karen A. "Harp Music Eases Pain from Lupus." *The Harp Therapy Journal* 4.1 (1999): 4.

Boenig, Robert and Kathleen Davis, eds. *Manuscript, Narrative, Lexicon Essays on Literary and Cultural Transmission in Honor of Whitney F. Bolton*. Lewisburg and London: Bucknell University Press and Associated University Presses, 2000.

Botterweck, Johannes. "Kinnor." *Theological Dictionary of the Old Testament*, vol. 7, 197–204. Edited by G. Johannes Botterweck, Helmer Ringgren, and Heinz-Josef Fabry. Grand Rapids: Wm. B. Eerdmans, 1995.

Braun, Joachim. *Music in Ancient Israel/Palestine: Archaeological, Written, and Comparative Sources*. Translated by Douglas W. Stott. Grand Rapids, MI: Wm. B. Eerdmans, 2002.

Burgh, Theodore W. *Listening to the Artifacts: Music Culture in Ancient Palestine*. New York: T & T Clark, 2006.

Burney, Charles. *A General History of Music, from the Earliest Ages to the Present Period. To which is Prefixed, A Dissertation on the Music of the Ancients*. London: printed for the author, 1776.

Burrows, Donald, ed. *Alexander's Feast*. Sevenoaks: Novello, 1982.

_____. "The Composition and First Performance of Handel's *Alexander's Feast*." *Music & Letters* 64.3/4 (Jul.–Oct. 1983): 206–11.

_____. "Handel and *Alexander's Feast*." *The Musical Times*, 123.1670 (Apr. 1982): 252–55.

Burrows, Donald, Helen Coffey, Anthony Hicks, and John Greenacombe, eds. *George Frideric Handel: Collected Documents (2), 1725-1734*. Cambridge: Cambridge University Press, 2015.

_____, eds. *George Frideric Handel: Collected Documents (3), 1734-1742*. Cambridge: Cambridge University Press, 2019.

Burrows, Donald, and Rosemary Dunhill, eds. *Music and Theatre in Handel's World: The Family Papers of James Harris 1732-1780*. Oxford: Oxford University Press, 2002.

Calmet, Augustin. *Antiquities Sacred and Profane: or, A Collection of Curious and Critical Dissertations on the Old and New Testament*. Translated and edited by Nicholas Tindal. London: printed for J. Roberts, 1724.

Campbell, Antony F. *The Ark Narrative (1 Sam 4–6; 2 Sam 6): A Form-Critical and Tradition-Historical Study*. Society of Biblical Literature Dissertation Series 16. Missoula, MT: Scholars Press, 1975.

_____. *1 Samuel*. Forms of the Old Testament Literature 7. Grand Rapids, MI, and Cambridge, UK: Eerdmans, 2003.

_____. *2 Samuel*. Forms of the Old Testament Literature 8. Grand Rapids, MI, and Cambridge, UK: Eerdmans, 2005.

Campbell, Antony F., and Mark A. O'Brien. *Sources of the Pentateuch: Texts, Introductions, Annotations*. Minneapolis: Fortress, 1993.

Cohen, Evelyn M. "Isaac Norsa's Hebrew Miscellany of 1523." *The Princeton University Library Chronicle* 64.1 (2002): 87–106.

Cohen, Judith. "Jubal in the Middle Ages." *Yuval* 3 (1974): 83–99.

Coke, David. "Roubiliac's Handel for Vauxhall Gardens: A Sculpture in Context." *Sculpture Journal* 16.2 (2007): 5–22

Coke, David, and Alan Borg. *Vauxhall Gardens: A History*. New Haven and London: Yale University Press, 2011.

Collier, Jeremy. *Essays upon Several Moral Subjects. Part II. The Seventh Edition Corrected.* London: printed for J. and J. Knapton, G. Strahan, F. Clay, D. Brown, B. Motte, and R. Williamson, 1731.

Creech, Thomas. *T. Lucretius Carus, Of the Nature of Things.* London: printed by J. Matthews for G. Sawbridge, 1714.

Cross, Frank Moore. "David, Orpheus and Psalm 151:3–4." *Bulletin of the American Schools of Oriental Research* 231 (1978): 69–71.

Crumb, R. *The Book of Genesis Illustrated.* New York: W.W. Norton, 2009.

Dalglish, E. D. *Psalm Fifty-One in the Light of Ancient Near Eastern Patternism.* Leiden: Brill, 1962.

Dan, Yosef. "The *Tefilah u-Dim'ah* Sermon of R. Judah Moscato." *Sinai* 76 (1975): 209–32. [Heb.]

Darwin, Charles. *The Expression of Emotions in Man and Animal.* New York: D. Appleton, 1886.

de Brossard, Sébastian. *A Musical Dictionary.* Translated by James Grassineau. London: printed for J. Wilcox, 1740.

de Jauregi, Miguel Herrero. *Orphism and Christianity in Late Antiquity.* Berlin: De Gruyter, 2010.

Dean, Winton. *Handel's Dramatic Oratorios and Masques.* London: Oxford University Press, 1959.

Debenham, Margaret, and Michael Cole. "Pioneer Piano Makers in London, 1737–74: Newly Discovered Documentary Sources." *Royal Musical Association Research Chronicle* 44.1 (2013): 55–86.

Dever, William G. *The Lives of Ordinary People in Ancient Israel: Where Archaeology and the Bible Intersect.* Grand Rapids: Wm. B. Eerdmans, 2012.

Diagram Group. *Musical Instruments of the World: An Illustrated Encyclopedia.* New York: Paddington, 1976.

Dimant, Devorah. "David's Youth in the Qumran Context (11 QPs 28:3–12)." *Prayer and Poetry in the Dead Sea Scrolls and Related Literature: Essays in Honor of Eileen Schuller on the Occasion of Her 65th Birthday*, 97–114. Edited by Jeremy Pener et al. Leiden: Brill, 2012.

Dingley, William. *Cathedral Service Decent and Useful, A Sermon Preach'd before the University of Oxford at St Mary's on Cecilia's Day, 1713.* Oxford: printed for Anthony Pelsley, 1713.

Doron, Aviva, ed. *Yehuda Halevi: A Selection of Critical Essays on His Poetry.* Tel Aviv: Hakibbutz Hameuchad, 1988. [Heb.]

Dowling Long, Siobhán. "Musical Instruments in Biblical Art." *Bible, Art, Gallery*, 97–121. Edited by Martin O'Kane. Sheffield: Sheffield Phoenix Press, 2011.

———. "'Why Weepest Thou? … And Why Is Thy Heart Grieved?' (1 Sam. 1:8): Grief and Loss in the Books of Samuel: A Musical Interpretation." *The Books of Samuel: Stories-History-Reception History*, 271–82. Edited by Walter Dietrich. Leuven: Peeters, 2016.

Dozeman, Thomas B. *The Pentateuch: Introducing the Torah*. Minneapolis: Fortress, 2017.

Dubzevitz, Abraham Dov. *Sefer ha-Mitsraf*. Odessa: Beilinson, 1871. [Heb.]

Dumbrill, Richard J. *The Archaeomusicology of the Ancient Near East*. Victoria, BC: Trafford, 2005.

———. *The Musicology and Organology of the Ancient Near East*. London: Tadema, 1998.

Durham, John I. *The Biblical Rembrandt: Human Painter in a Landscape of Faith*. Macon, GA: Mercer University Press, 2004.

Edwards, Owain, and Phyllis Kinney. "Parry, John (i)." *The New Grove Dictionary of Music and Musicians*, 2nd ed. Edited by Stanley Sadie and John Tyrrell. London: Oxford University Press, 2001.

Ellsworth, P. C., and C. A. Smith. "Shades of Joy: Patterns of Appraisal Differentiating Pleasant Emotions." *Cognition and Emotion* 2 (1988): 271–302.

Eshel, Hanan. "On Harps and Lyres: A Note on the Bronze Coins of the Bar Kokhba Administration." *Israel Numismatic Journal* 16 (2007–08): 118–30.

Even-Shoshan, Avraham, ed. *Ha-Millon Ha-`Ivri HaMrukaz*. Jerusalem: Kiriyat Sepher, 1988. [Heb.]

Feldman, Louis H. *Studies in Hellenistic Judaism*. Leiden: Brill, 1996.

Fernandez-Marcos, Natalio. "David the Adolescent: On Psalm 151." *The Old Greek Psalter:Studies in Honour of Natalio Albert Pietersman*, 205–17. Edited by Robert J. V. Hiebert. London: Bloomsbury, 2001.

Finesinger, Sol Baruch. "Musical Instruments in the OT." *Hebrew Union College Annual* 3 (1926): 21–76.

Finney, Paul Corby. "Orpheus David: A Connection in Iconography Between Greco-Roman Judaism and Early Christianity." *Journal of Jewish Art* 5 (1978): 6–15.

Fishbane, Michael. "The Inwardness of Joy in Jewish Spirituality." *In Pursuit of Happiness*, 71–88. Edited by Leroy S. Rouner. Notre Dame: University of Notre Dame Press, 1995.

Fleischer, Ezra. "The Sacred Poetry of Judah Halevi." *The Philosophical Teachings of Judah Halevi*. Edited by Haya Schwarz. Jerusalem: Ministry of Education, 1978.

Flesher, Paul V. M. "Rereading the Reredos: David, Orpheus, and Messianism in the Dura Europos Synagogue." *Ancient Synagogues: Historical, Analysis and Archaeological Discovery*, vol. 2, 2346–66. Edited by Dan Urman et al. Leiden: Brill, 1995.

Foxvog, D. A., and A. D. Kilmer. "Music." *International Study Bible Encyclopedia*, vol. 3, 436–49. Grand Rapids, MI: W. B. Eerdmans, 1980.

Franklin, John Curtis. "Lyre Gods of the Bronze Age Musical Koine." *Journal of Ancient Near Eastern Religions* 6.1 (2006): 39–70.

Freeman, L., et al. "Music Thanatology: Prescriptive Harp Music as Palliative Care for the Dying Patient." *American Journal of Hospital Palliative Care* 23.2 (2006):100–04.

Frevert, Ute, et al. *Emotional Lexicons: Continuity and Change in the Vocabulary of Feeling 1700–2000*. New York: Oxford University Press, 2014.

Friedheim, Emmanuel. "Jewish Society in the Land of Israel and the Challenge of Music in the Roman Period." *Review of Rabbinic Judaism–Ancient, Medieval, and Modern* 15.1 (2012): 61–88

Friedman, John B. *Orpheus in the Middle Ages*. Cambridge, MA: Harvard University Press, 1970.

Friedmann, Jonathan L. *Music in Biblical Life: The Roles of Song in Ancient Israel*. Jefferson, NC: McFarland, 2013.

Friedmann, Jonathan L., and Joel Gereboff, eds. *Qol Tamid: The Shofar in Ritual, History, and Culture*. Claremont: Claremont Press, 2017.

Fulton, Cheryl Ann. "Harp, V, Europe and the Americas, 5, Multi-rank harps in Europe outside Spain, i, The Instruments, iii, Wales and England." *The New Grove Dictionary of Music and Musicians*, 2nd ed. Edited by Stanley Sadie and John Tyrrell. London: Oxford University Press, 2001.

Gerson-Kiwi, Edith. "Musique dans la bible." *Dictionnaire de la Bible*, supp. 5, 1411–68. Paris: Letouzey and Ané, 1957.

Gerstenberger, Erhard S. *Psalms, Part 1, with an Introduction to Cultic Poetry*. Forms of the Old Testament Litrature 14. Grand Rapids, MI: Eerdmans, 1988.

Gioia, Ted. *Healing Songs*. Durham: Duke University Press, 2006.

Ginzberg, Louis. *Legends of the Jews*. Philadelphia: Jewish Publication Society, 2003.

————. *The Legends of the Jews, 4: Bible Times and Characters from Joshua to Esther*. Translated by Henrietta Szold. Philadelphia: The Jewish Publication Society of America, 1987.

————. *The Legends of the Jews, 6: Notes to Volume 3 and 4: From Moses in the Wilderness to Esther*. Translated by Henrietta Szold. Philadelphia: The Jewish Publication Society of America, 1987.

Glicksberg, Simon Jacob. *The Jewish Sermon*. Tel Aviv: n. p., 1940.

Glüxam, Dagmar. "Instrumentation, 9: Harp." *The Cambridge Handel Encyclopedia*, 341–42. Edited by David Vickers and Annette Landgraf. Cambridge: Cambridge University Press, 2009.

Goodenough, Erwin R. *Jewish Symbols in the Greco-Roman Period, vols. IX–XI: Symbolism in the Dura Synagogue*. New York: Pantheon, 1964.

Gorali, Moshe. *The Old Testament in Music*. Jerusalem: Maron, 1993.

Görg, M. "*Kinnôr*." *Theological Dictionary of the Old Testament*, 7:197–203. Edited by G. J. Botterweck et al. Grand Rapids, MI: Eerdmans, 1995.

Goscinny, René, and Albert Uderzo. *The Complete Asterix*. New York: Hachette, 2013.

Graetz, H. *Kritischer Commentar zu den Psalmen*, vol. 1. Breslau: Schottlaender, 1882.

Greenboym, Natan. "Yerushalayim Shel Zahav Ke'shir Koddesh." *Mayim Midalav* (1933): 27–32. [Heb.]

Grønbæk, Jakob H. *Die Geschichte vom Aufstieg Davids (1. Sam. 15–2 Sam. 5). Tradition und Komposition*. Acta Theologica Danica X. Copenhagen: Munksgaard, 1971.

Gross, Abraham. *R. Yosef ben Abraham Hayyun: Leader of the Lisbon Community and His Literary Work*. Ramat-Gan: Bar-Ilan University, 1993. [Heb.]

Gross, Benjamin. *L'Eternite d'Israel: La doctrine messianique de l'exil et de la redemption du Maharal de Prague (1512–1609)*. Strassbourg: n. p., 1968.

Grözinger, Karl E. *Musik und Gesang in der Theologie der frühen jüdischen Literatur: Talmud Midrasch Mystik.* Tübingen: J. C. B. Möhr, 1982.

Gunkel, Hermann. *Introduction to Psalms: The Genres of the Religious Lyric of Israel.* Compiled by Joachim Begrich. Macon, GA: Mercer University Press, 1998.

_____. *The Psalms: A Form-Critical Introduction.* Minneapolis, MN: Fortress Press, 1967.

Habel, Norman. *Job: A Commentary.* Old Testament Library. Philadelphia: Westminster, 1985.

Hadar, Adaya. "Music in the Thought of Rabbi Nahman of Braslav." Ph.D. diss. Bar Ilan University, Ramat Gan 2017. [Heb.]

Ḥaklîlî, Rāḥēl. *Ancient Jewish Art and Archaeology in the Diaspora.* Boston: Brill, 1998.

Halevi, Elimelech. *Aggadic Passages in Light of Greek Sources.* Tel Aviv: Armoni, 1973. [Heb.]

Halevi, Ephraim E. "Kinoro shel David." *Moznayim* 22 (1966): 334–36.

Halfpenny, Eric. "The Lyrichord." *The Galpin Journal* 3 (1950): 46–49.

Handy, Lowell K. "Review of *A Time to Mourn, a Time to Dance: The Expression of Grief and Joy in Israelite Religion* by Gary A. Anderson." *Journal of Near Eastern Studies* 55.3 (1996): 213–15.

Harbison, Peter. *The High Crosses of Ireland: An Iconographical and Photographic.* Bonn: Rudolph Habelt, 1992.

Harrán, Don. "The Levi Dynasty: Three Generations of Jewish Musicians in Sixteenth-century Mantua." *Rabbi Judah Moscato and the Jewish Intellectual World of Mantua in the 16th–17th Centuries*, 186–95. Edited by Giuseppe Veltri and Gianfranco Miletto. Boston: Brill, 2012.

_____. *Three Early Modern Hebrew Scholars on the Mysteries of Song.* Boston: Brill, 2014.

_____. "What Does *Halakhah* Say about Music? Two Early Rabbinic Writings on Music by Hai b. Sherira." *Hebrew Union College Annual* 84 (2014): 49–87.

Harris, Ellen T. "Handel and his Will." *Handel's Will: Facsimile and Commentary*, 9–20. Edited by Donald Burrows. London: The Gerald Coke Handel Foundation, 2009.

Hawkins, John. *A General History of the Science and Practice of Music.* London: printed for T. Payne and Son, 1776.

Hogwood, Christopher. "Thomas Tudway's History of Music." *Music in Eighteenth-Century England: Essays in Memory of Charles Cudworth*, 19–47. Edited by Christopher Hogwood and Richard Luckett. Cambridge: Cambridge University Press, 1983.

Humphreys, Samuel. *The Sacred Books of the Old and New Testament, Recited at large: and Illustrated with Critical and Explanatory Annotations, Carefully Compiled from the Commentaries and other Writings of Grotius, Lightfoot, Pool, Calmet, Patrick, Le Clerc, Lock, Burkitt, Henry, Pearse, and a Variety of other Eminent Authors, Ancient and Modern.* London: printed by R. Penny, 1735.

Idel, Moshe. "Judah Moscato: A Late Renaissance Jewish Preacher." *Preachers of the Italian Ghetto*, 41–66. Edited by David B. Ruderman. Berkeley: University of California Press, 1992.

————. "Kabbalah and Ancient Philosophy for Isaac and Judah Abravanel." *The Philosophy of Leone Ebreo: Four Lectures at the Colloquium of Haifa University, January 16, 1984*, 73–112. Edited by Menahem Dorman and Ze'ev Levy. Tel Aviv: Hakibbutz Hameuchad, 1985.

————. "The Magical and Theurgical Interpretations of Music from the Renaissance to Hasidism." *Yuval: Studies of the Jewish Music Research Center* 4 (1982): 33–62. [Heb.]

————. "Music and Prophetic Kabbalah." *Yuval: Studies of the Jewish Music Research Center* 4 (1982): 150–69.

————. "Music in Sixteenth Century Kabbalah in North Africa." *Yuval: Studies of the Jewish Music Research Center* 7 (2002): 154–70.

Idelsohn, Abraham Z. *Jewish Music: Its Historical Development.* New York: Dover, 1992.

Japhet, Sara. *1 and 2 Chronicles: A Commentary.* Old Testament Library. Louisville, KY: Westminster John Knox, 1993.

Jinbachian, Manuel. "Music and Musical Instruments in the Septuagint, the Peshitta and the Armenian Psalms." *Text Theology & Translation: Essays in Honour of Jan de Waard*, 53–77. Edited by Simon Crisp and Manuel Jinbachian. London: United Bible Societies, 2004.

Kafih, Yosef, trans. *R. Saadia Gaon's Commentary on the Torah.* Jerusalem: Mosad Harav Kook, 1963. [Heb.]

Kalat, J. W., and M. N. Shiota. *Emotion.* Belmont, CA: Thompson Wadsworth, 2007.

King, Paul J., and Lawrence E. Stager. *Life in Biblical Israel.* Louisville, KY: Westminster John Knox, 2001.

Kirsch, Jonathan. *King David: The Real Life of the Man who Ruled Israel.* New York: Ballantine, 2000.

Koehler, Ludwig, and Walter Baumgartner. *The Hebrew and Aramaic Lexicon of the Old Testament.* Leiden: Brill, 1995.

Kolyada, Yelena. *Compendium of Musical Instruments and Instrumental Terminology in the Bible.* London: Taylor and Francis Group, 2014.

Kraeling, Carl H. *The Synagogue: Excavations at Dura-Europos, Final Report 8, Part I.* New Haven, CT: Yale University Press, 1956.

Kruger, Paul A. "Emotions in the Hebrew Bible: A Few Observations on Prospects and Challenges." *Old Testament Essays* 28.2 (2015): 395–420.

Kuehn, J. *Die Musik in den Heiligen Schriften im Talmud und in der Kabbalah.* Wien: Kuehn, 1930. [Heb.]

Lasater, Philip Michael. "'The Emotions' in Biblical Anthropology? A Genealogy and Case Study with ירא." *Harvard Theological Review* 110.4 (2017): 520–40.

Lawergren, Bo. "Distinctions between Canaanite, Philistine, and Israelite Lyres, and Their Global Lyrical Contexts." *Bulletin of the American Schools of Oriental Research* 309 (1998): 41–68.

Leman, Marc, and Pieter-Jan Maes. "Music Perception and Embodied Music Cognition." *The Routledge Handbook of Embodied Cognition,* 81–89. Edited by Lawrence Shapiro. New York: Routledge, 2014.

Levarie, Siegmund. "Philo on Music." *Journal of Musicology* 9 (1991): 124–30.

Leveen, Jacob. *The Hebrew Bible in Art.* The Schweich Lectures of the British Academy 1939. Reprint ed. New York: Hermon Press, 1974.

Luzzatto, Samuel David. *Torah Commentary,* vol. 1. Translated by Eliyahu Munk. Jerusalem/New York: Lambda, 2012.

Martin, Benjamin. *The General Magazine of Arts and Sciences, Philosophical, Philological, Mathematical, and Mechanical.* London: printed for W. Owen, 1755–65.

McAdams, Stephen, Chelsea Douglas, and Naresh M. Vempala. "Perception and Modeling of Affective Qualities of Musical Instrument Sounds Across Pitch Registers." *Frontiers in Psychology* 8 (2018): 1–19.

McKinnon, James W. *Music in Early Christian Literature.* Cambridge: Cambridge University Press, 1989.

Menn, Esther M. "Praying King and Sanctuary of Prayer, Part II: David's Deferment and the Temple's Dedication in Rabbinic Psalms Commentary (Midrash Tehillim)." *Journal of Jewish Studies* 53 (2002): 299–323.

Meshel, Z. "The Painting of the Harp Player in Kuntilat Adjaroud in Sinai." *Tatslil* 9 (1977): 109–10. [Heb.]

Miletto, Gianfranco. "The Human Body as a Musical Instrument in the Sermons of Judah Moscato." *The Jewish Body: Corporality, Society and Identity in the Renaissance and Early Modern Period*, 277–94. Edited by Maria Diemling and Giuseppe Veltri. Leiden: Brill, 2009.

Mirguet, Françoise. "What is an 'Emotion' in the Hebrew Bible? An Experience that Exceeds Most Contemporary Concepts." *Biblical Interpretation* 24 (2016): 442–65.

Montagu, Jeremy. *Musical Instruments of the Bible*. Lanham, MD: Scarecrow, 2002.

_____. *The World of Medieval & Renaissance Musical Instruments*. Woodstock, NY: The Overlook Press, 1976.

Morrison, Steven J., and Steven M. Demerost. "Cultural Constraints on Music Perception and Cognition." *Progress in Brain Research* 178 (2009): 67–77.

Moscato, Yehuda. *Nefutsot Yehudah*. Bnei Berak/New York: Mishor, 2000.

_____. *Sermons*, vol. 1. Edited and translated by Gianfranco Miletto and Giuseppe Veltri. Leiden: Brill, 2011.

Muffs, Yochanan. "Joy and Love as Metaphorical Expressions of Willingness and Spontaneity in Cuneiform, Ancient Hebrew, and Related Literature: Divine Investitures in the Midrash in the Light of Neo-Babylonian Royal Grants." *Judaism, Christianity, and Other Greco-Roman Cults: Studies for Morton Smith at Sixty*, 1–36. Edited by Jacob Neusner. Leiden: Brill, 1975.

_____. "Love and Joy as Metaphors for Volition in Hebrew and Related Literatures, Part II: The Joy of Giving." *The Journal of the Ancient Near Eastern Society of Columbia University* 11 (1979): 91–111.

Mucznik, Sonia. "Musicians and Musical Instruments in Roman and Early Byzantine Mosaics of the Land of Israel: Sources, Precursors and Significance." *Gerión* 29.1 (2011): 265–86.

Neusner, Jacob. *Judaism's Theological Voice: The Melody of the Talmud*. Chicago: University of Chicago Press, 1995.

Nihan, Christophe. "Saul Among the Prophets (1 Sam 10:10-12 and 19:18-24): The Reworking of Saul's Figure in the Context of the Debate on 'Charismatic Prophecy' in the Persian Era." *Saul in Story and Tradition*, 88–118. Edited by Carl S. Ehrlich and Marsha C. White. Tübingen: Mohr Siebeck, 2006.

Nissinen, Martti. *Prophets and Prophecy in the Ancient Near East*. Atlanta: Society of Biblical Literature, 2003.

Noth, Martin. *The Deuteronomistic History*. JSOTSup 15. Sheffield: JSOT Press, 1981.

Nulman, Macy. *Concise Encyclopedia of Jewish Music*. New York: McGraw-Hill, 1975.

Oppenheimer, Aharon. "The Attempt of Hananiah, Son of Rabbi Joshua's Brother to Intercalate the Year in Babylonia: A Comparison of the Traditions in the Jerusalem and the Babylonian Talmuds." *Between Rome and Babylonia: Studies in the Leadership in Jewish Societies*, 255–64. Edited by Nili Oppenheimer. Tubingen: Mohr Siebeck, 2005.

Ovadiah, Asher. "Excavations in the Area of the Ancient Synagogue at Gaza." Preliminary Report. *Israel Exploration Journal* 19.4 (1969): 193–98.

_____. "The Symbolic Meaning of the David-Orpheus Images in the Gaza Synagogue Mosaic." *Liber Annuus* 59 (2009): 301–07.

Petersen, David L. *Late Israelite Prophecy*. Society of Biblical Literature Monograph Series 23. Missoula, MT: Scholars Press, 1977.

_____. "Portraits of David: Canonical and Otherwise." *Interpretation* 40:2 (1986): 130–42.

Provenza, Antonietta. "Soothing Lyres and *Epodai*: Music Therapy and the Cases of Orpheus, Empedocles and David." *Music in Antiquity: The Near Eastern and the Mediterranean*, 298–307. Edited by Joan Goodnick Westenholz, Yossi Maurey, and Edwin Seroussi. Berlin: Walter de Gruyter, 2014.

Rabinowitz, Isaac. "The Alleged Orphism of 11 Q Pss 28:8-12." *Zeitschrift fur die Alttestamentliche Wissenschaft* 76 (1964): 193–200.

Ratzaby, Yehuda. *A Dictionary of Judaeo-Arabic in R. Saadya's Tafsir*. Ramat-Gan: Bar-Ilan University, 1985.

Recanati, Menachem. *Commentary on the Torah*. Lublin, 1595; offset, Jerusalem, 1961.

_____. *Sefer ha-Peli'ah*, vol. 2. Przemyśl, 1883.

Reevy, Gretchen M. *Encyclopedia of Emotion.* Santa Barbara: Greenwood, 2010.

Roberts, John H. "The Composition of Handel's *Esther,* 1718–1720." *Händel Jahrbuch* 55 (2009): 353–90.

Römer, Thomas. *The So-Called Deuteronomistic History: A Sociological, Historical, and Literary Introduction.* London and New York: T and T Clark, 2007.

Rosenblum, Noah. *ha-Malbim: Interpretation, Philosophy, Science and Mystery in the Writings of R. Meir Leibush Malbim.* Jerusalem: Mosad Harav Kook, 1988. [Heb.]

Sachs, Curt. *The History of Musical Instruments.* New York: W. W. Norton, 1940.

Safiullinna, Liliya Garifullovna, and Gulnara Ibragimovna Batyrshina. "Musical Images as a Reflection of the Artistic Universalism of Marc Chagall." *Terra Sebus: Acta Musei Sabesiensis* (2014): 67–104.

Sanders, James. *The Psalms Scroll of Qumran Cave 11, Discoveries in the Judean Desert 4.* Oxford: Clarendon, 1965.

Sandler, Peretz. *The Be'ur of Moses Mendelssohn: Origin and Influence.* Jerusalem: Rubin Mass, 1984. [Heb.]

Sarna, Nahum. *Genesis.* JPS Torah Commentary. Philadelphia: Jewish Publication Society, 1989.

Schumm, W. R. "Satisfaction." *Encyclopedia of Human Emotions,* 583–90. Edited by D. Levinson, J. J. Ponzetti, and P. F. Jorgenson. New York: Macmillan, 1999.

Schwartz, Dov. *Kinor Nishmati: HaMusika BeHagut HaYehudit.* Ramat Gan: Bar Ilan University Press, 2012. [Heb.]

Sellers, Ovid R. "Musical Instruments of Israel." *Biblical Archaeologist* 4.3 (1941): 33–47.

Sendrey, Alfred. *Music in Ancient Israel.* New York: Philosophical Library, 1969.

Sendrey, Alfred, and Mildred Norton. *David's Harp: The Story of Music in Biblical Times.* New York: New American Library, 1964.

Seroussi, Edwin. "Music in Medieval Ibero-Jewish Society." *Hispania Judaic* 5 (2007): 5–67.

Shiloah, Amnon. *The Musical Legacy of Jewish Communities.* Tel Aviv: Open University, 1985–1987. [Heb.]

Shirt, David John. "'Sing Psalms to the Lord with the Harp': Attitudes toward Musical Instruments in Early Christianity – 680 AD." *Journal of Early Christian History* 6 (2016): 97–115.

Simerly, Meeka. "Naomi Shemer's Artistic Expression: Poetry, Prayer, or Both?" *Emotions in Jewish Music: Personal and Scholarly Reflections*, 5–29. Edited by Jonathan L. Friedmann. Lanham, MD: University Press of America, 2012.

Smith, John Arthur. *Music in Ancient Judaism and Early Christianity*. Burlington, VT: Ashgate, 2013.

Smith, Morton. "Psalm 151, David, Jesus and Orpheus." *Zeitschrift fur die Alttestamentliche Wissenschaft* 93.2 (1981): 247–53.

Smith, Ruth. "The Argument and Contexts of Dryden's *Alexander's Feast*." *SEL: Studies in English Literature* 18 (1978): 465–90.

_____. "Early Music's Dramatic Significance in Handel's *Saul*." *Early Music* 35 (2007): 173–89.

_____. *Handel's Oratorios and Eighteenth-Century Thought*. Cambridge: Cambridge University Press, 1995.

_____. "Timotheus, Alexander, Semele and Handel." *Handel Institute Newsletter* 14.1 (Spring 2003): unnumbered 1–4.

Spencer, F. Scott. "Getting a Feel for the 'Mixed' and 'Vexed' Study of Emotions in Biblical Literature." *Mixed Feelings and Vexed Passions: Exploring Emotions in Biblical Literature*, 1–41. Edited by F. Scott Spencer. Atlanta, GA: Society for Biblical Literature, 2017.

Sperber, Daniel. *Material Culture in Eretz Israel During the Talmudic Period*, vol. 2. Ramat-Gan: Bar-Ilan University, 2006. [Heb.]

Stern, H. "The Orpheus in the Synagogue of Dura Europos." *Journal of the Warburg and Courtauld Institutes* 21.1/2 (Jan.–Jun.1958): 1–6.

Stern, Samuel. *Poetry and Melody in the Worship of God*. Jerusalem: Machon Leb Bratslav, 2006. [Heb.]

Stillingfleet, Benjamin. *Principles and Power of Harmony*. London: printed by J. and H. Hughs, 1771.

Strack, H. L., and Gunter Stemberger. *Introduction to the Talmud and Midrash*. Minneapolis, MN: Fortress Press, 1996.

Sweeney, Marvin A. *Isaiah 1-39, with an Introduction to Prophetic Literature*. Forms of the Old Testament Literature 16. Grand Rapids, MI: Eerdmans, 1996.

_____. *1 and 2 Kings: A Commentary*. Old Testament Library. Louisville, KY: Westminster John Knox, 2007.

_____. *King Josiah of Judah: The Lost Messiah of Israel*. Oxford and New York: Oxford University Press, 2001.

_____. *The Pentateuch*. Core Biblical Studies. Nashville, TN: Abingdon, 2017.

_____. *Reading Ezekiel: A Literary and Theological Commentary*. Reading the Old Testament. Macon, GA: Mercer University Press, 2013.

Talgam, Rina. *Mosaics of Faith: Floors of Pagans, Jews, Samaritans, Christians, and Muslims in the Holy Land*. Jerusalem: Yad Ben-Zvi Press; University Park, PA: The Pennsylvania State University Press, 2014.

Tobi, Yosef. *Between Hebrew and Arabic Poetry: Studies in Spanish Medieval Hebrew Poetry*. Boston: Brill, 2010.

Uzziel, Ben-Zion Meir Hai. *Hegiyonei Uzziel*, vol. 2. Jerusalem: Va'ad le-Hotsa'at Kitvei ha-Rav, 1992. [Heb.]

Varka, Natassa. "Charles Jennens's Collection of Handel's Sacred Oratorios from *Saul* to *Jephtha*: Sources, Contexts, and Revisions." Ph.D. diss., University of Cambridge, 2017.

von Hornbostel, Erich Moritz, and Curt Sachs. "Systematik der Musikinstrumente." *Zeitschrift für Ethnologie* 46 (1914): 553–90.

Warner, Mira. "Aspects of Music Culture in the Land of Israel during the Hellenistic, Roman and Byzantine Periods: Sepphoris as a Case Study." *Music in Antiquity: The Near East and Mediterranean*, 273–96. Edited by Joan Goodnick Westenholz et al. Berlin: De Gruyter, 2014.

Weiss, Zeev. "'The House of Orpheus': Another Villa from the Late Roman Period in Sepphoris." *Qadmoniot: A Journal for the Antiquities of Eretz-Israel and Bible Lands* 126 (2003): 94–101.

Westermann, Claus. *Genesis 1–11: A Commentary*. Continental Commentary. Minneapolis: Augsburg, 1984

White, H. G. Evelyn. *Hesiod, Homeric, Hymns and Homerica*. Adelaide: University of Adelaide, 2014.

Williams, Sarajane. "Patients with Parkinson's Disease Find Relief with Harp Music." *The Harp Therapy Journal* 6.1 (2001): 6–7.

Wilson, John, ed. *Roger North on Music*. London: Novello, 1959.

Winternitz, Emanuel. *Musical Instruments and their Symbolism in Western Art*. New York: W. W. Norton, 1967.

Xeravits, Geza. "The Reception of the Figure of David in Late Antique Synagogue Art." *Figures who Shaped Scriptures, Scriptures that Shaped Figures: Essays in Honour of Benjamin G. Wright III*, 71–90. Edited by Geza Xeravits et al. Berlin: De Gruyter, 2018.

Young, Percy M. *Saul: Kritischer Bericht, Hallische Händel Ausgabe, Kritische Gesamtausgabe* 1.13. Kassel: Bärenreiter, 1964.

Zettler, Richard L., and Lee Horne, ed. *Treasures from the Royal Tombs of Ur.* Philadelphia: University of Pennsylvania, 1998.

Scripture Index

Genesis

1:26–31	33
2:4–4:26	33
4:20	51
4:21	4, 6–7, 19, 23, 32–33, 51, 77
4:22	51, 77
19:36–37	52
22	106
29–31	54
31:27	4, 33, 46, 47, 54

Exodus

15	38
15:20	20, 46

Numbers

10:1–10	45

1 Samuel

1:8	95
4–6	35
6:16	102
9:1–10:16	34
10:5	4, 32, 57
10:10–12	58
16	95
16:1–13	34
16:14	34
16:14–23	34, 35
16:16	4, 20, 53, 87, 121, 122
16:16–23	32, 53
16:21–23	95, 97
16:23	4, 54, 119
17	117
17:1–58	34
17:55–58	129
18	95
18:6	46
18:6–8	129

18:10	87, 121, 122
18:10–11	95, 97, 130
18:10–12	54
19:9–10	54
19:18–24	58
30–31	35

2 Samuel

5:11	105
6	35, 100
6:1–11	100, 122
6:3	101
6:5	4, 57, 101
6:13	101
12–15	100, 122
23:2	105

1 Kings

10	36
10:11–12	41
10:12	4, 52
12	37
16	37
22	37

2 Kings

3	32, 36
3:15	57, 71
13	37
14	37

Isaiah

5	32
5:2	55
5:8–30	38
5:11–12	69
5:12	4, 38, 55, 69
5:12–14	61
5:13	69, 93
11:1–3	93
11:6–9	91

12:3	63	68	117
15–16	38	71	39, 56
16:11	4, 38, 52, 73	71:22	4, 39, 56
		80	117
23	32	81	39
23:16	4, 38, 55	81:1–4	56
24	52	81:3	4, 39, 46, 47, 68
24:1–23	38		
24:8	4, 38, 46, 47, 52	92	24, 56, 73, 150
24:9	67, 71	92:1–4	56
30	38	92:3	52
30:32	4, 38, 57	92:4	4, 39, 66, 73, 75
		96	36
Ezekiel		97	117
2:10	66	98	4, 39, 56
26	38, 52	98:5	39, 56, 73
26:13	4, 38	100	68
32:16	66	105	36
		106	36
Hosea		108	39
9:1	71	108:3	4, 39
		114:9	52
Amos		119:62	58, 71
6:5	103, 122	127:2	63
		134	63
Psalms		137	15, 23, 39, 52, 61, 74, 112
1	24, 113, 116		
12:1	65, 79	137:2	4, 25, 39, 74, 86
16:11	65, 79		
30	23	137:4	74
33	24, 39, 56, 120	137:5	74
		147	40, 56
33:1–3	73	147:7	4, 39, 56
33:2	4, 24, 38, 52, 56, 65, 80	148	25, 148
		149	25, 40
37:2	108, 110	149:3	4, 40, 56
42–43	39, 56	149:5–6	75
43	56	150	25, 40, 56
43:4	4, 39, 56	150:3	4, 40, 56
49	51	151	8, 147, 160
49:5	4, 39		
52	93		
57	39	**Job**	
57:8–9	56	21:9–13	66
57:9	4, 39, 71	21:12	4, 23, 40, 55
67:2	121		

29–31	40
30:31	4, 23, 40, 52
39:24-25	40

Daniel

3	25

Nehemiah

12:27	4, 40, 56

1 Chronicles

13	102
13:8	4, 40, 57
15	102
15:15	102
15:16	4, 22, 47
15:16–24	102
15:19–22	22
15:21	4, 51
15:28	4, 57, 102
16	36
16:5	4, 51–52
25:1	4
25:3	4
25:6	4, 52
25:9	63

2 Chronicles

5:2–6:2	41
5:12	4, 22, 52
9:11	4
20	41
20:28	4, 57
29	41
29:25	4, 41, 52

1 Maccabees

3:45	8
4:54	8, 26
11–12	123
13:51	8, 27

Matthew

2:12–13	116

1 Corinthians

14:7	19, 27

Revelation

4:4	27
14:2	28
15:2	28
18:22	19, 28

Subject Index

Aaron, 22
Abijah, 94
Abinadab, 100
Abner, 130
Abot R. Natan, 72
Abrabanel, Yizhak, 77
Abraham, 73, 95, 108
Achilles, 88
Adah, 32
Adam, 33, 72–73
Africa, 4, 13, 19, 21, 22, 153
Aha bar Bizna, 72
Ahaz, 94
Ahio, 101
Akedah, 62
Alexander Balus, 123
Alexander's Feast, 123–125, 136–143
Alexandria, 8, 91, 92
Alfasi, Isaac, 14
Almug, 22, 36, 41, 52
Amora, 67–71
Amsterdam Haggadah, 116
Aphek, 35
Apollo, 19, 28, 58, 78, 88–89, 126, 155
Aquinas, 120
Arabic, 14, 16, 32
Aramaic, 3, 26, 31–32, 152
Aristobulos, 9
Aristotle, 89, 138
Ark of the Covenant, 21, 35–36, 40–41, 57, 100–103, 117, 122
Armenian Bible, 5, 152
Artapanus, 9
Asa, 94
Asaph, 40, 102, 105
Asor, 24, 52, 66
Assyria, 38, 57
Assyrian, 26, 33, 57, 88
Asterix, 7
Athens, 28
Augustine, 120
Avenary, Hanoch, 1

Babylonia, 13, 15, 25, 26, 28, 36, 52, 74, 112
Bain, Alexander, 56
Baker, Kyle, 6
Bar Kokhba, 9–10, 19, 25, 65, 148, 154
Barbieri, Giovanni Francesco, 96
Basil, 120
Batya, Bayer, 77
Beethoven, 44
Berlin, Zvi Yehuda, 82
Bethlehem, 20
Boenig, Robert, 120
Boethius, 139
Braun, Joachim, 2, 4, 44, 146
Broda, Moses Judah Leib ben Wolf, 115
Brown, Thomas, 49
Brydges, James, 124
Buckeridge, Henry Baynbrigg, 137
Burney, Charles, 132
Burrows, Donald, 140–141
Byzantium, 28

Cacofonix the Bard, 7
Cain, 20, 51
Callistus, 92
Calmet, Augustin, 133–135, 139, 142
Cavallino, Bernardo, 96
Chagall, Marc, 6, 96, 101–102, 122, 157, 158
Chananiah, 70
Charles the Bald, 102
Charlotte Rothschild Haggadah, 116
Clement of Alexandra, 12, 91–92
Cleopatra, 7
Cohen, Evelyn M., 112, 120–121
Cole, Michael, 142
Collier, Jeremy, 137–138
Common Sense, 127, 142
Coptic, 32
Corelli, 44
Cronos, 138
crosses 121

Crumb, R., 6–7
Cyrus, 36

Damascus Gate, 90
Darwin, Charles, 56
David, 1, 6, 8–9, 10, 11–13, 17, 20–21,
    22, 23, 25, 27–28, 32, 34–35, 40, 44,
    51, 53–54, 55, 56, 57, 58, 61–62, 65,
    71–72, 73, 75, 76, 79–81, 84–86, 87–
    122, 128–132, 135–136, 143, 146,
    147, 148, 149, 150, 151, 152, 157,
    158, 159, 160, 161, 162
David and Bathsheba, 7
de Gelder, Aernt, 96
Dead Sea Scrolls, 8, 10, 147
Dean, Winston, 124
Debenham, Margaret, 142
Demetrius and the Gladiators, 7
Domenichino, 112
Dowling Long, Siobhán, 17, 147
Dryden, John, 136–141
Dubsewitz, Abraham Dov, 81
Dumas b. Labrats, 14–15
Dura-Europos synagogue, 10–12, 72,
    91, 148

Eden, 33, 62, 72, 75
Edom, 36–37, 41
Egypt, 19, 26, 32, 57, 66, 79, 81, 96,
    116, 123, 152
Elijah, 37
Elisha, 32, 37, 57–58
Esh Qadechu, 15
Eshel, Hanan, 9–10, 65, 148
Esther, 123–124, 135, 141
Ethan, 102, 105
Ethiopic, 31
Eurydice, 89
Eve, 32

Fieschi Psalter, 116
Fleisher, Ezra, 85
Flesher, Paul, 11–13, 148
Friedheim, Emmanuel, 67–68
Friedmann, Jonathan L., 17, 150

Gaon, Saadia, 82
Gaza synagogue, 6, 10–11, 72, 89–90,
    145, 157, 161

The Gentleman's Magazine, 126–127,
    128–129
Geonim, 9, 13, 145
Gereboff, Joel, 17
Gerson-Kiwi, Edith, 2
Gibeon, 34
Gilboah, 35
Gilead, 54
Ginzberg, Louis, 105, 106, 107, 113
Giulio Cesare, 123
Giveat ha- Eloqim, 34
Goliath, 93, 96, 108, 117, 129
Goodenough, Erwin, 11
Gorali, Moshe, 6
Goscinny, René, 7
Greco-Roman, 11, 64, 72, 148, 154
Greek, 3, 5, 8, 10–13, 19, 21, 26–28, 32,
    53, 55, 78, 87–91, 119, 135, 139, 145,
    146, 148, 149, 150, 151, 152, 153,
    155, 156, 157, 158, 161
Gregory XV, 112

Hai b. Sherira, 13–14
Halakhah, 13–14, 61, 62
Halevi, Judah, 14, 15, 85–86
Ḥalil, 2, 3, 14, 15, 20
Hammer, Zevulun, 86
Handel, George Frideric, 5, 17, 123–
    143
Harbison, Peter, 95
Harrán, Don, 13–14, 16, 151–152
Harris, James, 131–132
Hasidism, 16, 80, 152
Ḥatzotzrah, 2–3, 22, 45
Hearpe, 29
Hellenism, 10, 26, 43, 89, 146, 148,
    157, 161
Heman, 40, 102, 105
Hermes, 28, 88, 150, 153, 156
Hezekiah, 41, 52, 57, 94
Higgayon BeKhinnor, 5, 17, 78, 80, 84,
    151, 152, 156
Hilarius of Potiers, 120
Hiram of Tyre, 21
Hittite, 32, 152
Hiyya bar Abba, 24, 69
Holbien, Hans, 95
Hollywood, 7, 20
Homer, 21, 28, 150, 160

Hume, David, 49
Hunterian Psalter, 103–104

Iamblichus, 89
ibn Ezra, Abraham, 112
ibn Ezra, Moshe, 14, 15
ibn Gabirol, Solomon, 14–15
ibn Shaprut, Chisdai, 14
Idel, Moshe, 16, 152
Iduthin, 102
Iliad, 21
Isaac, 73, 95
Istar, 58
Italy, 5, 16–17, 57, 77, 80, 84, 112, 114, 120–121, 127, 139, 142, 151–152

Jacob, 54, 95
Jans, Geertgen tot Sint, 93–94
Jeduthun, 40
Jehoram, 94
Jehoshaphat, 36–37, 41, 57, 94
Jehu, 37–38
Jennens, Charles, 128, 130–131
Jesse, 20, 93–95
Joachim, 120
Jonathan, 130
Jones, Thomas, 124
Josephson, Ernst, 96
Josephus, 31, 64, 69, 73, 106
Jotham, 94
Jubal, 1, 4, 6–7, 19, 20, 23, 32, 51, 77–78, 151
Julius Caesar, 7
Kabbalah, 1, 13, 16, 17, 78–79, 83, 151, 152
Karna, 26
Karo, Joseph, 14
Keren, 26
Khenanyahu, 22
King James Bible, 5, 21–23
King of Kings, 7
Kinor Nishmati, 16
Kinura, 5, 27, 32
Kithara, 5, 8, 26–28, 87, 153, 154, 157
Kohanim, 22, 27, 63
Kraeling, Carl H., 11
Kronberg, Julius, 96

Laban, 54–55

Lamech, 32
Lamentations Rabbah, 68
Leveen, Jacob, 112
Levites, 1, 2, 20, 22, 23, 28, 39–40, 51–52, 55, 56, 57, 58, 61, 62–63, 68, 72, 101–102, 106
The London Daily Post, 127
Lowe, Judah (Maharal), 82–84
Luzzatto, Shmuel David, 78
Lyra, 21, 87, 103, 133, 134–135, 160

Macedonia, 92
Maimonides, Moses, 14, 16, 105
Manasseh, 94
Mar Uqba, 71
Mari, 31, 58
Masoretes, 23
Master of the Ingeborg Psalter, 98–98, 118
McKinnon, James K., 9, 155
Mekhilta de Rabbi Ishmael, 66
mena'anim, 3, 21
Mendelssohn, Moses, 84
Mesha, 36–37
Mesopotamia, 19, 58, 88, 149, 150, 154
Messianism, 11–13, 17, 24, 61–62, 65–66, 68, 73–74, 76, 79, 82–84, 91, 148, 151, 157
Metziltayim, 2–3, 22, 52
Mezeritsch, Eliezer Sussman, 116
Michal, 102, 129–131, 135,
Midrash, 17, 61, 62, 66, 68–69, 73–75, 77, 78, 80, 83
Mijwiz, 7
Miletto, Gianfranco, 16, 151, 156
Miletus, 138
Mirguet, Françoise, 49
Miriam, 20
Mishnah, 2, 13, 25, 61, 62, 67, 68
Mizmor, 55
Moab, 32, 36–38, 52, 73
Montagu, Jeremy, 17, 134, 156
Moriah, 106, 108
Moscato, Judah, 5, 16–17, 57, 78, 80, 84, 151, 152, 156
Moses, 9, 22, 45
Mukannisum, 31

Naamah, 51, 77
Nabla, 5, 27, 64
Near East, 1, 7, 13, 31, 33, 43, 58, 149, 150, 156, 157, 159
Nebuchadnezzar, 74
Nebuchadrezzar, 25, 26
Nefutsot Yehuda, 80
Nero, 28
Nevel, 2–3, 5, 10, 14, 20, 21–23, 24–25, 26–27, 52, 61, 62–66, 68–69, 73, 75, 87, 120
Norsa, Isaac, 120
Norton, Mildred, 44, 159

Obed-edom, 101
Odyssey, 21
Organon, 5
Orpheus, 8–9, 10–13, 53, 72, 88–93, 96, 103, 113, 121, 126–127, 137, 145, 147, 148, 152, 156, 157, 158, 160, 161, 162
Ovadiah, Asher, 11–12, 90, 157

pa'amonim, 3
Pan, 91
Paris Psalter, 92–93
Parry, John, 124
Philistines, 35, 57, 93, 154
Philo of Alexandria, 8, 9, 148, 155
Phoenician, 31, 58
Pistis Sophia, 3
Plain Dealer, 142
Plato, 88–89, 100, 147
Porphyry, 89
Portugal, 27, 112
Powell, William, 123
Psalmos, 55
Psalms of Ascents, 23
Psalmterion, 5
Psaltery, 5, 6, 19, 103, 116, 119–122
Purcell, Henry, 126
Pythagoras, 77–78, 89, 147, 151

Queen of Sheba, 21–22, 36, 41, 124
Qumran, 8, 65, 147, 158, 160

R. Abbahu, 69, 70
R. Ami, 71
R. Chanina b. Dosa, 73

R. Eleazer, 62
R. Eleazar b. Menachem, 71
R. Hisda, 71
R. Hunna, 24, 71
R. Isaac, 73
R. Joshua, 64, 70
R. Levi, 71
R. Pinchas, 71
R. Shabbetai, 75
R. Simeon b. Laqish, 71
R. Yohanan, 68
R. Zerikan, 71
Rachel, 54
Rav Joseph, 24
Rav Judah, 24, 64–65, 79, 81–82
Rav Papa, 24
Reed Sea, 20
Rehoboam, 93
Rembrandt, 97
The Robe, 7
Rome, 2, 7, 11, 12, 25, 28, 78, 120
Roshim, 21
Rothschild, Amschel Mayer, 116
Rothschild, Charlotte, 116
Rothschild Miscellany, 112–114
Roubiliac, Louis-François, 125–126, 136, 143

Sachs, Curt, 3, 44, 45–46, 47, 87, 100, 158
St. Cecilia, 136–137
St. Jerome, 26, 87
Samuel, 20, 105
Sanders, James, 8
Sanskrit, 32
Saul, 6, 20–21, 23, 28, 32, 34–35, 53–54, 67, 87, 89, 95–100, 112, 117, 121–122, 161
Saul, 123–124, 128–132, 135–136, 141, 149
Scandinavia, 19, 28, 153
Schwartz, Dov, 16, 17
Sendrey, Alfred, 44, 46, 47, 159
Sennacherib, 88
Sepphoris mosaics, 10–11, 72, 161
Septuagint, 3, 4–5, 8, 26–27, 87, 120, 147, 148, 152
Shabbat (Sabbath), 1, 39, 55, 63, 6, 73, 106

Shekhinah, 68
Shemer, Naomi, 6
Sheminit, 51, 65, 82
Sheol, 39
Shiloh, 35
Shofar, 1, 2–3, 4, 43, 51, 57, 79, 154
Sibylline Oracles, 8
Simeon b. Eleazar, 63
Six-Day War, 6
Smith, Ruth, 17
Solomon, 6, 20, 21, 36, 41, 52, 93
Song of the Vineyard, 69
Spain, 5, 13–14, 27, 77, 112, 159, 160
Spartans, 138
Spock, 7
Star Trek, 7
Sutton Hoo, 28
Sweeney, Marvin A., 17
Syriac, 32, 152

Tabernacle, 20, 22
Talgam, Rina, 92
Talmud, 2, 13, 17, 24, 25, 63, 68–72,
    78–82, 146, 158, 160
Tanna, 61, 62 – 64, 66–68, 81–82
Targum, 3, 26
Temple (Jerusalem), 2, 4, 8, 9–10, 20,
    21, 22–24, 25, 27, 32, 36, 38–39, 40–
    41, 46, 56, 61–64, 67–69, 70, 71, 74,
    75–76, 83, 90, 102, 121, 149
Timotheus, 125, 133, 137–142
Tobi, Joseph (Yosef), 14, 16, 160
Toph, 2, 3, 14, 20, 21, 102
Tosefta, 61, 62, 63, 67
Tsiyyon halo tishali, 15
Tubal-Cain, 51, 77–78, 131, 132, 135
Tyers, John, 127

Uderzo, Albert, 7
Ugaritic, 31, 58, 146, 149, 150, 153
Ugav, 2, 4, 7, 20, 23, 33, 51, 147
Ur, 88
Utrecht Te Deum, 128–129
Uzziah, 93, 100
Uzziel, Ben-Zion Meir Hai, 85–86

Valley of Blessing, 41
van den Hoecke, Jan, 96
van Leyden, Lucas, 96

Vauxhall Gardens, 126–127, 128, 136
Vikings, 28
Vincent, P.H., 90
Virgin Mary, 94
Von Geldern Haggadah, 115
von Hornbostel, Erich Moritz, 3, 44
Vulgate, 3, 23, 26, 87–88, 101, 116

Westminster Abbey, 143
Woolley, Leonard, 88
Wynn II, Watkins Williams, 124

Xena: Warrior Princess, 7
Xeravits, Geza, 1, 2–13, 161–162

"Yerushalayim shel Zahav," 6
Yigzol shena, 15

Zeus, 138
Zimri-Lim, 31
Zophar, 40